Marx's Concept of
the Alternative to Capitalism

Historical Materialism Book Series

The Historical Materialism Book Series is a major publishing initiative of the radical left. The capitalist crisis of the twenty-first century has been met by a resurgence of interest in critical Marxist theory. At the same time, the publishing institutions committed to Marxism have contracted markedly since the high point of the 1970s. The Historical Materialism Book Series is dedicated to addressing this situation by making available important works of Marxist theory. The aim of the series is to publish important theoretical contributions as the basis for vigorous intellectual debate and exchange on the left.

The peer-reviewed series publishes original monographs, translated texts, and reprints of classics across the bounds of academic disciplinary agendas and across the divisions of the left. The series is particularly concerned to encourage the internationalization of Marxist debate and aims to translate significant studies from beyond the English-speaking world.

For a full list of titles in the Historical Materialism Book Series
available in paperback from Haymarket Books, visit:
www.haymarketbooks.org/category/hm-series

Marx's Concept of the Alternative to Capitalism

Peter Hudis

Haymarket Books
Chicago, IL

First published in 2012 by Brill Academic Publishers, The Netherlands
© 2012 Koninklijke Brill NV, Leiden, The Netherlands

Published in paperback in 2013 by
Haymarket Books
P.O. Box 180165
Chicago, IL 60618
773-583-7884
www.haymarketbooks.org

ISBN: 978-1-60846-275-9

Trade distribution:
In the US, Consortium Book Sales, www.cbsd.com
In Canada, Publishers Group Canada, www.pgcbooks.ca
In the UK, Turnaround Publisher Services, www.turnaround-psl.com
In Australia, Palgrave Macmillan, www.palgravemacmillan.com.au
In all other countries, Publishers Group Worldwide, www.pgw.com

Cover design by Ragina Johnson.

This book was published with the generous support of
Lannan Foundation and the Wallace Global Fund.

Printed in the United States.

10 9 8 7 6 5 4 3 2 1

Library of Congress Cataloging-in-Publication data is available.

Contents

Acknowledgements

This work is not the product of mere solitary reflection, since it arose and developed as a result of a series of discussions and debates with numerous friends and colleagues over the course of the last decade, many of them associated with the philosophy of 'Marxist-Humanism'. I wish to especially single out Richard Abernethy, Dave Black, Dan Buckley, Dale Heckerman, Karel Ludenhoff, Eli Messinger, Marilyn Nissim-Sabat, James Obst, Sandra Rein, Ali Reza, Sekou Samateh and Stephen Sarma-Weierman. I wish to especially thank Frieda Afary and Kevin Anderson for their insights, expressed in numerous conversations and letters, and for their careful and studious commentary on the manuscript.

I am no less indebted to the thoughts and suggestions provided by a number of scholars at Loyola University Chicago, who commented on earlier versions of this work. These include Andrew Cutrofellow, David Ingram, Lauren Langman, David Schweickart, Dan Vaillancourt and Thomas Wren. While any faults contained in this work are my responsibility alone, I could not have come this far without their assistance.

Why Explore Marx's Concept of the Transcendence of Value-Production? Why Now?

The object and purpose of this study

Two decades after the collapse of statist Communism in the USSR and Eastern Europe, which many claimed had consigned Marx's work to the dustbin of history, a new climate has emerged in which his ideas are subject to renewed discussion and re-examination. This change is due, in part, to the phenomenon of capitalist globalisation, which has sparked interest in Marx's analysis of the inherently expansionary and global nature of capital, which he defined as 'self-expanding value'. It is also due to the emergence of a global-justice movement over the past two decades, which has called attention to the economic inequality, social instability and environmental destruction that have accompanied the global expansion of capitalism. Most of all, the new climate of discussion on Marx's work is due to the worldwide financial and economic crisis that began in 2008, the most serious to afflict the global economy in the past seventy years. The crisis has not only revealed the deep fault-lines that prevent capitalism from supplying the most basic of human needs for hundreds of millions of people worldwide; it has also made it clear that the system has little to offer humanity except years and indeed *decades* of economic austerity, reductions in public services, and eroding living conditions. Capitalism has clearly exhausted its historic initiative and *raison d'être* when all it can offer the future of humanity are social and natural conditions that are bound to become worse than those afflicting us today.

As a result of these and related developments, a number of new works on Marx have appeared, many of which explore hitherto neglected aspects of his thought – such as his writings on the world-market, economic crisis, race and gender, non-Western societies, and the philosophical underpinning of his analysis of the logic of capital. These studies have appeared while a new edition of Marx's complete works, the *Marx-Engels Gesamtausgabe* (known as *MEGA²*), is being issued by an international team of scholars co-ordinated from Berlin. *MEGA²* will make Marx's entire body of work available for scholarly analysis for the first time, in 114 volumes.[1] It provides us with a new vantage-point for exploring Marx's work unencumbered by uninformed claims about Marx's work that have governed generations of earlier discussions of Marx's theoretical contribution.

Although the literature on Marx over the past one hundred years is immense, most of it has focused on his analysis of the economic and political structure of capitalism, the 'materialist conception of history', and his critique of value-production. There has been very little discussion or analysis, however, of his conception of what constitutes an alternative to capitalism. The lack of discussion of this issue has persisted in the face of the growth of the global-justice movement, which has sponsored a series of fora, gatherings and conferences in Brazil, Venezuela, Kenya, Senegal and elsewhere since the 1990s, devoted to the theme 'Another World is Possible'. This diverse movement indicates that despite the notion, which became widely voiced after 1989, that 'there is no alternative'[2] to capitalism, increasing numbers of people around the world are searching for such an alternative. However, there appears to be little or no consensus within the global-justice movement as to what such an alternative might consist of. It is even hard to find consensus as to what theoretical resources would need to be explored in thinking one out. As a result, the discussion of alternatives to capitalism at events sponsored by the global-justice movement tends to remain rather abstract and limited to statements of intent.

---

1. The first Marx-Engels *Gesamtausgabe* was issued in 12 volumes from 1927–35. It is known as *MEGA¹*. The new *Gesamtausgabe*, or *MEGA²*, began appearing in East Germany in 1972 and has been issued since 1990 by a more international group of scholars. It will eventually include everything Marx ever wrote, including his voluminous excerpt-notebooks, most of which were unknown until recently. It is the only edition of Marx's writings that meets the rigorous standards of modern textual editing.

2. Former British Prime Minister Margaret Thatcher popularised this phrase in the early 1980s. For a discussion of its ideological impact, see Mészáros 1995.

In some respects, today's situation has not changed much since 1918, when Otto Neurath of the Vienna Circle became the planning minister of the short-lived Bavarian Socialist Republic. Shortly after the collapse of this early effort to develop a postcapitalist social system he wrote:

> At the beginning of the [1918] revolution people were as unprepared for the task of a socialist economy in Germany as they had been for a war economy when war broke out in 1914…Any preparation for consciously shaping the economy was lacking. The technique of a socialist economy had been badly neglected. Instead, only pure criticism of the capitalist economy was offered and the Marxist pure theory of value and history was studied.[3]

It would be no exaggeration to say that nearly one hundred years later, the situation described by Neurath continues to largely define contemporary discussions of the issues raised by Marx's work.

There are several reasons for the lack of theoretical reflection on and discussion of Marx's view of the alternative to capitalism. Perhaps of foremost importance is the claim that he simply never addressed the issue. It has long been assumed that Marx's criticism of some of the utopian socialists[4] and his strictures against inventing 'blueprints about the future', meant that he was not interested in commenting about a postcapitalist society. Marx did not indulge in speculations about the future, it is widely assumed, because he believed that socialism would emerge quasi-automatically from the inherent contradictions of capitalist society. Another reason for the paucity of discussion of Marx's view of the alternative to capitalism is that many defenders and critics of Marx took it for granted that socialism is defined by the abolition of the market and private property, and the formation of centralised, state-planned economies. Many assumed that a socialist society consists of simply 'taking over' monopolised and semi-planned capitalism and running it 'in the interests of the masses'. To many, it therefore seemed superfluous to take the trouble to sort out what Marx might have had to say about an alternative to capitalism when the 'socialism' he strove for was presumably already in existence. This attitude persisted long after it became clear that the societies that called themselves 'socialist' or 'communist' were dismal failures. Given the widespread discrediting of the régimes that *claimed* to rule in the name

---

3. Neurath 1973, p. 18. Kurt Eisner, the leader of the Bavarian Socialist Republic, asked Neurath to become planning minister at the end of 1918; he continued to serve under the short-lived Bavarian Soviet Republic, which was installed in early 1919 following Eisner's assassination.

4. While Marx was very critical of some utopian socialists, he heaped considerable praise upon others – especially Fourier and Owen.

of Marx, it seemed pointless to pour old wine into new bottles by inquiring anew into what Marx had to say about alternatives to capitalism.

In the twenty-first century we face a radically changed situation. Now that the state-powers that ruled in Marx's name have largely passed from the scene, at the same time that the entire corpus of his work is finally becoming available for study, it becomes possible to take a closer look at his *œuvre* to see if the assumptions that have traditionally governed the understanding of Marx's view of the alternative to capitalism are in fact accurate.

Four lines of inquiry guide this work. First, although Marx never wrote a book devoted to the alternative to capitalism, and he was extremely wary about indulging in speculation about the future (especially in his published writings), numerous comments and suggestions are found throughout his works about the transcendence of value-production and the contours of a postcapitalist future. How significant are they? One of my purposes is to subject these comments to systematic and critical examination.

Second, even if it were true that Marx never wrote a word about a postcapitalist future, it does not follow that his work fails to speak implicitly or indirectly to the matter in important ways. Is it plausible that Marx's analysis of capital was a purely empirical and scientific endeavour that was not in some way informed by presuppositions concerning the kind of society he hoped would one day come into being? One of the claims that I will aim to substantiate is that the very content of Marx's analysis of capital, value-production and wage-labour rests upon an implicit understanding on his part of what human existence would consist of in their absence. Allan Megill puts it thusly in a recent analysis of Marx's philosophical legacy: 'In fact, it is perhaps better not to call Marx's method a method at all: it is much more an *approach to the material*, a pre-established interpretative perspective. It is an approach that "always already" contains within itself a certain conviction about capitalism, namely, that capitalism is doomed to destroy itself'.[5] Although Megill is correct that Marx's work exhibits a 'pre-established interpretative perspective', even if it is often only implicit in much of it, I believe he is incorrect in conterposing it to the presence of a distinctive Marxian *method*. Marx remained deeply indebted to Hegel's dialectical philosophy throughout his life, and it directly informed his methodological approach to a host of issues. One of my claims is that Marx's dialectical method cannot be fully grasped or appreciated apart from the specific vision of the future that grounded his critique of capital and capitalism.[6]

---

5. Megill 2002, p. 240.
6. It has likewise been claimed that Hegel's dialectical method cannot be fully grasped or appreciated apart from his concept of 'the Absolute'. For more on this,

Third, although most of Marx's work consists of an analysis and criticism of capital, the critique is hardly a purely *negative* one that fails to posit implicit (and sometimes explicit) notions of a positive alternative to it. Marx never denied his indebtedness to Hegel's dialectic of negativity, and negativity in Hegel does not lead to a nullity; instead, the positive emerges from the negation of the negation, which Hegel termed 'absolute negativity'. Thus, Marx's undeniable debt to Hegel's dialectic[7] offers any serious student of Marx a further reason to attempt to discern and analyse the indications of the future that flow from his critique of the capital and other social forms that define present-day society.

Fourth, relatively few scholarly readers of Marx today would contend that his philosophical perspective had much to do with the totalitarian, single-party states that ruled in his name. His emphatic support for democracy, free association, and critique of statist domination, found from his earliest to his last writings, offers strong support for this claim. What is far less clear, however, is what Marx envisaged as the specific form of society that could live up to his *liberatory* ideals. Does he ever address this directly?

Despite the voluminous literature on Marx, there have been surprisingly few attempts to examine his body of thought as a whole in terms of what it suggests about a future, postcapitalist society. It does not seem possible to fully evaluate the contributions or limitations of Marx's legacy in the absence of such an investigation. I will seek to fill this gap by exploring Marx's concept of the transcendence of value-production through an examination of his body of work, as found in his major published writings as well as unpublished ones that are now being compiled as part of the *MEGA*² project.

This does not pretend to be a comprehensive study of Marx. Nor does it attempt to put forwards a specific model of a postcapitalist society. Although I consider efforts to produce the latter to be of great importance, I have a more modest aim: to survey *Marx's* work with *one* aim: to see what implicit or explicit indications it contains about a future, non-alienating society.

Why, one might ask, begin here at all? The reason is that Marx is not simply one of a number of important thinkers but the founder of a distinctive

---

see Rose 1981, written from outside the Marxian tradition, and Dunayevskaya 2003, written from within it.

7. This debt permeated his entire work, including his 'mature' critique of political economy. As Marx stated in 1875 a passage in Volume II of *Capital* that Engels left out of the published version, 'In my zealous devotion to the schema of Hegelian logic, I even discovered the Hegelian forms of the syllogism in the process of circulation. My relationship with Hegel is very simple. I am a disciple of Hegel, and the presumptuous chattering of the epigones who think they have buried this great thinker appear frankly ridiculous to me'. See Marx 2008, p. 32.

approach to the understanding of capitalism that retains its historical relevance so long as capitalism remains in existence. Marx's body of work is one of those rare historical achievements that represent the crossing of a conceptual threshold; it marks a new *philosophical moment* that radically transforms all subsequent approaches to the object of investigation. This is as true of those who criticise Marx as much as those who claim to follow him. Marx's work (to borrow Michel Foucault's phrase) is *transdiscursive*, in that it produces 'the possibilities and the rules for the formation of other texts'.[8] His work delineates the parameter of possibilities for the study of capital – as well as of the alternative to it. In Marx, we encounter a thinker who possesses a deep and profound emancipatory conception that radically separates him from his predecessors. Although no Marxist himself, Michael Polanyi captured the sense of the 'irrevocable' threshold that is crossed by an original thinker in a way that addresses why any effort to think out an alternative to capitalism today *must* come to grips with Marx's philosophical contribution:

> We call their work creative because it changes the world as we see it, by deepening our understanding of it. The change is irrevocable. A problem that I have once solved can no longer puzzle me; I cannot guess what I already know. Having made a discovery, I shall never see the world again as before. My eyes have become different; I have made myself into a person seeing and thinking differently. I have crossed a gap, the heuristic gap which lies between problem and discovery...We have to cross the logical gap between a problem and its solution by relying on the unspecifiable impulse of our heuristic passion, and must undergo as we do so a change of our intellectual personality.[9]

This work focuses on Marx's concept of the transcendence of *value*-production because he held that capitalism is defined by the production of value and surplus-value. Value is not the same as material wealth; it is wealth computed in monetary terms. Marx acknowledges that value 'exists initially in the head, in the imagination, just as in general ratios can only be *thought* if they are to be fixed, as distinct from the subjects which are in that ratio to each other'.[10] However, this does not mean that Marx considered value to be a purely *mental* category, let alone a dialectical illusion. Value, he held, expresses a *real* social relationship, since 'As value, the commodity is at the

---

8. Foucault 2003, p. 387.
9. Polanyi 1962, p. 143.
10. Marx 1986a, p. 81. The editors of the English-language *Marx and Engels Collected Works* have chosen to entitle what has been known as the *Grundrisse* as *Outlines of the Critique of Political Economy (Rough Draft of 1857–58)*. For the sake of convenience, I will refer to it by its better-known name, the *Grundrisse*.

same time an equivalent for all other commodities in a particular ratio'.[11] Value is the name given for a real, *material* relationship, insofar as 'value is a commodity's quantitatively determined exchangeability'.[12]

The peculiar feature of capitalism, Marx held, is that *all* social relations become governed by the drive to augment value, irrespective of humanity's actual needs and capacities. He therefore treats value-production not as a transhistorical feature of human existence but rather as a specific characteristic of *capitalist* society. Marx was of course fully aware that commodity-exchange predates the existence of capitalism. He does not, however, simply equate value-production with the exchange of equivalents on the market. In precapitalist societies, he argues, goods and services were primarily exchanged on the basis of their material *utility*, not on the basis of their (abstract) exchange-*value*. Only with capitalism – that is, only when commodity-exchange becomes the primary and indeed *universal* medium of social interaction through the commodification of *labour-power* – does value becomes the defining principle of social reproduction. Marx did not hold that labour is *the* source of *value* in *all* forms of society; labour (along with nature) in precapitalist societies is a source of *material wealth*, not of value. As Marx states in the *Grundrisse*, 'The economic concept of value does not occur among the ancients...The concept of value wholly belongs to the latest political economy, because that concept is the most abstract expression of capital itself and of the production based upon it'.[13]

Marx also denied that value-production would characterise a *postcapitalist* society. In response to one of the few critiques of his theoretical corpus that appeared in his lifetime, he wrote: '*Value*. According to Mr. Wagner, Marx's

---

11. Marx 1986a, pp. 78–9.
12. Marx 1986a, p. 78. Since value only exists in *objectified* form, the subject of *Capital*, Marx takes pains to note, is not value itself but rather the commodity. Marx does not treat the commodity, however, merely as a material thing or as a form of material wealth. He treats the commodity as the 'simplest social form' in which *value* manifests itself. In sum, the commodity-form is inseparable from value-production. For more on this, see Marx 1989h, pp. 544–5.
13. Marx 1987a, pp. 159–60. In his sometimes valuable recent study of dialectics, Paul Paolucci is surprisingly imprecise on this point: 'Although labor relations might be different in various modes of production, it nevertheless remains true that labor is the source of social value under tribal, slave, feudal, and capitalist modes of production, though it may not have crystallized in the former to the point of there being able to be discovered and conceptualized in the same way capitalism makes possible'. See Paolucci 2007, p. 87–8. The passage conflates value with material wealth, presenting the former as a transhistorical feature of human existence. He also contends that capitalism reveals what prior modes of production conceal – the socially determinative role of value. However, for Marx, capitalism is a *mystifying* system, especially in comparison with precapitalist ones, precisely because it is defined by value-production.

theory of value is the *"cornerstone of his socialist system"*. As I have never established a *"socialist system"*, this is a fantasy of Wagner, Schäffle *e tutti quanti.'*[14]
He added, 'In my investigation of value I have dealt with bourgeois relations,
not with the application of this theory of *value* to a 'social state not even constructed by me but by Mr. Schäffle for me'.[15] According to Marx, social relations were not governed by the drive to augment value *prior* to capitalism and
they would not governed by it *after* capitalism.

Popularisations of Marx often reduce his theory of value to the notion that
labour is the source of all value. However, Marx never claimed originality for
this idea; he adopted it from classical-political economists like Adam Smith.
Marx's main object of concern is not with the *source* of value. His primary
concern is with the way social relations in modern society take on the *form* of
value. His main object of critique is the *inverted* character of social relations
in capitalism, wherein *human* relations take on the form of relations between
things. There is little doubt that Marx's critique of capitalism centres upon a
critique of value-production. What is far less clear, however, is exactly what
is needed, in Marx's view, to surmount value-production. My aim is to discover the elements, however implicit, that he thought are needed to overcome
value-production.

My approach is to investigate Marx's theoretical corpus on its own terms.
In doing so I will avoid conflating it with that of his close colleague and follower, Friedrich Engels. There is no question that Engels was Marx's closest colleague and follower. However, although Marx and Engels's names are
often hyphenated and many have even treated their writings as interchangeable, Marx was, by Engels's own admission, a far deeper and more rigorous thinker. On many issues their views are far from identical. Marx often
expressed surprise that he and Engels were viewed as identical twins. As he
wrote to Engels in 1856, 'What is so very strange is to see how he treats the
two of us as a *singular*: "Marx and Engels *says* etc."'.[16] Since this is not the
place to enter into a comparative examination of whether or not Engels's comments on a postcapitalist society coincided with those of Marx, I will bracket
out Engels's contribution by focusing primarily on the philosophical works
composed by Marx himself.[17]

---

14. Marx 1989h, p. 533.
15. Marx 1989h, pp. 536–7.
16. See Marx 1983a, p. 64.
17. An exception this will be when there is direct textual evidence that Marx
approved of specific formulations of Engels on postcapitalist relations, such as Engels's
discussion of workers' cooperatives and labour-time in *Anti-Dühring*.

Objectivist and subjectivist approaches to Marx's philosophical contribution

Over the past two decades, two major strains of thought have sought to come to grips with the contemporary relevance of Marx's critique of capitalism. One strain contends that Marx's most important contribution lies in his understanding of capital as an autonomous force that takes on a life of its own, totally subsuming the will and actions of the human subject. In this perspective, Marx analyses capital as a peculiar object of knowledge invested with characteristics that parallel Hegel's delineation of the logic of the concept in the *Science of Logic*. These thinkers hold that capital, like Hegel's doctrine of the concept, possesses the distinct ontological property of complete indifference to anything that lies outside its logic of self-movement. They therefore view capital not only as the subject of Marx's theoretical work but also as the *Subject* of modern society. I call these theorists *objectivist Marxists*, because they contend that Marx's critique of capital is best understood as an analysis of objective forms that assume complete self-determination and automaticity. The objectivist Marxists include several distinct groupings: (1) the Japanese theorist Kozo Uno and his followers, which include Thomas Sekine, Robert Albritton, and John Bell; (2) the German philosopher Hans-Georg Backhaus and US social theorist Moishe Postone, both heavily indebted to the work of the Frankfurt school; and (3) the proponents of 'systematic dialectics' in the US and Western Europe, such as C.J. Arthur, Patrick Murray, Geert Reuten and Tony Smith.[18]

At the other end of the philosophical spectrum, a second and radically different strain of thinkers contends that Marx's most important contribution lies in his understanding of the subjective human forces that struggle against and strive to annul capital's drive for hegemony.[19] They emphasise not the self-determining and automatic character of capital but the *limits* and *barriers* that it repeatedly encounters. I call these theorists *subjectivist Marxists* because they emphasise the subjective human forces that seek to subvert and contain

---

18. Although Tony Smith is part of the 'systematic-dialectics' school that has emerged in the last decade, as will be discussed below, he has a radically different interpretation of the Hegel-Marx relation from the other theorists of this tendency.

19. This divide between subjectivist and objectivist readings of Marx has earlier antecedents – such as in the debates in the early twentieth century between Georg Lukács and Rosa Luxemburg, who each tended to emphasise subjectivity and mass self-activity, and Karl Kautsky, Georgii Plekhanov and other 'orthodox' Marxists who emphasised the importance of objective material conditions. In some respects, this debate was replayed in Jean-Paul Sartre's exchange with Althusser and Lévi-Strauss in the mid-twentieth century. Debates within Marxist theory, as is the case with philosophy as a whole, often take the form of matters of *philosophia perennis*.

the logic of capital. Prominent among the subjectivist Marxists are 'autonomist Marxists' such as Mario Tronti, John Holloway, Antonio Negri, and Michael Hardt.

While these schools of thought have made a number of important contributions to the understanding of Marx's work over the past few decades, I will critically examine them in terms of how they worked to unearth Marx's concept of the transcendence of capitalist value-production.

The version of objectivist Marxism found in the work of Kozo Uno and his followers holds that Marx analysed capitalism as a self-contained logical system. The *logic of capital*, they contend, is not the same as *historically-existing* capitalism since, as Thomas L. Sekine puts it, 'the subsumption of real economic life by the commodity-economy is never perfect or absolute'.[20] There is no direct homology between capitalism as it historically exists and the logic of capital. The latter is the real object of Marx's critique, since Marx aims to show that generalised commodity-production is defined by a 'dehumanising logic, which, once it catches on, pervades the world until much of direct human contact or community is obliterated'.[21] Commodity-economic logics 'seem to have a certain automaticity'[22] and an expansiveness that can only be properly understood by discerning its abstract universal 'laws'.

Sekine therefore argues that capital is best understood from the vantage-point of the logic of capital rather than from the proletariat, non-commodified social relations, or precapitalist modes of production. When capital is viewed, 'from without, as, for instance, from the point of view of the revolutionary proletariat, one ends up assuming the position of the blind man touching an arbitrary part of the elephant. In the dialectic of capital the teller of the story (the subject) is capital itself, and not "we" the human being'.[23]

What is achieved by focusing on the pure, abstract logic of capital? We learn that capitalism becomes the more 'perfect' the more value-production overcomes restrictions imposed by use-values. The more efficient capital is in achieving this, the higher the rate of profit. The drive for profit is the absolute idea of capital, it is the quest for an infinite surpassing of all limits: 'As soon as the rate of profit becomes the 'subjective notion' (in the Hegelian sense) of capital, every individual firm strives for a maximum rate of profit, by the mercantile practice of buying cheap and selling dear'.[24]

---

20. Sekine 1997b, p. 212.
21. Sekine 1990, p. 131.
22. Albritton 1999, p. 13.
23. Sekine 1990, pp. 129–30.
24. Sekine 1997b, p. 7.

The Unoists argue that before we can begin to envisage a future free of capitalism we must 'first come to grips with the inner law of motion (or logic) of capitalism'. If the idea of capital remains unclear, the understanding of its transcendence would be 'haphazard and arbitrary'. Hence, we should follow Marx who 'forgets about blueprints for the future and concentrates on economics'.[25]

There is much to be said for the view that Marx does not analyse a *historically*-existing capitalism but rather a chemically-pure capitalism that does not exist and never will exist. He utilised this approach in order to discern capital's 'law of motion', instead of getting bogged down in secondary or non-essential features. However, questions can be raised about whether Uno and his followers succeed in correctly identifying the essential features of capital.

Sekine argues that '[c]apitalism is based on self-regulating markets and anarchic production of commodities'.[26] Robert Albritton likewise contends that '[e]conomic reification implies a market-governed society: a society in which the actions of human agents are directed and subsumed by market forces beyond their control'.[27] There is no doubt that self-regulating markets and anarchic production were important factors in capitalism's *historical* development. But is this the same as claiming that the existence of an anarchic market serves as a *defining feature* of the *logic* of capital? Moreover, is it the *market* that generates 'economic reification' or is it produced, instead, by the alienation of labour?

One of my aims is to investigate whether Marx considered the existence of the market and private property to be defining factors of the logic of capital. Albritton and other followers of Uno clearly insist that they are *intrinsic* to the logic of capital: 'Pure capitalism involves the subsumption of labour and production-process to a system of interlocking markets that are self-regulating in the sense that no extra-economic force (state, monopoly, trade-unions and so on) can interfere with the markets'.[28] Albritton writes, 'Pure capitalism is based on the absolute right of private property'.[29]

Since the Unoists contend that unregulated markets, anarchic competition and private property serve as the inner core of the logic of capital, they conclude that contemporary society is no longer capitalist – since unregulated markets and anarchic competition are a thing of the past. As Sekine puts it,

---

25. Sekine 1990, pp. 128–9.
26. Sekine 1990, p. 135.
27. Albritton 1999, p. 17.
28. Albritton 1999, p. 18.
29. Albritton 1999, p. 20.

the contemporary world 'cannot constitute a world-historic stage of development of capitalism, since it fails to embody the logic of capital'.[30] One is left wondering what theoretical significance Marx's work still has if this is in fact the case.

Most importantly, the great stress that the Unoists place on unregulated markets, anarchic competition, and private property leads them to deny that alienated labour constitutes the defining feature of capitalism. Sekine writes, 'Marx wrote a great book on capital (or commodities) not a book on labour (or production)'.[31] For the Unoists, forms of labour and the struggles against it are *not* intrinsic to the logic of capital: 'What we are trying to determine is the material reproduction of social life entirely through a commodity-economic logic without any human resistance or intervention of any form of extra-economic force'.[32]

This view is not easily reconciled with the connection Marx makes between the alienation of labour, value-production and capital. Marx held that capital is not simply an instrument of production; it is the expression of a specific kind of *labour* – abstract or undifferentiated labour. As he wrote in the *Economic and Philosophical Manuscripts* of 1844, capital is the expression of 'a special sort of work which is indifferent to its content, of complete being-for-self, of abstraction from all other being'.[33] In capitalism 'all the natural, spiritual and social variety of labour' is extinguished. This makes humanity 'ever more exclusively dependent on labour, and on a particular, very one-sided machine-like labour at that'. As a result, the individual becomes 'depressed spiritually'; from 'being a man [he] becomes an abstract activity'.[34] In Volume I of *Capital*, Marx further developed this with his concept of the 'dual character of labour'. All labour, he held, is simultaneously the *concrete* exertion of particular kinds of labour and undifferentiated, *abstract* labour. Abstract labour is the substance of value and capital is self-expanding value. Marx considered this concept of the dual character of labour so important that he referred to it as his original contribution, also terming it 'the pivot on which a clear comprehension of political economy turns'.[35]

This poses problems for the Unoists, who see the logic of capital as freeing itself from such contingent factors as forms of labour. They are especially uncomfortable with the discussion of the dual character of labour in Chapter

---

30. Sekine, 1997b, p. 216.
31. Sekine 2000, p. 130.
32. Albritton 1999, p. 38.
33. Marx 1975r, p. 286.
34. Marx 1975r, pp. 236–8.
35. See Marx 1976e, p. 132.

One of *Capital*, which they leave out of their reconstructions of the dialectic of capital.[36]

This is not to suggest that Uno and his followers set aside labour altogether. They seek to take account of it by utilising *levels-theory*. The logic of capital corresponds to one level of analysis. The other level is actual history, which only approximates the logic of capital. Contingent factors like conditions of labour, production-relations, and resistance to capital occur on the level of historical analysis. For example, Albritton seeks to account for subjective resistance even though his understanding of the logic of capital completely abstracts from it: 'Thus, although capital's logic is always a totalizing force in modern history, to the extent that it runs up against resistances, it can never consummate a totality that is unified around an essence at the level of history'.[37]

There are benefits to such a levels-approach, since a major problem faced by many thinkers is the temptation to conflate the *logical* analysis of a phenomenon with its *actual* development. Kierkegaard addressed this: 'A person can be a great logician and become immortal through his services and yet prostitute himself by assuming that the logical is the existential and that the principle of contradiction is abrogated in existence because it is indisputably abrogated in logic; whereas existence is the very separation that prevents the logical flow'.[38]

As Albritton and other followers of Uno emphasise, the actual historical development of capitalism often upsets the 'logical flow' of capital's drive to self-expand irrespective of human resistance or natural limitations. Marx seems to have been conscious of this as well, as seen from his comment in *Capital*:

> Capitalist production...ruthlessly enforces its will despite obstacles which are in any case largely of its own making. At all events, in order to portray the laws of political economy in their purity we are ignoring these sources of friction, as is the practice in mechanics when the frictions that arise have to be dealt with in every particular application of its general laws.[39]

---

36. See Sekine 1997a, which proceeds from 'The Pricing of Commodities' in Chapter One to 'The Functions of Money' in Chapter Two to 'The Operation of Capital' in Chapter Three, without bringing in the issue of labour. Labour and the production-process are brought in later, in discussing the historical development of the capitalist method of production.

37. Albritton 1999, pp. 24–5.

38. Kierkegaard 1992, p. 55.

39. Marx 1976e, p. 1014. This is from the famous 'Chapter Six' of *Capital*, 'Results of the Immediate Process of Production', published only after Marx's death.

Nevertheless, the way in which Albritton views the relation between the logical and historical raises many questions. Although Marx analysed capital as a product of specific conditions of production in which concrete labour becomes dominated by abstract labour, Albritton defends Uno's view that 'value must be thoroughly established and understood as a circulation form before its substantive grounding in the production process can be understood'.[40] In doing so, he takes issue with Marx for what he calls the 'weak and at times ambiguous presentation of the labour theory of value in the early pages of *Capital*'.[41] He argues that Marx was 'not fully cognisant of the above points and hence does not theorize capital's inner logic as a rigorous dialectical logic'.[42]

The view that forms of circulation and the market define the logic of capital leads Uno and some of his followers to conclude that the key to transcending capitalism is to abolish markets and establish state control of production.[43] Albritton writes, 'The USSR represented a huge effort to realise socialism and its failure to do so is tragic. It was relatively successful in some areas and less so in others...I disagree with [the] view that a planned economy can be capitalist'.[44]

The Unoists are not wrong to contend that grasping the logic of capital predetermines the understanding of its alternative. The problem is that their view of the logic of capital comes to grief in light of this very insight. Their claim that alienated labour is extrinsic to the logic of capital, whereas market-anarchy and private property is intrinsic to it, leads them to conclude that the abolition of the latter is the central precondition for a postcapitalist society. This leads them to hold onto a rather traditional view of 'socialism', one that is not likely to spark the imagination of a humanity that has absorbed the disastrous experiences of centrally planned economies in Eastern Europe and the USSR.[45]

---

40. Albritton 1999, p. 75.
41. Ibid.
42. Albritton 2008, p. 88.
43. See Albritton 1999, p. 180: 'The capitalist epoch will come to be seen as one which relied on incredibly crude economic mechanisms called "markets".' This tends to overlook the fact that markets existed before capitalism and that the market is far from being the *distinguishing* or *defining* feature of capitalism.
44. Albritton 2004, p. 89.
45. Sekine has a more critical attitude towards the former USSR, and a more expansive view of socialism as consisting of transformed ecocommunities based on a balance of production and consumption. It is not clear, however, if such a position meshes with his overall attitude to the determining role of markets. See Sekine 1990.

Another version of objectivist Marxism is found in the work of a number of thinkers associated with the latter-day Frankfurt school, such as Hans-Georg Backhaus. They seek to critically build on the insights of such pioneering figures of the Frankfurt school as Adorno, Horkheimer, Marcuse and Habermas while placing greater emphasis than they did on political economy and the exegesis of Marx's *Capital*. In his influential and comprehensive work *Dialektik der Wertform. Untersuchungen zur Marxschen Ökonomiekritik*, Backhaus argues that Marx's object of critique is not an empirically existing capitalism but rather the abstract logic of capital.[46] Like Uno and his followers, he emphasises that, for Marx, the universal forms of capital are the object of investigation, not its actual unfolding in history. Backhaus considers this of cardinal importance, since failure to grasp this leads to making the *personifications* of capital (businessmen, speculators, etc.) the object of critique, instead of capital's deep structure. For Backhaus, the determining force of modern society is not the capital*ists* but rather capital, which takes on a life of its own in a manner analogous to Hegel's concept of the absolute subject. He writes, 'The fusion of the subject-object inversion with the problem of the concept of capital is the fundamental theme of Marx's *œuvre*'.[47] He further specifies, 'Marx's basic thought, hitherto ignored by all economists, is that human beings confront their own generic forces, that is their "collective forces" or "social forces" as an autonomous, alien being. This thought culminates in the conception of the autonomous totality of social capital as a real total subject, which abstracts itself from the weal and woe of individual subjects and is "indifferent" to them'.[48]

Backhaus attempts to show that 'Marx describes capital as subject or as self-relation'.[49] In an argument that parallels the position of Uno and his followers, he contends that Hegel's Absolute Idea is 'adequate' to the Marxian concept of capital. *Capital*, he argues, is not Marx's *least* Hegelian work but his *most* Hegelian work – even more 'Hegelian' than the 1844 *Manuscripts*.

Despite his affinity with some positions of the Unoists, there are major differences between Backhaus and their approach. The most significant is that Backhaus contends that the core of the logic of capital is not the market and private property but the social form of labour. He argues that capital can take the form of a self-determining subject that disregards contingency only because the labour that produces it is subsumed by an abstraction. Whereas

---

46. See Backhaus 1997.
47. Backhaus 1992, p. 68.
48. Backhaus 1992, p. 81.
49. Backhaus 1992, p. 71.

the Unoists downplay the category of the dual character of labour in explaining capital's drive for self-expansion, Backhaus posits the concept of abstract labour as central to it.[50]

These themes are further elaborated in Moishe Postone's *Time, Labor and Social Domination: A Reinterpretation of Marx's Critical Theory*.[51] Postone's work centres on a critique of what he calls the central flaw of 'traditional Marxism': its *transhistorical* view of labour. By this he means the view of labour as an instrumental and socially-mediating activity that expresses the natural, species-essence of humanity. Although this view has been widely attributed to Marx by both his critics and followers, Marx himself held, as Postone shows, that labour in this sense exists only in capitalism. Only in capitalism does labour become the all-determining social relation, because only in capitalism does labour take on a *dual* character.[52] Its dual character lies in the opposition between concrete labour and abstract labour. Concrete labour is the array of differentiated forms of exertion that create useful products; abstract labour is undifferentiated human labour, 'labour in general'. The subsumption of concrete labour by abstract labour through the medium of socially-necessary labour-time reduces the former to a monotonous, repetitive, and routinised activity. It comes to dominate all social interaction. For Marx, abstract labour is the basis of value-production, which is *specific* to capitalism.

The problem with traditional Marxism, Postone suggests, is that it *naturalises* the form of labour specific to capitalism by viewing it in *metaphysical* terms. Traditional Marxism becomes so enamoured of the expansive power of labour in transforming conditions of natural existence that it adopts an affirmative attitude towards the very object of Marx's critique – the reduction of human contingency to the exigencies of abstract labour. It assumes that the source of capitalism's contradictions lies not in its alienating mode of labour but, rather, in unequal forms of *distribution*. The market and private property become seen as the main problem. Instead of grasping value as the expression of the specific *kind* of labour *in capitalism*, it becomes understood as a

---

50. Backhaus suggests that Hegel's writings, especially his *First Philosophy of Spirit*, anticipated Marx's concept of abstract labour. See Backhaus 1992, pp. 64–7.

51. Although Backhaus' *Dialektik der Wertform* was not published until 1997, several initial chapters of it appeared earlier, in the 1970s, and were widely discussed in Germany. Very little of his work is currently available in English.

52. It is important not to conflate Marx's famous contention that all forms of human society possess a particular mode of production with the claim that 'labour as such' is the defining and determining relation of all forms of society. Ancient Greek society, for instance, had a particular mode of production, but the notion that 'labour as such' was the determining social form was so far from view that Aristotle contended that 'action and production differ in kind...Life consists in action, not production'. See Aristotle 1998, p. 7 [1254a6–7].

'blind' mechanism regulating the exchange of commodities. For traditional Marxism, the abolition of this blind mechanism through state-planning and nationalised property is 'socialism'. The 'new society' is defined as having the nature of labour under capitalism – its role as a rational regulator of social relations – come into its own, unimpeded by 'market anarchy'. According to 'the interpretation of value as a category of the market', avers Postone, 'the same forms of wealth of labor that are distributed mediately in capitalism would be coordinated in socialism'.[53] Traditional Marxism assumes that 'in socialism the ontological principle of society appears openly, whereas in capitalism it is hidden'.[54]

Postone's critique of traditional Marxism illuminates important dimensions of the contemporary period. Many presume that the crisis of the welfare-state in the West and the collapse of 'actually existing socialism' in the East provide ample proof that capitalism has irretrievably triumphed over 'socialism' and that 'Marxism' is dead. Yet such a viewpoint is valid only *if* the aporiae of traditional Marxism are accepted. Marx held that the production of wealth is not the same as the production of value. The latter is historically specific and emerges only when labour assumes a dual character. This, not the existence of private property or the market, constitutes the core of the logic of capital. Whether surplus-value is appropriated by the state or the market is of secondary importance. Capitalism exists wherever the defining principle of social organisation is the reduction of human labour to ever-more abstract forms of value-creating labour. In this sense, what passed for 'socialism' turns out to be the very object of Marx's critique of capitalism. Postone concludes, 'Far from demonstrating the victory of capitalism over socialism, the recent collapse of "actually existing socialism" could be understood as signifying the collapse of the most rigid, vulnerable and oppressive form of state-interventionist capitalism'.[55]

Postone also contends that traditional Marxism errs in proclaiming the working class as the subject of social transformation. He argues, as do other objectivists, that the *subject* of modern society is not the human-being but *capital*. Capital takes on a life of its own *because* the subjectivity of workers becomes subsumed by abstract labour. Neither the workers nor any other social force can therefore be considered subjects of liberation. Since self-initiative and creative unfolding characterises capital and not labour, we must look not to proletarian class-struggle but to *capital* to point the way towards

---

53. Postone 1993, p. 49.
54. Postone 1993, p. 61.
55. Postone 1993, p. 14.

the transcendence of capitalism. Postone goes as far as to contend that *dead labour is the emancipatory alternative.*

Postone grounds this argument in the claim that the individuality of the labourer cannot be distinguished from the value-form of labour-power. Since workers cannot be separated from the value-form of their labouring activity (at least insofar as they function as workers) subjecting capitalism to critique from the standpoint of the labourer leads to adopting an affirmative attitude towards the value-form of labour-power. Such a standpoint makes unequal forms of distribution, instead of the nature of labour under capitalism, the object of critique. Traditional Marxism goes no further than stressing the difference between the value of labour-power and the value of the total product created by wage-labour. While such a standpoint may appear 'radical', it really goes no further than the position of such classical-political economists as David Ricardo. Postone argues, 'The identification of the proletariat (or the species) with the historical Subject rests ultimately on the same historically undifferentiated notion of "labor" as does Ricardian Marxism'.[56]

But if the working class or any other human agent is not the principle of emancipation, *how* can capitalism be overcome? It is overcome, Postone submits, by capital itself. He addresses this by focusing on 'the central contradiction of capitalism' – the drive to increase material wealth versus the drive to augment value. Capitalism is driven not only to produce material goods and services but also to augment value. Labour is the source of value and the magnitude of value is determined by the amount of socially-necessary labour-time it takes to produce a commodity. There is a continual contradiction between the drive to produce material wealth and to augment value. As productivity rises, more goods are produced in the same unit of time. Therefore, the value of each commodity falls. The increase in material wealth corresponds to a decline in the magnitude of value. Costs of production fall and prices tend to fall as a result. This presents capitalists with a knotty problem: the relative fall in the value of each commodity risks leaving them short of the funds needed to maintain their level of productive output. They respond by trying to further boost productivity, since the greater the quantity of goods produced, the better the opportunity to realise the value of his initial investment. The best way to increase productivity is to invest in labour-saving devices. The resulting growth in productivity, however, reproduces the problem, since the increase in material wealth leads to a further decrease in the relative value of each commodity. Thus, capitalism is based on a kind of treadmill-effect in

---

56. Postone 1993, p. 80.

which it is constantly driven towards technological innovation regardless of the human or environmental cost. The result is as follows:

> A growing disparity arises between developments in the productive powers of labor (which are not necessarily bound to the direct labor of the workers), on the one hand, and the value frame within which such developments are expressed (which *is* bound to such labor), on the other. The disparity between the accumulation of historical time and the objectification of immediate labor time becomes more pronounced as scientific knowledge is increasingly materialized in production…a growing disparity separates the conditions for the production of material wealth from those for the generation of value.[57]

The resulting 'shearing pressure' renders the system unstable. But how *exactly* does this lead to an emancipatory future? Postone does not say. On the one hand, he is trying to counter what is often seen as the pessimism of earlier theorists of the Frankfurt school like Adorno and Marcuse by insisting that capital is a two-dimensional entity that does not foreclose the possibility of liberation. On the other hand, he leaves us with little sense of how to close the gap between is and ought – especially since, as he emphasises, there is no reason to presume that capitalism will 'automatically collapse'. He writes, 'overcoming the historical Subject' – i.e. capital – 'would allow people, for the first time, to become the subjects of their own liberation'.[58] However, by refusing to identify human agents *in the present* who could help realise such a future, it becomes hard to see how capital can actually be 'overcome'. Posing *dead labour as the emancipatory alternative* by pointing to the 'shearing pressure' could hardly suffice so long as an automatic collapse of capitalism is ruled out of consideration.

Postone therefore has little to say about either a postcapitalist future or how to get there. What may be making it hard for him to do so is the theoretical conception he is most attached to – that *capital is the subject*. Postone's view of this is based on a specific reading of Hegel. As he sees it, Hegel's concept of the absolute subject bears a striking similarity to the concept of capital, since it is a self-moving substance that 'grounds itself.' He argues that Hegel's Absolute, as a self-referential entity, expresses the logic of capital as self-expanding value. He contends that Marx based his analysis of capital on this Hegelian notion, as seen in the chapter on 'The General Formula of Capital', in *Capital*, Volume I. There Marx writes, 'value is here the subject', 'an automatic

---

57. Postone 1993, p. 297.
58. Postone 1993, p. 224.

subject'; he calls value 'the dominant subject [*übergreifendes Subjekt*] of this process...'.[59]

Though this may appear to confirm the claim that Marx views capital as the absolute subject, the appearance is deceptive. It is important to keep in mind the context of 'The General Formula of Capital'. Marx is discussing the process of *circulation*, as embodied in the movement from money to commodity to more money (M-C-M'). This movement creates, by necessity, the *appearance* that value 'has the occult ability to add value to itself'.[60] However, Marx later shows that this appearance is dispelled once we enter the labour-process and encounter capital's dependence on living labour. As Marx shows in the next chapter, '*Contradictions* in the General Formula', value *appears* to self-expand on its own account so long as we restrict ourselves to the process of circulation. When we move to the production-process, however, we find that capital's claim to be the self-moving subject encounters internal *limits*, flowing from the dual character of labour. This is why Marx did not use the phrase 'value as subject' when he moved into the analysis of the production-process of capital.[61] As Marx wrote in the *Grundrisse*, capital 'cannot ignite itself anew through its own resources. *Circulation therefore does not carry within itself the principle of self-renewal*...Commodities therefore have to be thrown into it anew from the outside, like fuel into a fire. Otherwise it flickers out in indifference'.[62]

These and other passages indicate that Marx does think that capital takes on the form of a self-moving substance or subject – *insofar as we view capital from the viewpoint of the process of circulation*. Postone, as noted above, criticises 'traditional Marxism' for emphasising the process of circulation at the expense of the forms of production. In opposition to this standpoint of 'traditional Marxism', he seeks to redirect radical theory towards a thoroughgoing critique of the *production*-relations of contemporary society. In doing so, however, Postone *imports* a category that Marx uses to express the *circulation*-process into an effort to highlight the dynamics of the *production*-process. Despite his emphatic opposition to theoretical approaches that view production-relations as a mere reflection of the process of circulation, he prioritises a category that is actually adequate to the sphere of circulation. In a

---

59. Marx 1976e, p. 255.
60. Ibid.
61. The *development* of Marx's *Capital* further raises questions about Postone's claim that Marx posed capital or 'dead labour' as the subject. Marx revised *Capital* substantially when he issued the French edition in 1872–5 and stated that it possesses a 'scientific value independent of the original'. In the French edition, Marx removed all three references to capital and value as subject. See Marx 1989c, p. 124.
62. Marx 1986a 28, p. 186. Emphases are in the original.

word, by conflating Marx's discussion of value as '*an* automatic subject' at a specific point in the analysis of capitalist circulation with value as *the* absolute subject in Marx's analysis of capitalism as a whole, Postone contravenes his own insistence concerning the importance of not elevating the sphere of distribution or circulation above that of production.

Since Postone thinks that *capital* is the subject of modern society, and not the workers or other human forces of liberation, he is led to argue that the alternative to capital will ultimately emerge not from the development of *human* agents like the proletariat but rather from capital itself. *Capital is indeed the emancipatory alternative for Postone.* Yet what are the emancipatory forms that we could expect to see emerge from the self-development of capital? Is there a role for *human* subjectivity in overcoming capital, and if so, what is it? Aside from mentioning in passing the way in which capital generates new needs and desires, he does not say. Postone reaches something of an impasse when it comes to addressing the *specific* forms of life which can replace the logic of capital, especially since he (correctly) emphasises that simply abolishing the market is not a solution.

The third grouping of objectivist Marxists are those who subscribe to 'systematic dialectics', an independent school of thought developed over the past two decades. The most prominent of these theorists is C.J. Arthur, author of *The New Dialectic and Marx's 'Capital'*. Arthur's work falls in between the positions of the Unoists and Postone. Like the Unoists, he emphasises the distinction between the logic of capital and capitalism's historical development. Like Postone, he emphasises the homology between Marx's delineation of the logic of capital and Hegel's logic of the concept. However, he differs from Postone in placing more emphasis on forms of circulation and monetary relations than on production-relations, and he differs from the Unoists in placing more emphasis on subjective forms of resistance to capital.

Arthur contends that most commentators on Marx have failed to come to grips with the complexity of his ideas because they conflate *historical* dialectics with *systematic* dialectics. Historical dialectics deals with the rise and fall of actual social systems. Systematic dialectics, on the other hand, deals with 'a given whole and demonstrates how it reproduces itself: thus the ordering of the categories is in no way determined by the recapitulation of a historical chain of causality; it is articulated on the basis of purely systematic considerations'.[63] Marx's *Capital*, he argues, is best understood as 'the articulation of categories to conceptualize an existent concrete whole'. The order in which Marx presents the categories does not correspond to 'the order of

---

63. Arthur 2002, p. 64.

their actual appearance in history'.[64] Capital consists of a *sequential* ordering of abstract categories, not a *consequential* ordering of how they actually unfold in history.

Arthur convincingly shows that conflating the historical with the systematic has led to gross misunderstandings of Marx's work, beginning with Marx's closest colleague and follower, Friedrich Engels. Marx's discussion in Chapter One of *Capital* on the commodity-form and the forms of value is notoriously difficult, and has given rise to numerous efforts to justify or reject the apparent reliance on what Rosa Luxemburg once called 'its Hegelian rococo'.[65] An early attempt to make sense of these difficulties was offered by Engels, who held that the development from the 'simple' to the 'general' or universal commodity-form in Chapter One referred to the historical development from small-scale commodity-production to more complex forms in advanced industrial capitalism. He held that Chapter One is best understood by discerning the *historical sequence* implied by Marx's analytical categories. Arthur finds this highly specious. Chapter One, he says, has nothing to do with a historical delineation of commodity-production. Although it begins with the 'simple' exchange of one product of labour for another, Marx is referencing not a particular historical stage (like small-scale or petty commodity-exchange) but rather the determinate *social form* that characterises a chemically-pure capitalism. Marx begins with the most simple or abstract expression of the social form that characterises capitalism in order to draw out the developmental logic of capital as a whole. Just as Hegel begins his *Science of Logic* with the most elementary and barren category, 'Being', that nevertheless implicitly contains the whole, so Marx begins *Capital* with the most elementary expression of the commodity-form that contains within itself the elements that call for systematic elaboration. Marx's historical account of capitalism appears only at the end of Volume I of *Capital*, not at the beginning, because the historical phenomenon of capitalism can only be comprehended from the vantage-point of the systemic and abstract *logic* of capital.[66]

The impatience to leap from the abstract to the concrete, from the systematic to the historical, explains why many have found Marx's *Capital* difficult to grasp. Even Engels conceded in letters to Marx, as he was reading the galley-proofs of Chapter One, that he found it hard to follow the argument. Arthur

---

64. Arthur 2002, p. 4.
65. See Luxemburg 1978, p. 184.
66. This is not to suggest that Marx makes references to historical development only at the conclusion of *Capital*. In discussing money in Chapter Two, Marx does discuss the historical sequence by which precious metals came to serve as money. This does not, however, constitute a historical rendition of the development of capitalism itself.

writes that to adequately comprehend Marx, we need to recognise that 'The key transition in *Capital* is not from simple commodity production to capitalist production, but from the "sphere of simple circulation or the exchange of commodities" to "the hidden abode of production".'[67]

Like other objectivist Marxists, Arthur sees a homology between Marx's *Capital* and Hegel's *Science of Logic*. The homology may not be self-evident, since Arthur assumes that 'Hegel was an idealist' whereas Marx was a 'materialist'.[68] The homology nevertheless exists, he argues, because capitalism is above all a *monetary* economy characterised by the same kind of 'immanent abstractness' found in Hegel's delineation of the logic of the concept. He writes, 'In value-form theory it is the development of the forms of exchange that is seen as the prime determinant of the capitalist economy'.[69] Hence, the forms of value and capital analysed by Marx 'are in effect of such abstract purity as to constitute a real incarnation of the ideas in Hegel's logic'.[70] On these grounds 'capital may be seen as the avatar of Hegel's absolute concept'.[71]

This places Arthur closer to the Unoists than to Postone, who contends that production rather than exchange or monetary relations constitutes the inner core of the logic of capital. Whereas Postone ties value-production to the dual character of labour, Arthur asks 'but can it make sense to speak of value where there are no markets?'[72] As Arthur sees it, labour can be brought into the dialectic of capital only *after* the general form of value, or money, has been delineated. He denies that the social form of labour is the defining or constitutive feature of capital: 'Labour and value are not to be positively identified with each other'.[73] As he sees it, it is not that labour becomes abstract in the process of production which *then* lends an abstractive character to value and capital; instead, it is monetary or exchange-relations that render labour abstract: 'It may still be the case that labour becomes "abstract" only when products are priced'.[74]

On these grounds, Arthur takes issue with Chapter One of *Capital*, which discusses the dual character of labour *prior* to discussing the forms of value and money. Arthur writes, 'It is notorious that Marx dives down from the phenomenon of exchange-value to labour as the substance of value in the first

---

67. Arthur 2002, p. 24.
68. Arthur 2002, p. 10.
69. Arthur 2002, p. 11.
70. Arthur 2002, p. 82.
71. Arthur 2002, p. 141.
72. Arthur 2002, p. 94.
73. Arthur 2002, p. 40.
74. Arthur 2002, p. 46. See also 157: 'It is *through* exchange that abstraction imparts itself to labour, making it abstract human labour'.

three pages of *Capital* and people rightly complain that they do not find any proof there'.[75] In contrast to Marx's approach, he thinks that it is best to

> ...leave aside initially any labour content – in this way I am departing from Marx who analyzed both together...I differ from Marx in that I refuse to find it necessary to come to labour until after conceptualizing capital as a form-determination. Bringing in labour too early risks giving the appearance of model-building.[76]

He contends that, in *Capital*, 'Marx has a dogmatic beginning in so far as he presupposes the items exchanged are labour products'.[77]

Given the overriding importance that Marx ascribed to his category of the dual character of labour, this raises the question of whether Arthur fully does justice to the content of *Capital*. How do we square Arthur's claim that his 'systematic-dialectical' approach is best-suited to understanding Marx's actual aim and intent in *Capital*, when that very approach compels him to call into question Marx's exposition of what he called his 'original contribution' which is 'crucial to an understanding of political economy'?[78]

Arthur also distances himself from the Unoists by arguing that labour is not extrinsic to the dialectic of capital. Although he thinks that Marx was mistaken to bring forms of labour into Chapter One of *Capital*, he thinks that the *logic* of capital never succeeds in completely freeing itself from dependence on living labour. 'The problem for capital', he writes, 'is that it needs the *agency* of labour'[79] in order to create *surplus*-value. In his view, labour needs to be brought into the logic of capital in order to explain how the capitalist manages to compel workers to produce more value than they themselves consume. At *this* level of the logic of capital – that of the discrepancy between the value of labour-power and the value of the total product – resistance is bound to occur:[80]

> The former 'subjects' of production are treated as manipulable objects; but it is still a question of manipulating their activity, not of depriving them of all subjectivity. They act for capital, indeed *as capital*, but still in some sense *act*...Thus, even if Marx is right that the productive power of labour

---

75. Arthur 2002, p. 12.
76. Arthur 2002, pp. 79–80, 85.
77. Arthur 2002, pp. 157–8.
78. Marx 1976e, p. 132.
79. Arthur 2002, p. 52.
80. Albritton responds thus: 'Because of the way Arthur inserts class struggle into the dialectic of capital, it becomes impossible to theorize capital's inner logic as a whole dialectically...Class struggle, strictly speaking, is outside the theory'. See Albritton 2005, pp. 179, 182.

is absorbed into that of capital to all intents, it is necessary to bear in mind that capital still depends on it. Moreover, the repressed subjectivity of the workers remains a threat to capital's purposes in this respect.[81]

What does Arthur's 'systematic dialectics' suggest about a possible alternative to capitalism? Like most objectivists, he prefers to say little about the future on the grounds that the main burden of a Marxian critique consists of tracing out the trajectory of *capital*. Although he finds a place for subjective resistance within the logic of capital, he refrains from suggesting that it contains any immanent indication of the content of a new society. Still, the considerable emphasis that he places on market and monetary relations suggests that he considers the abolition of the market the *pons asini* of the negation of capitalism. On these grounds, he rejects Postone's characterisation of the USSR and other state-command economies as 'state-capitalist'. At the same time, he is very critical of Soviet-type régimes because their reliance on extra-economic force to spur economic growth led to gross inefficiencies. He writes, 'A negation of capital that fails to go beyond capital is necessarily a negation of capital that falls behind capital'.[82] What might constitute a negation of capital that truly *transcends* capital, however, is a matter that his work leaves largely unaddressed.

A diverse group of thinkers who have developed a very different approach from the objectivists are *autonomist* Marxists. I refer to them as *subjectivists* because they contend that the focus of Marx's work is delineating the forms of subjective resistance that arise against the logic of capital. They distance themselves from the arguments of the objectivists in a number of important ways. First, instead of viewing labour and capital as distinct, externally-connected entities, they hold that capital emerges and develops in response to struggles against oppression and exploitation. Workers not only *resist* the *development* of capital, but their resistance is also responsible for the very *constitution* of capital. Mario Tronti articulated this position as early as 1964: 'We too have worked with a concept that puts capitalist development first, and workers second. This was a mistake. And now we have to turn the problem on its head, reverse the polarity and start again from the beginning: and the beginning is the class struggle of the working class'.[83]

Each stage of capitalist production, Tronti and other autonomists argue, took shape in response to specific forms of mass resistance. Though it *appears*

---

81. Arthur 2002, p. 52.
82. Arthur 2002, p. 211.
83. Tronti 1979, p. 1.

that capital is in control of modern society, it is actually a reactive, not creative force.[84]

Second, instead of viewing capital as a self-determining movement that effaces barriers to its self-expansion, they argue that it is an inherently unstable and antagonistic form constantly torn between the drive to augment value and the struggles that resist value-production. Antonio Negri writes, 'The focus in Marx is always the actuality and the determinacy of the antagonism'.[85] John Holloway develops these issues as follows:

> The defining feature of Marxist economics is the idea that capitalism can be understood in terms of certain regularities (the so-called laws of motion of capitalist development). These regularities refer to the regular (but contradictory) pattern of the reproduction of capital, and Marxist economics focuses on the study of capital and its contradictory reproduction...The attempts to use Marx's own categories to develop a theory of capitalist reproduction are, however, always problematic, in so far as the categories of Marxism derive from a quite different question, based not on the reproduction but on the destruction of capitalism, not on positivity but on negativity...By a strange twist, Marxism, from being a theory of the destruction of capitalist society, becomes a theory of its reproduction.[86]

Third, whereas the objectivists emphasise Marx's contributions to economics and the intersections between philosophy and economics, the autonomists see Marx's project primarily in *political* terms. Negri writes, 'Clearly, profit and wage continue to exist, but they exist only as quantities regulated by a relation of power...If anything, the marketing of labour-power today has become a totally political operation'.[87]

Fourth, whereas all of the objectivists agree that Marx is deeply indebted to Hegel, the autonomists often see Marx's philosophical lineage quite differently. Negri argues that Marx's thought draws most of all from the pre-Kantian philosophy of Spinoza. Holloway argues that Marx's work can best be understood from the vantage-point of Frankfurt-school Marxist Theodor Adorno's *Negative Dialectics*.

---

84. As Holloway 2002, p. 143 puts it: 'Class struggle does not take place within the constituted forms of capitalist social relations; rather the constitution of those forms is itself a class struggle'.
85. Negri 1988, p. 221.
86. Holloway 2002, pp. 134, 136.
87. Negri 1988, pp. 224–5.

Since the writings of the autonomist Marxists are numerous and diverse, I will focus on what many consider a defining text of the tendency: Antonio Negri's *Marx Beyond Marx: Lessons on the 'Grundrisse'*.[88]

Negri's influential work consists of a close analysis of Marx's *Grundrisse*, his 'rough draft' of *Capital* which was written in 1857–8. Marx's massive nine-hundred-page tome was unknown prior to the 1930s, and it has long been considered one of Marx's most enigmatic and difficult texts. Negri focuses on this work because it is 'the point where the objective analysis of capital and the subjective analysis of class behavior come together'.[89] It is a counter to what he considers 'the blind objectivism of a certain Marxist tradition'.[90] As he sees it, the *Grundrisse* is superior to *Capital* because the latter suffers from precisely what the Unoists and the theorists of systematic dialectics find attractive in it – 'a certain objectivism' in which economic categories take on a life of their own:

> The movement of the *Grundrisse* toward *Capital* is a happy process; we cannot say the same of the reverse movement. The *Grundrisse* represents the summit of Marx's revolutionary thought... *Capital* is this text which served to reduce critique to economic theory, to annihilate subjectivity in objectivity, to subject the subversive capacity of the proletariat to the reorganizing and repressive intelligence of capitalist power.[91]

The *Grundrisse*, writes Negri, is 'an essentially open work... the categories are not flattened out, the imagination does not stagnate'.[92] What many find forbidding about this work – what Marx once called 'its sauerkraut and carrots shapelessness' – is seen by Negri as a virtue, since it allows the *antagonistic* and unstable nature of the Marxian value-categories to come more readily to the fore.

This is most directly seen in how 'in the *Grundrisse* work appears as immediately abstract labour'.[93] Although the book begins with a lengthy chapter on 'Money', Marx makes it clear (more so than in *Capital*, according to Negri) that money can serve as a universal equivalent of commodity-exchange only if living labour is already subsumed by a disembodied abstraction. Money *conceals* this process, since (as Marx put it) 'all inherent contradictions of bourgeois society appear extinguished in money relations as conceived in a simple

---

88. I have addressed Holloway's work in more detail elsewhere. See Hudis 2004b.
89. Negri 1984, p. 9.
90. Negri 1984, p. 13.
91. Negri 1984, pp. 18–19.
92. Negri 1984, p. 12.
93. Negri 1984, p. 10.

form'.[94] Negri contends that Marx's genius is expressed in his ability to analyse the fetishised forms of money in light of the hidden social relations of
labour. Money can become the universal equivalent only if concrete labour
is subsumed by abstract labour; but abstract labour is produced in the same
instant as concrete labour by the living labourer. An *internal tension* is built
into all of Marx's value-theoretical categories, including such abstract ones
as money. The subjectivity of the labourer can therefore never be abstracted
from the logic of capital. Negri writes, 'Marx characterizes the working class
as a solid subjectivity...as an historical and social essence...its essence as
creator of value is engaged in a continual struggle'.[95]

Negri argues that this subject-object dynamic is especially pronounced in
Marx's theory of crisis, which was first formulated in the *Grundrisse*. Central
to this theory of crisis is the concept of the tendency for the rate of profit
to decline. In the *Grundrisse*, Negri writes, the decline in profit-rates is not
treated as a function of quasi-automatic economic laws operating on their
own. Capitalists try to maintain or boost profit-rates by increasing the proportion of *surplus*-labour (labour-time that is *beyond* that needed to reproduce
the labourer) relative to *necessary* labour (labour-time needed to reproduce the
labourer). However, there are 'rigid limits' beyond which necessary labour
cannot be further reduced, since capital needs the living labourer to produce
value. Capital nevertheless pushes against this rigid limit, and the labourers
respond by intensifying their resistance to the drive to diminish the sphere of
necessary labour. As a result, capitalism is unable to extract as much surplus-
value as previously, leading to a decline in the rate of profit. Negri concludes,
'The law of the tendency to decline represents, therefore, one of the most lucid
Marxist intuitions of the intensification *of the class struggle* in the course of
capitalist development'.[96]

As Negri acknowledges, Marx further developed his concept of the tendency of the rate of profit to decline in what was to become *Capital*, Volume III.
There, Marx ties the decline not only to the contradiction between necessary
and surplus-labour, but also to the rising organic composition of capital. As
capitalists invest in greater amounts of technology and labour-saving devices,
the amount of value-creating labour declines relative to constant capital, pre-
cipitating a decline in profit-rates. Negri finds this to be a step backwards
from the *Grundrisse*, since it attributes the decline in profit rates to purely
objective factors. In *Capital*, he contends, 'The entire relation will be dislocated

---

94. Marx 1986a, p. 172.
95. Negri 1984, p. 73.
96. Negri 1984, p. 101.

on an economistic level and objectified improperly'. It is an approach that 'eliminates the class struggle as a fundamental and rigid variable'.[97]

No part of the *Grundrisse* better exemplifies Marx's prioritisation of subjective resistance, he argues, than the discussion of the cooperative form of labour. Marx indicates that the 'real' or total subsumption of labour by capital does not efface agency, since workers forge bonds of association and cooperation as they are brought together in productive enterprises. The centralisation of capital *necessitates* a greater socialisation of labour. The more that labourers are socialised, the more they learn how to cooperatively battle capital: 'This objective process, dominated by capital, begins to reveal *the new subjective level of the working class*. A qualitative leap occurs: the unity of working class behaviors begins to be self-sufficient.'[98] Living labour develops from being a component part of capital to taking on 'constituent power'. This 'power is established politically on that social cooperation that is congenital to living labour...in the cooperative immediacy of living labour, constituent power finds its creative massification'.[99]

This reading of the *Grundrisse*, which informs all of his later work, takes Negri far from objectivist readings of Marx. He sums up his position as follows: 'In so far as we refuse the objectivist interpretations of the *"school of capital-logic"* – which infinitely assert the power of capital to possess and command all development – in so far as we reject this, it seems to us that we must also avoid the *path of subjectivity* which imputes capital to an objectification *tout court*'.[100] Instead of focusing one-sidedly on capital-as-subject, Negri holds, we should recognise that all of the categories employed by Marx are two-dimensional and inherently antagonistic. Hence, capital cannot 'self-expand' unless labour does as well: 'The other subject, the worker, must emerge, since capitalist subsumption does not efface its identity but just dominates its activity: this subject must emerge precisely at the level to which the collective force of social capital has led the process. *If capital is a subject on one side, on the other labour must be a subject as well'*.[101]

---

97. Ibid. Negri's claim is highly questionable, however, since the last chapter of the *Grundrisse* also ties the decline in the rate of profit to such 'objective' and 'economic' factors as the organic composition of capital.

98. Negri 1984, p. 124.

99. Negri 1999, p. 32. Although the term 'constituent power' is not found in *Marx Beyond Marx*, Negri's later use of this term flows directly from this earlier work's discussion of the cooperative form of labour. In his more recent work 'constituent power' is not restricted by Negri to the industrial working class, but is applied to the 'multitude' that resists the dominating framework of 'Empire'.

100. Negri 1984, p. 132.

101. Negri 1984, p. 123.

Although Negri's effort to account for agency illuminates important aspects of Marx's work, one can ask whether his interpretation takes matters too far. Is it really the case that *every* stage of capitalist development is a product of heightened subjective resistance? Negri thinks so, as seen from his analysis of the major changes in contemporary capitalism. In *Empire* and *Multitude*, Negri and Hardt identify two such shifts: one is the 1970s, when capitalism abandoned the 'Fordist' model of mass-industrial production stimulated by Keynesian fiscal policies, and the other is the 1990s and 2000s, when the axis of power shifted from imperial nation-states towards an integrated global system. Both changes, they contend, represented capital's response to intensifying subjective resistance. The first came in response to the increased bargaining power and strikes of workers as well as the mass-movements of the 1960s, while the second, they contend, came in response to more diffuse forms of resistance as proletarian or industrial labour was replaced by struggles of the 'mass' or 'social worker' – those employed in the service-sector, the domestic sphere, etc. It seems highly questionable, however, that the move towards a globally-integrated world-capitalism was a response to intensifying struggles by 'new forms of constitutive power', given the political quiescence that has prevailed in the dominant capitalist nations, especially over the last several decades. It also seems questionable whether the decline of corporate profit-rates claimed by some analysts has come as a direct result of intensified social struggles.

Even more questions can be raised about whether the autonomist approach takes us further than the objectivists when it comes to envisaging an alternative to capitalist value-production. According to Negri 'there is no value without exploitation'; hence, a postcapitalist society is 'the destruction at the same time of the law of value itself, of its capitalist or socialist variants'.[102] A new society can only mean 'the destruction of capital in every sense of the term. It is non-work, it is the subjective, collective and proletarian planning of the suppression of exploitation. It is the possibility of a free constitution of subjectivity'.[103]

But what *specific* forms of social organisation are needed to end value-production and capital? What model or arrangement of society can allow for the 'free constitution of subjectivity'? Negri thinks it is pointless to try to answer such questions, since a new society can only emerge from the forms of socialisation and cooperation arising from spontaneous struggles: 'In [Marx's] materialist methodology the only kind of anticipation allowed is the one that moves in the rhythm of the tendency. This is therefore a complete refusal of

---

102. Negri 1984, p. 83.
103. Negri 1984, p. 169.

utopia and a limitation on his research on the contemporary historical limits of capitalist development'.[104]

Negri and Hardt make this explicit in *Empire* by suggesting that the quest for a new society is so immanent in everyday struggles that there is no need to *theoretically* articulate an ultimate goal: 'Empire creates a greater potential for revolution than did the modern régimes of power because it presents us...with an alternative: a multitude that is directly opposed to Empire, *with no mediation* between them'.[105] The transcendence of capital occurs quasi-automatically, from the exuberance of the multitude overflowing the boundaries of capital.

Although Negri is highly critical of theories that emphasise the automaticity of capital's self-expansion, he seems to fall prey to embracing automaticity in another guise, insofar as he thinks that an alternative to capitalism will arise spontaneously, without the mediation of *theoretical* labour that tries to envisage future modes of social organisation.[106] 'Exuberance', after all, has no necessary connection to *thought* – let alone *conceptual* thought that tries to envisage the *future*. Despite (or perhaps *because of*) his subjectivist approach, he does not have much more to say about a postcapitalist society than the objectivists do.

Although most of the re-examinations of Marx's work over the last several decades can be characterised as primarily objectivist or subjectivist, the work of several thinkers does not fall neatly into these categories, even if they share some similarities with them. One such thinker is Tony Smith. Although he advocates what I have termed the objectivist position of systematic dialectics, he has major differences with some of its proponents. He places much more emphasis on labour and resistance than Arthur does, and he also has a very different view of the Hegel-Marx relation. In contrast to all of the objectivists reviewed in this study, Smith does not agree that there is a homology between the logic of capital and Hegel's logic of the concept in the *Science of Logic*. He writes,

> The picture of Hegel trying to deduce the content of nature and spirit from his logical categories is a myth that caricatures what we now know of his actual working procedures...Those who go to the chapter on the Absolute Idea looking for some metaphysical supersubject will be disappointed; it

---

104. Negri 1999, p. 264.
105. Hardt and Negri 2000, p. 393.
106. The same problem is exhibited in the work of C.L.R. James, who once proclaimed that 'the new society already exists; we merely have to record the facts of its existence'. For a critical evaluation of James's legacy, see Hudis 2005b.

consists entirely of an account of the dialectical methodology used in the *Logic* as a whole.[107]

Smith does not deny that capital is a 'supersubject'. He *does* deny that Marx based his view of capital on Hegel's logic of the concept, since the latter does not blot out or annul particularity and contingency.

This has important ramifications for envisaging a new society, since Smith contends that the concluding book to Hegel's *Science of Logic*, the 'Doctrine of the Concept' [Notion], which centres on his concept of the Syllogism, actually 'provides the framework for comprehending socialism, not capitalism'.[108] Through a close textual reading of the *Science of Logic*, Smith argues that Hegel does not privilege any of the three terms of the syllogism – Universal, Particular, and Individual – but, rather, presents them as irreducible components. Universality does not 'blot out' the particular or the individual; it rather enables both to be expressed and cognised. Therefore, he argues, the logic of the concept cannot be the correlate of capital's abstract universality, which is completely indifferent to particularity and contingency. As he sees it, Hegel, like Marx, 'wants a totality that does not blot out the principle of subjectivity, individuality, personality. And this is what is termed socialism'.[109]

The implication is that we can gain greater insight into Marx's concept of a new society – and perhaps even further explain that concept for today's realities – by exploring more closely the actual content of Hegel's most abstract works, including the conclusion of his *Science of Logic*.[110]

Another thinker who does not readily fit into the category of subjectivist or objectivist is Raya Dunayevskaya. Not unlike the autonomists, she stresses that all of Marx's value-theoretical categories are tightly tied to conditions of labour and struggles that challenge the hegemony of value-production. She writes that 'Economics is a matter not only of the economic laws of breakdown of capitalism, but of the strife between the worker and the machine against dead labour's domination over living labour, beginning with hearing the worker's voice, which has been "stifled in the storm and stress of the process of production".'[111] However, unlike Negri and the autonomists, she does not deny that capital is defined by a 'law of motion' that develops indepen-

---

107. Smith 1993, pp. 18, 29.
108. Smith 1993, p. 29.
109. Smith 1993, p. 31.
110. Although there are few direct references to the last chapter of Hegel's *Science of Logic* in Marx's works, he directly commented, and at considerable length, on the concluding chapter of Hegel's *Phenomenology of Spirit*, 'Absolute Knowledge.' Although Marx's notes on this chapter are of considerable importance, they have long been neglected. An English translation is found in the Appendix, below, pp. 216–21.
111. Dunayevskaya 1981, p. 140.

dent of the will of the producers (Note her use of the phrase 'not only of the economic laws' in the above.) Instead of reducing *every* stage of capitalism to a response to subjective revolt, she argues that Marx has a more nuanced view that avoids posing a one-to-one relation between the objective and subjective. Moreover, she rejects Negri's contention that *Capital* is more 'objectivist' and 'economistic' than the *Grundrisse*, even though she acknowledges that it analyses a chemically-pure capitalism. She writes, 'In the last part of the work, "Accumulation of Capital", as we approach the most "economist" and "scientific" development – "the organic composition of capital" – Marx reminds us all over again that this organic composition cannot be considered outside of its effects "on the lot of the labouring classes'.[112] Marx, she contends, traces out the logic of capital as an *objective* movement while keeping his finger on the pulse of *human* relations.

Dunayevskaya also has a distinctive view of the Hegel-Marx relation. First, she does not accept the prevailing assumption that Hegel is an 'idealist' and Marx is a 'materialist'. She notes that Hegel has a materialist dimension and that there are idealist components in Marx. Second, she argued (even more forcefully than Smith) that Hegel's 'Doctrine of the Concept' does not annul particularity and contingency. She particularly calls attention to the inclusion of the chapter on 'Life' near the end of the 'Doctrine of the Concept' in the *Science of Logic*. She notes that Hegel wrote that his logic of the concept (to use his own words) should be viewed not as 'a mere abstract Universal, but as a Universal which comprises in itself the full wealth of Particulars'.[113] Hegel in fact repeatedly emphasises that the 'Idea has its reality in some kind of matter'.[114] As she sees it, the 'whole Logic (both logic and *Logic*) is a logic of self-determination', but that does not mean that it annuls objectivity. The logic of the concept cannot be so easily reduced to the logic of capital. Third, she argues that the last chapter of the *Logic*, the 'Absolute Idea', which centres on the 'the negation of the negation', is of great importance in illuminating Marx's concept of a new society, since both the 1844 *Manuscripts* and *Capital* explicitly refer to the transcendence of capitalism in terms of 'the negation of the negation.'[115] On these grounds, she argues that the realities of our era make it imperative to return *directly* to Hegel's Absolutes in working out a conception of the alternative to capitalism. Fourth, she denies that Hegel's Absolutes represent a closure or the 'end of history'. So imbued are Hegel's

---

112. Dunayevskaya 1981, p. 140.
113. Hegel 1979, p. 58.
114. Hegel 1979, p. 759. See also Dunayevskaya 2002, p. 71.
115. In the 1844 *Manuscripts* Marx writes, 'Communism is the position as the negation of the negation'. See Marx 1975r, p. 306. See also Marx 1976e, p. 929.

Absolutes with negativity that each high point is but the jumping-off point for new beginnings:

> Whatever Hegel said, and meant, about the Owl of Minerva spreading its wings only at dusk simply does not follow from the *objectivity* of the drive, the *summation* in which the advance is immanent in the present. While he neither gave, nor was interested in, any blueprints for the future, he was not preoccupied with death, the 'end' of philosophy, much less of the world...When subjected to the dialectical method from which, according to Hegel, no truth can escape, the conclusion turns out to be a new beginning. There is no trap in thought. Though it is finite, it breaks through the barriers of the given, reaches out, if not to infinity, surely beyond the historic moment.[116]

At the same time, Dunayevskaya does not argue that Marx's work is a mere application of Hegelian categories. Although *Capital* owes much to Hegel's *Logic*, she argues that it also represents a sharp departure from it. This is because the *subject* of Hegel's dialectic is disembodied thought, whereas the *subject* in *Capital* is the human-being who resists capital's 'process of suction'. She writes,

> *Capital*...is the Great Divide from Hegel, and not just because the subject is economics rather than philosophy...It is that Great Divide because, *just because*, the Subject – not subject matter, but Subject – was neither economics nor philosophy but the human being, the masses. Because dead labour (capital) dominates over living labour, and the labour*er* is the 'gravedigger of capitalism', all of human existence is involved. *This* dialectic is therefore totally new, totally internal, deeper than ever was the Hegelian dialectic which had *de*humanized the self-development of humanity in the dialectic of Consciousness, Self-Consciousness, Reason. Marx could transcend the Hegelian dialectic not by denying that it was 'the source of all dialectic'; rather, it was precisely because he began with that source that he could make the leap to the live Subject who is the one who transforms reality.[117]

According to the above interpretation, the problem that Marx has with Hegel is not that Hegel is an idealist who ignores empirical realities like economics or the labour-process. Nor is Marx distinguished from Hegel in being an economist, instead of a philosopher. Instead, Marx departs from Hegel over the latter's failure to pose the labour*er* as the active subject of the dialectical process. In doing so, Hegel is led to violate his own principle insofar as he

---

116. Dunayevskaya 2002, p. 184.
117. Dunayevskaya 1981, p. 143.

is compelled to reach for an force standing outside and above the historical process – disembodied 'absolute spirit' – to resolve its contradictions. Marx's effort to correct this deficiency in Hegel leads him to posit workers as the actual subject.

The philosophical literature on Marx over the past several decades clearly reveals a wide disparity of interpretations and approaches. It should only be expected that Marx would be subject to such widely varying interpretations, given the expansive and contentious nature of his philosophical project. What is clear, however, is that many of the approaches towards Marx settle for analysing one aspect of his *œuvre* at the expense of others. Except for Back-haus, all of the objectivists considered in this study focus on *Capital* while passing over the work of the young Marx, especially the 1844 *Manuscripts*. Negri and the autonomists, on the other hand, emphasise the *Grundrisse* at the expense of *Capital* and say little about Volumes II and III of *Capital*. Almost none of the thinkers surveyed say anything about the last decade of Marx's life, when he turned his attention to the study of precapitalist societies. The tendency to *fragment* Marx by studying aspects of his work in isolation from others has not only made it difficult to evaluate whether or not Marx's body of work is internally coherent, it has created a major obstacle to coming to grips with Marx's concept of the transcendence of value-production. Since Marx never devoted a work to the alternative to capitalism, and since any implicit or explicit suggestions on his part about an alternative have to be gleaned from a careful study of an array of diverse and difficult texts, the tendency to analyse one part of Marx's *œuvre* at the expense of others has made it all the harder to discern whether he has a distinctive concept of a new society that addresses the realities of the twenty-first century.

Bertell Ollman addresses this problem in noting that the theorists of systematic dialectics are unable to take account of the *whole* of Marx's *Capital*, since it clearly contains not only logical but also historical analysis. He writes, '*Capital* I contains whole sections that, according to the proponents of Systematic Dialectics...simply don't belong there or are simply out of place'.[118] I would add that this also applies to many of the subjectivist theorists who cannot account for parts of Marx's work that emphasise systematic and objective approaches. It is possible, of course, that different philosophical tendencies can latch onto one or another angle of Marx's thought because he was an inconsistent and contradictory thinker who invites divergent interpretations. Yet it is also possible, as Ollman notes, that many interpretations of his work represent 'misguided attempts to reduce Marx's varied strategies to a single

---

118. Ollman 2003, pp. 183–4.

one...at the expense of the others'.[119] It is possible that Marx employed a host of argumentative and conceptual strategies based on his specific concerns and object of investigation, and it is all too easy to fall into one-sided readings which fail to take account of his work as a whole. However, if we cannot make sense of Marx's work as a whole, is it really possible to discern whether or not his work contains a concept of a new society that is worth re-examining today? With this in mind, it is time to return to the whole of Marx, with new eyes.

---

119. Ollman 2003, pp. 187–8.

Chapter One

The Transcendence of Alienation in the Writings of the Young Marx

> *In the general relationship which the philosopher sees between the world and thought, he merely makes objective for himself the relation of his own particular consciousness to the real world.*
>
> Karl Marx (1841)[1]

Marx's beginnings, 1837–41

Two aspects of Marx's early work are of concern to us here. One aspect is the values and principles that the young Marx upheld and brought to bear on his subsequent analysis of capitalist production.[2] It is hardly conceivable that Marx could have developed such a thoroughgoing and virulent criticism of capitalism merely on the basis of a descriptive analysis of contemporary conditions. What normative standpoint led him to call into question the central principles and practices of capitalism in the first place?

---

1. Marx 1975d, p. 42.

2. The writings of the young Marx may not appear to be the best place to begin a study of his conception of the alternative to capitalism. Marx's writings from 1837 to 1843 were largely composed when he was still a liberal democrat who had not yet broken with capitalism, and they contain little or no explicit critique of capitalist value-production. Moreover, the numerous writings composed by him in the years immediately following his break with capitalism (1843/4 to 1847) do not contain the extensive analyses and criticisms of value-production that defines his later work, such as *Capital*.

Nevertheless, I will seek to show that these early writings constitute the *basis* of Marx's conception of the alternative to capitalism that became fleshed out in his later work.

Why did he come to find such formations as private property, alienated labour, class-society, and the separation of the state and civil society so objectionable? An analysis of Marx's early writings – including those composed *before* his break with capitalism – are of indispensable importance in answering these questions. The second aspect is the specific indications provided by his early writings, especially those composed from 1843/4 to 1847, as to what might constitute an alternative to capitalism. Although his early works rarely specify the *institutional* forms needed to replace capitalism,[3] Marx's philosophical engagement with the social and intellectual realities of the 1840s led him to develop a specific conception of the transcendence of alienation that is of indispensable importance in understanding his overall understanding of the alternative to capitalism.

I will seek to demonstrate this by beginning with Marx's earliest extant writings. One of the first, an 1837 letter to his father, represents a kind of statement of philosophical conversion. After having been under the 'spell' of Kant and Fichte, the 19 year-old Marx declares that he has now become committed to Hegelianism. What drives this change of mind is his dissatisfaction with the 'opposition between what is and what ought to be'.[4] Attacking his earlier views as 'entirely idealistic' and 'formalist', he proclaims that 'the object must be studied in its development; arbitrary divisions must not be introduced, the rational character of the object itself must develop as something imbued with contradictions in itself and find its unity in itself'.[5] He considers his prior philosophical standpoint, which counterposed form and matter, an egregious error and contends that he has now 'arrived at the point of seeing the idea in reality itself. If previously the gods had dwelt above the earth, now they became its center'.[6]

This conception of the idea as immanently contained within the real does not mean that Marx has decided to reject 'idealism' in favour of 'materialism'. As he writes a few years later in his doctoral dissertation on ancient Greek

---

3. As David Leopold has argued, 'the most that can be extracted' along these lines from Marx's early writings are 'quasi-institutional threads'. While I concur with this assessment, I will aim to demonstrate that these 'threads' are of considerable importance – both in their own right and for understanding Marx's subsequent development. See Leopold 2007, p. 246.

4. Marx 1975b, p. 12.

5. Ibid. Marx's comment hews closely to Hegel's formulation in the *Science of Logic*: 'This is what Plato demanded of cognition, that it should consider things in and for themselves, that is, should consider them partly in their universality, but also that it should not stray away from them by catching at circumstances, examples and comparisons, but should keep before it solely the things themselves and bring before consciousness what is immanent in them'. See Hegel 1979a, p. 830.

6. Marx 1975b, p. 18.

philosophy, 'Idealism is no figment of the imagination, but a truth'.[7] Marx is searching for a way to conceptualise the ideal as integrally connected to the real. This is but the first expression of a theme that will show up again and again in Marx's work and which will largely determine his attitude towards efforts to propose alternatives to existing realities.

This is not to suggest that the integrality of ideality and reality are the *only* normative concerns of the young Marx. His very earliest writings also display a powerful feeling for *social justice*. As he wrote in his very first extant piece, 'The chief guide which must direct us in the choice of a profession is the welfare of mankind and our own perfection... man's nature is so constituted that he can attain his own perfection only by working for the perfection, for the good, of his fellow men'.[8]

What is important to watch is how these two seemingly separate[9] concerns – social justice and a philosophical commitment to the immanence of the ideal within the real – helped to predetermine and shape Marx's approach to a host of different problems.

Marx's interest in the relation between philosophy and reality dictated the subject-matter of his first theoretical work, his doctoral dissertation *On the Difference Between the Democritean and Epicurean Philosophy of Nature*. Although a detailed analysis of the work is beyond the confines of the present book, several aspects of it are worth re-examination. Marx is drawn to Epicurus because he 'applauds sensuous existence' while highlighting the idea of freedom in his theory of declination of the atom. Whereas Democritus's theory, in which atoms fall in straight lines, stresses predictability and determinism, Epicurus, who focuses on the *swerving* of the atom from straight lines, emphasises chance and free will. Marx sees Democritus as 'throw[ing] himself into the arms of positive knowledge' whereas Epicurus has philosophy 'serve freedom itself'.[10] He singles out Seneca's summation of Epicurus: 'It is wrong to live under necessity; but no man is constrained to live under necessity... On all sides lie many short and simple paths to freedom'.[11]

---

7. Marx 1975d, p. 28.
8. Marx 1975a, p. 8.
9. By 'separate' I do not mean to suggest that they are separate in *Marx's* understanding, but that there is no *logical* reason that commitment to one should necessarily involve commitment to the other.
10. Marx 1975d, pp. 40, 41.
11. Marx 1975d, p. 82. The phrase is from Seneca's *Ad Lucilium epistolae*. See Inwood and Gerson 1988, p. 68, where the passage is rendered more elegantly as: 'It is bad to live under necessity, but there is no necessity to live with necessity. Everywhere the paths to freedom are open'.

What is perhaps more telling is Marx's *critique* of Epicurus. Marx contends that, while Epicurus strives to emphasise sensuous reality *and* freedom, 'the concept of the atom and sensuous perception face each other as enemies'.[12] The declination of the atom is posed as an *abstraction* from determinant being: 'The atom abstracts from the opposing being and withdraws itself from it'.[13] His atomic theory posits the *ideal* side, 'according to which all relation to something else is negated and motion is established as self-determination'.[14] Epicurus's concept of freedom is that *of abstract individuality:* 'abstract individuality is freedom from being, not freedom in being. It cannot shine in the light of being... Epicurus grasps the contradiction at its highest peak and objectifies it'.[15]

Marx considers Epicurus's position an advance over that of Democritus, who fails to posit the 'ideal side' – the principle of *freedom*. Yet Epicurus 'objectifies' a kind of *dualism*, in that freedom becomes defined only *negatively*, as absence of pain and undue stress [*ataraxy*]. Whereas Democritus submerges subject into substance, Epicurus *detaches* subject from substance. Epicurus 'has carried atomistics to its final conclusion, which is its dissolution and conscious opposition to the universal'.[16]

Although Marx does not always make this explicit in the text of the dissertation,[17] he is clearly exploring the aporiae of post-Aristotelian Greek philosophy, with an eye to more contemporary realities. As one important study of Marx's dissertation put it,

> The atom is 'the full' as opposed to 'the empty': it is matter. It is subject to 'dependent motion,' to falling down. But at the same time as an absolute unit the atom is free and independent. In emphasizing the distinction, Marx had in mind the contrast between material necessity and formal civic liberty, or, in the language of the Young Hegelians, between 'bourgeois society' and 'the political state'. Figuratively speaking, the atom as an aspect of materiality is nothing but a bourgeois; as an absolute form of existence it is a citizen of the French Revolution. Epicurus had emphasized the principle of atomicity, that is, independence and hence individual freedom; but the contradictions of this principle were obvious even in this 'atomistic science'.[18]

---

12. Marx 1975d, p. 39.
13. Marx 1975d, p. 51.
14. Marx 1975d, p. 53.
15. Marx 1975d, p. 62.
16. Marx 1975d, p. 73.
17. Marx does make it explicit that his study of Democritus and Epicurus is driven by his concern with the fate of philosophy in the aftermath of Hegel in his 'Notebooks on Epicurean Philosophy'.
18. Lifshitz 1973, pp. 23–4.

As Marx sees it, the central problem with Epicurus is that his philosophy mirrors the contradictions of the modern world insofar as freedom and self-determination are posited at the expense of maintaining a substantial connection with the material world. The idea of freedom and sensuous reality confront each other as mortal enemies. Post-Aristotelian Greek philosophy therefore typifies the pitfall that Marx had earlier indicated that he sought to extricate himself from: the separation of ideality and reality.

In sum, just as stoicism, scepticism, and Epicureanism constituted a *regression* from the 'acme' of philosophy reached with Aristotle, so post-Hegelian philosophy constitutes a subjectivist regression from the Hegelian synthesis.[19] Marx is exploring this as part of envisaging a *reversal* of such regression: 'The modern rational outlook on nature must first raise itself to the point from which ancient Ionian philosophy, in principle at least, begins – the point of seeing the divine, the Idea, embodied in nature'.[20]

Marx sees this breakdown of Hegelianism as inevitable, since the unity of reason and reality proclaimed by his philosophy now confronts a new set of realities that it cannot account for. Reason and reality oppose each other as 'two worlds', 'one edge turned against the world, the other against philosophy itself'. 'The party of the concept', which turns against reality, battles it out with 'the party of reality', which turns against philosophy.[21] Both sides 'place themselves behind a philosophical giant of the past' – but, Marx notes, 'the ass is soon detected under the lion's skin'.[22]

Marx is, of course, far from reconciled to this situation. He seeks a *new beginning* to overcome the diremption of reason and reality – although he is still feeling his way as to how to go about it. He recalls how 'Themistocles, when Athens was threatened with destruction, tried to persuade the Athenians to abandon the city entirely and found a new Athens at sea, in another element'.[23] He has not yet discovered what that new 'element' might be. Yet he sees the path forwards in 'turning' philosophy *towards the material world* – in a way that would not represent its *abandonment* but rather its

---

19. As Marx puts it in his 'Notebooks on Epicurean Philosophy', 'The world confronting a philosophy total in itself is therefore a world torn apart. This philosophy's activity also appears torn apart and contradictory; its objective universality is turned back into the subjective forms of individual consciousness in which it has life'. See Marx 1975c, p. 491.

20. Marx 1975c, pp. 423–4.

21. Marx 1975d, p. 86.

22. Marx adds, 'Thus we obtain hair-, nail-, toe-, excrement-philosophers and others, who have to represent an even worse function in the mystical world man of Swedenborg'. See Marx 1975d, p. 87.

23. Marx 1975c, p. 492.

realisation.[24] In noting 'there are moments when philosophy turns its eyes to the external world',[25] he adds: 'But the *practice* of philosophy is itself *theoretical*. It is the *critique* that measures the individual existence by the essence, the particular reality by the idea'.[26]

As we shall demonstrate, Marx's effort to discern the idea of freedom 'in reality itself' is a theme that will govern all of his subsequent work, and it has a direct bearing on his understanding of how to posit an alternative to capitalist value-production. Although that can be demonstrated only through the course of exploring his later work, there is another concept in his dissertation that becomes especially important for understanding his subsequent development. This concept is *inversion*.

A great deal of Marx's criticism of both capitalism and speculative philosophy will centre on the notion of the inversion of subject and predicate, in which the products as well as the *actions* of people take on the form of an autonomous power that determine and constrain the will of the subjects that engender them. Although many commentators assume that Marx drew the concept of inversion from Feuerbach's critique of religion,[27] Marx's use of the concept actually predates Feuerbach's *Essence of Christianity*, in which the concept of inversion takes on considerable importance.[28] Marx first utilises the concept of inversion in his dissertation, in the course of a critique of Plutarch's *Colotes*. Marx takes issue with Plutarch for writing, 'so that of every quality we can truly say, "It no more is than is not"; for to those affected in a certain way the thing is, but to those not so affected it is not'. Marx notes that in doing so Plutarch 'speaks of a fixed being or non-being as a predicate'. However, 'the being of the sensuous' is *not* a predicate; it is a *subject*. Marx concludes, 'Ordinary thinking always has ready abstract predicates which it separates from the subject. All philosophers have made the predicates into subjects'.[29]

Marx also discusses inversion in criticising those who adhere to 'the party of reality' – that is, those who turn away from philosophy in light of the 'duality of self-consciousness' that characterises the contemporary world. Despite

---

24. Marx's position on this issue represents a reversal of Plato's standpoint, which centres on a 'turning' from the material world to the ideal world of the Forms. See Plato 1961a, pp. 750–1 [518c4–518d1].

25. Marx 1975c, p. 491.

26. Marx 1975d, p. 85.

27. This claim is made, among many others, by Arthur 1986.

28. Feuerbach's *Essence of Christianity* was published in 1841, shortly after Marx finished his dissertation. Marx was aware of Feuerbach's work from as early as 1837 and he made use of his *Geschichte der neuern Philosophie* in his dissertation. However, the concept of inversion – also known as 'transformative criticism' – does not figure in this early work of Feuerbach.

29. Marx 1975c, p. 458.

the one-sidedness of the 'party of the concept', it nevertheless 'makes real progress' since it takes responsibility for developing ideas. The 'party of reality', in contrast, makes no progress because it imputes its ideas to 'reality', instead of taking responsibility for developing them. Marx writes that for this party 'the inversion, we may well say the madness, appears as such'.[30] Marx is making a pun out of the fact that *Verkehrtheit* [inversion] is often identified with *Verrücktheit* [madness]. An inverted world is indeed a *mad world*, insofar as the subject becomes the predicate and the predicate becomes the subject.[31]

This is not in any way to suggest that the critique of an inversion of subject and predicate is *original* to Marx, since it has a long trajectory in the history of philosophy.[32] It is to suggest, however, that Marx *utilised* this concept from very early on – and not simply on the basis of such figures as Feuerbach. The critique of subject-predicate inversion is one of the major normative principles that Marx will bring to bear on his understanding of both philosophy and reality as he increasingly turns his attention to 'material matters' in the period following the completion of his dissertation.

Marx's critique of politics and philosophy, 1842–3

Marx turned to 'material matters' following the completion of his dissertation by directly engaging in active politics, becoming a radical journalist. The choice was not completely of his own making. March 1842 represented a critical turning point in Marx's life because the increasingly conservative turn in the German (and especially Prussian) political scene closed off any hope of an academic career. In that month, young-Hegelian associates of Marx such as Bruno Bauer were fired from their positions in the universities; new censorship-restrictions were imposed; and Friedrich Wilhelm II of Prussia

---

30. Marx 1975d, p. 86.

31. Marx will often make much of the correspondence between 'inversion' and 'madness'. See Backhaus 1992, pp. 60–1: 'Marx here intentionally makes use of the ambiguity of this word which is innate to the German language alone. Thus, on the one hand, money is a 'deranged [*verrückte*] form' in the sense that it is the 'most nonsensical, most unintelligible form,' that is, it is 'pure madness [reine *Verrücktheit*].'

32. The critique of subject-predicate inversion – also known as the reversal of ontological priority – goes back at least as far as Aristotle's criticism of Plato's theory of Forms. Aristotle takes issue with Plato for posing particulars as the dependent entities and the Forms as the independent entities. Aristotle argues, in contrast, that particulars are ontologically prior. See *Posterior Analytics*: 'Things are prior and more familiar in two ways; for it is not the same to be prior by nature and prior in relation to us, nor to be more familiar and more familiar to us. I call prior and more familiar in relation to us what is nearer to perception, prior and familiar *simpliciter* what is furthest away'. See Aristotle 1984, pp. 115–16 [71b34–72a6].

made it clear that he would rule in the name of absolutism. The liberals' response to these events was a great disappointment to Marx and his associates, since they essentially capitulated to Friedrich Wilhelm II without a fight. Propelled by the philosophical problematic formulated in his doctoral dissertation, as well as by the actual social conditions, Marx threw himself into an intense engagement with political realities.

Marx's main political concerns in 1842–3 centred on a virulent defence of freedom of the press, a critique of religion, and an opposition to social inequality. He takes issue with the 'shallow, superficial rationalism'[33] of the censor, calling it a 'bureaucracy of intelligence'.[34] He opposes any form of press-censorship on the grounds that a free press is 'the spiritual mirror in which a people can see itself, and self-examination is the first condition of wisdom'.[35] He makes a critique of religion on the grounds that 'Morality is based on the autonomy of the human mind, religion on its heteronomy'.[36] Although Marx had earlier expressed hostility to religion in his dissertation,[37] his objection to linking religion with politics now became much more pronounced: 'Just as you do not ask the physician whether he is a believer, you have no reason to ask the politician either'.[38] He opposes social inequality – though this is not yet his *main* concern – by taking issue with viewing 'freedom as merely an individual property of certain persons and social estates'.[39]

These political positions are underpinned by a thick set of normative or even *ontological* considerations. Marx does not oppose press-censorship on pragmatic or utilitarian grounds – for instance, by suggesting that it is not effective, or that it violates the greater good of the greater number. He contends that press-censorship is wrong because 'Freedom of the will is inherent in human nature'.[40] Since 'we must take the essence of the inner ideas as the measure to evaluate the existence of things', it follows that 'from the standpoint of the idea, it is self-evident that freedom of the press has a justification quite different from that of censorship because it is itself an embodiment of the idea, an embodiment of freedom, a positive good'.[41] He develops this by

---

33. Marx 1975e, p. 117.
34. Marx 1975e, p. 126.
35. Marx 1975f, p. 165.
36. Marx 1975e, p. 119.
37. In discussing the various proofs of God's existence in the dissertation, he argued that 'such *proofs are proofs of the existence of essential human self-consciousness, logical explanations for it*...Taken in this sense all proofs of the existence of God are proofs of his *non-existence*'. See Marx 1975d, pp. 104–5.
38. Marx 1975g, p. 201.
39. Marx 1975f, p. 151.
40. Marx 1975f, p. 137.
41. Marx 1975f, p. 154.

arguing that 'no man combats freedom; at most he combats the freedom of others'.[42] Since to be free defines our nature as human-beings, not even the censor opposes freedom: instead, he proclaims *his* freedom in acting as one. The censor affirms freedom as a *particular* privilege, instead of as a *universal* right. This distinction between particular and universal interests will later come to play a central role in Marx's critique of capitalism.

The normative stance adopted by Marx in his early writings is that freedom is an *ontological* characteristic of human-beings, as against something that *ought* to exist. He asks, 'Is there no *universal human* nature, as there is a universal nature of plants and stars? Philosophy asks what is true, not what is held to be true. It asks what is true for all mankind, not what is true for some people. Its metaphysical truths do not recognise the boundaries of political geography'.[43]

It is therefore not surprising that Marx returns – *within* these political writings – to the central theme of his doctoral dissertation: the relation between ideality and reality. The ideality posited by Marx is that human-beings are *inherently* free beings. In these early political writings, he is trying to 'measure' political realities by the ideality that resides *within* them. He therefore writes,

> Philosophy does not exist outside the world any more than the brain exists outside man because it is not situated in the stomach...Since every true philosophy is the intellectual quintessence of its time, the time must come when philosophy not only internally by its content, but also externally through its form, comes into contact and interaction with the real world of its day...philosophy has become worldly and the world has become philosophical...[44]

This understanding of the relation of philosophy and reality also underpins Marx's conception of *law*. Marx affirms the importance of laws and legal statutes on the grounds that they serve as the 'positive, clear, universal norms in which freedom has acquired an impersonal, theoretical existence independent of the arbitrariness of the individual. A statutebook is a people's bible of freedom'.[45] However, legal statutes are adequate to their concept only insofar as they correspond to 'the natural laws of [humanity's] own reason'.[46] He adopts an attitude to the law and political actuality that is largely drawn from natural-law theory; indeed, Marx readily cites such thinkers as Hobbes,

---

42. Marx 1975f, p. 155.
43. Marx 1975g, pp. 191–2.
44. Marx 1975g, p. 195.
45. Marx 1975f, p. 162.
46. Marx 1975g, p. 202.

Spinoza, Grotius and Rousseau in discussing how natural laws are rationally 'deduced'. He writes, 'The legal nature of things cannot be regulated according to the law; on the contrary, the law must be regulated according to the legal nature of things'.[47]

This conception in turn serves as Marx's standpoint for criticising the elevation of particular over universal interests – a theme that will become more pronounced in his later work. As early as his first articles against press-censorship, Marx took issue with those who defend freedom of the press on the grounds of freedom of commerce – even though he had not turned his attention to economic issues. He argues that 'freedom of trade' is a particular freedom that must not be used to measure other freedoms, since 'every particular sphere of freedom is the freedom of a particular sphere, just as every particular mode of life is the mode of life of a particular nature'.[48] The elevation of the private over the general strikes Marx as unacceptable, because it disturbs the 'natural' ability of human-beings as a whole to express their aspirations for *free* development: 'Interest by its very nature is blind, immoderate, one sided; in short, it is lawless natural instinct, and can lawlessness lay down laws? Private interest is no more made capable of legislating by being installed on the throne of the legislator than a mute is made capable of speech by being given an enormously long speaking-trumpet'.[49]

It is important to note that, as of the start of 1843, Marx had neither turned to a study of political economy nor had he broken from capitalism. His first mention of 'communism' appears in an essay of October 1842, but he mentions it only to dismiss it.[50] He appears to have studied Fourier, Leroux, Considérant, and Proudhon by early 1843, but he takes only passing note of their criticisms of capitalism. Although he attacks 'pseudo-liberalism' on several occasions,[51] he remains a radical democrat. It is not until late 1843 – when Marx makes direct contact with French socialists and members of secret societies of German communists – that he breaks decisively with capitalist society.

That Marx remains within the parameters of a radical but not anti-capitalist critique of politics in 1842–3 has important ramifications for his effort to turn philosophy to 'material matters'. Although he is still seeking to overcome the philosophical dualities criticised in his doctoral dissertation, he has not yet found the 'new element' upon which to do so. Despite feelings of sympathy for those of the 'poorest estates', he does not accord them any special role in

---

47. Marx 1975i, p. 227.
48. Marx 1975f, p. 173.
49. Marx 1975i, p. 261.
50. See Marx 1975h, pp. 215–21.
51. See Marx 1975d, p. 110.

transforming society, nor does he indicate *how* political conditions can actually be changed. His effort to connect ideality and reality therefore suffers from a tendency to abstractness, as when he writes: 'In a true state there is no landed property, no industry, no material thing, which as a crude element of this kind could make a bargain with the state... The state pervades the whole of nature with spiritual nerves'.[52] By 'true state', of course, Marx means one in conformity with the idea of freedom. However, since he has not yet discovered a material force that can *realise* this idea, he dismisses 'material' entities such as *things* and *industry* as 'crude'. Marx's political-philosophical project therefore remains quite incomplete as of this point.

Although it is unclear whether Marx was fully aware of these limitations, in the spring of 1843 he decided to deepen his understanding of the problems associated with political reality as well as philosophy, by engaging in both further studies of modern politics[53] and a critical commentary on Hegel's *Philosophy of Right*. The latter should not be viewed as a departure from his earlier political concerns. Instead, he turns to the *Philosophy of Right* because it represents the most comprehensive *philosophical* analysis of the political realities that he began to analyse in 1842–3.[54]

Marx's 'Contribution to the Critique of Hegel's *Philosophy of Right*' is one of his most extensive treatments of Hegel and has become the subject of a considerable body of scholarly work.[55] My aim here is not to engage in a detailed analysis of the *Critique*, nor is it to assess the merits or demerits of Marx's interpretation of Hegel. My aim is rather to draw out the central ideas of Marx's *Critique* that help disclose the normative principles that he will subsequently employ in his criticism of capitalism as well as in his elaboration of a possible alternative to it.

Marx's critique of the *Philosophy of Right* centres on Hegel's view of the relation of civil society and the state. Marx *credits* Hegel with having sharply

---

52. Marx 1975j, p. 306.
53. Many of Marx's political studies in early and mid-1843 can be found in his 'Kreuznach Notebooks', in which an examination of the French Revolution of 1789 and the history of modern European politics play a central part. See Marx 1981d, pp. 9–60. In this period, Marx also carefully studied such thinkers as Rousseau, Montesquieu, Chateaubriand, Ranke, and Machiavelli.
54. Leopold claims that Marx's 1843 *Critique* represents a shift in his concerns in that it reflects a growing interest in the modern state. However, since he makes no effort to analyse the political writings that precede the *Critique*, his claim remains to be substantiated. The ensuing analysis will contend that Marx's critique of the *Philosophy of Right*, while marking an important *development* in his thought, represented a continuation and indeed culmination of the concerns that characterised his writings of 1842–3.
55. See especially Avineri 1969, Cohen 1989, Dupré 1966, and Mészáros 1970.

differentiated them – something absent in the writings of Hobbes, Locke, or Rousseau. At one and the same time, Marx makes a *critique of* Hegel for *inverting* the relation between civil society and the state. Whereas civil society, in Marx's view, governs the formation of the state, Hegel makes the state govern the formation of civil society. Hegel posits the state as an 'external necessity' that is *above* civil society – even though the 'abstract' character of the private sphere of civil society is responsible for the 'abstract' character of the modern state. Marx is not satisfied with simply criticising Hegel for presenting civil society as the expression of the state, instead of the state as an expression of civil society. He asks *why* Hegel does so. The answer, Marx contends, is that Hegel posits the *idea* as the subject, instead of as the predicate of the 'real subject' – living men and women. He writes, 'The idea is made the subject, and the actual relation of family and civil society to the state is conceived as its imaginary activity'.[56]

In Hegel, Marx contends, everything becomes a mere 'attribute of the idea, a result, a product of the idea'. And since the idea is made the subject, 'the real subjects, namely civil society, family...become unreal objective elements of the idea with a changed significance'.[57] It therefore follows that in Hegel 'it is always on the side of the predicate...that development takes place'.[58] Marx writes,

> Hegel transforms the predicates, the objects, into independent entities, but divorced from their actual independence, their subject. Subsequently the actual subject appears as a result, whereas one must start from the actual subject and look at its objectification...the real subject appears as something else, as an element of the mystical substance.[59]

Marx sees a number of problems with Hegel's inversion of subject and predicate when it comes to the relation of civil society and the state. First, it makes the state the active agent and civil society the passive object. Second, although Hegel treats the state as an 'organism' (which Marx sees a 'great advance')[60] he fails to explain exactly *how* the state is the organic expression of the idea. Third, since the state is presented as the expression of the idea, Hegel adopts an uncritical attitude towards the state. The state necessarily becomes viewed uncritically, if it is assumed ahead-of-time that it is an instantiation

---

56. Marx 1975k, p. 8.
57. Ibid.
58. Marx 1975k, p. 11. Marx means here, of course, the predicate as *Marx* would define it – the idea or the state. Hegel himself poses these as the subject, which is why Marx objects to the 'inversion'.
59. Marx 1975k, p. 23.
60. Marx 1975k, p. 11.

of the self-determining idea. Fourth, in presenting the state as the subject and civil society as the predicate, Hegel fails to explain what mediates their inter-relation. Hegel at times presents forms of political representation as the mediation *between* civil society and the state, while at other times he identifies such forms *with* the state.

Although the bulk of Marx's *Critique* focuses on his disagreements with the *Philosophy of Right*, it soon becomes clear that Marx does not just object to Hegel's *ideas*. He objects to the way in which the relation between subject and predicate becomes inverted in *real life* – a situation, as noted earlier, that Marx finds akin to *madness*. Although civil society, in Marx's view, is the active principle that brings the modern state into being, the latter becomes a 'person apart' that dominates, controls, and restricts civil society. Nor does such real inversion stop here. The law is a result and manifestation of human activity; yet, over time, it takes on a life of its own and treats the actual subject, human-beings, as its object. The same is true of bureaucracy: a product of subjective human interaction becomes 'a circle from which no one can escape' – it becomes 'the imaginary state alongside the real state'.[61] This is also true of political forms of representation: the legislators present themselves as the subjects who *make* the law, when in fact 'the legislature does not make the law; it only discovers and formulates it'.[62] The critique of inversion extends to Marx's view of civil society. Although Marx views civil society as logically *prior* to the state, he subjects it to critical examination: 'Present day civil society is the realised principle of *individualism*; the individual existence is the final goal: activity, work, content are mere means...Instead of the individual function being a function of society, it turns, on the contrary, the individual function into a society for itself'.[63] For Marx, civil society also becomes a 'person apart' insofar as it is a product of humanity's social, *communal* being – and yet the latter is prevented from being realised because of civil society's fostering of individual egoism and self-interest. Marx may consider civil society the subject of modern society, but it is an *abstract subject* in that it represents the *separation* or *alienation* of humanity from its communal essence. As a result, its product, the state, must necessarily assume an abstract form as well. As he puts it, 'In modern times the idea of the state could not appear except in

---

61. Marx 1975k, pp. 46–7.
62. Marx 1975k, p. 58. This statement indicates that Marx has not moved away from his attachment to natural-law theory at the time he composes his critique of the *Philosophy of Right*.
63. Marx 1975k, p. 81.

the abstraction of the *"merely* political state" or the abstraction of civil society from itself'.[64]

Critical as Marx is of Hegel, it would be wrong to conclude that Marx sees him as failing to grasp the realities of the modern era. *Rather, Marx's view is that Hegel captures the realities of the modern era all too well.* Hegel expresses in thought the inverted reality of the social relations of modernity. By identifying the state with the idea – with an *abstraction* – Hegel adequately conveys the *abstract* (or *separate*)[65] nature of the state. Hegel creates a veritable monument to present-day reality in the form of a philosophical system. His philosophy thereby does a tremendous service insofar as it helps bring to consciousness the realities of the world of which it is the expression.

Marx writes, 'Hegel is not to be blamed for depicting the nature of the modern state as it is, but for presenting that which is as the *nature of the state'*.[66] He adds, 'Hegel has often been attacked for his exposition of morality. He has done no more than expound the morality of the modern state and modern civil law'. Marx refers to this as Hegel's 'great merit'.[67] Marx actually praises Hegel on many occasions in the *Critique*.[68]

What Marx's *Critique* does *not* do is accuse Hegel of being an 'idealist', instead of a 'materialist'. Although many commentators have presumed that Marx attacks Hegel for 'inverting' the ideal and the real in privileging the former at the expense of the latter, the criticism never appears once in the 1843 *Critique*.[69] Marx does not accuse Hegel of neglecting reality, nor does he coun-

---

64. Marx 1975k, p. 113.

65. The modern state, for Marx, is 'abstract' insofar as it is *separate* and *independent* from the social relations that engender it. It *hovers over* civil society even though it is its product. The view of the state as abstract has a long lineage in both philosophy and literature. See Paz 1974, p. 513:

> I speak of towers, bridges, tunnels, hangers, wonders, and disasters, / the abstract state and its concrete police, the schoolteachers, jailers, preachers, / the shops that have everything, where they spend everything, and it all turns to smoke...

66. Marx 1975k, p. 63.

67. Marx 1975k, p. 108.

68. Despite claims to the contrary by numerous writers, Marx does *not* accuse Hegel of being an apologist for the existing Prussian state. Although it is a commonplace in much of the secondary literature on Marx to claim that he accused Hegel's *Philosophy of Right* of being an apology for Prussian absolutism, no such claim on Marx's part appears in any of his writings. Marx criticised Hegel for accommodating to existing reality because he seeks a philosophical justification for the *relation* of civil society and the state; but he does not accuse Hegel of justifying the *specific political practices* of the Prussian government. It was not Hegel, but the late Schelling, whom Marx considered an apologist for Prussian absolutism: 'Schelling's philosophy is Prussian policy *sub specie philosophiae'*. See Marx 1975n, p. 350.

69. Sidney Hook entitles his discussion of the 1843 *Critique* in *From Hegel to Marx: Studies in the Intellectual Development of Marl Marx* as 'Systematic Philosophical Idealism versus Scientific Materialism' and states, 'As contrasted with Hegel, Marx's

terpose idealism to materialism. Instead, he writes that 'abstract *spiritualism* is *abstract materialism; abstract materialism* is the *abstract spiritualism* of matter'.[70] Marx does not criticise Hegel for treating *reality* abstractly; he criticises him for treating the *subject* abstractly – that is, as a mere embodiment of predicates of consciousness. The latter defect enables Hegel to provide an *adequate* description of the actual (abstract) political realities of modern society.

While inversion is a major theme of Marx's 1843 *Critique*, it is not the only one. Marx also makes a critique of modern society for treating 'activity, work, content' as mere means to an end, instead of as ends in themselves. As far back as his 1842 writings on freedom of the press, Marx wrote, 'An end which requires unjustified means is no justified end'.[71] He added, 'The writer does not look on his work as a *means*. It is an *end in itself*; it is so little a means for him himself that, if need be, he sacrifices *his* existence for *its* existence'.[72] This echo of the second formulation of Kant's categorical imperative is no accident: Marx explicitly refers to the principle on numerous occasions.[73] The principle becomes integral to his 'On the Jewish Question', written shortly after the *Critique*. Marx refers to 'life in civil society, in which he acts as a private individual, regards men as a means, degrades himself into a means, and becomes a plaything of alien powers'.[74] In the modern world, 'political life declares itself to be a mere *means*, whose purpose is the life of civil society'.[75] On this

---

philosophy of history is at once realistic and dynamic, empirical yet hostile to the belief that 'social facts' exist ready made *in rerum natura*.' See Hook 1968, p. 41. This dubious counterposition of Marx's 'realism' to Hegel's lack of realism characterises many traditional interpretations of Marx up to the present moment.

70. Marx 1975k, p. 88.

71. Marx 1975f, p. 164.

72. Marx 1975f, p. 175.

73. Marx's first explicit reference to the categorical imperative appears in the 'Notebooks on Epicurean Philosophy'. See Marx 1975c, p. 439. That Marx made use of this concept neither makes him a Kantian nor prevents him from having serious criticisms of Kant's position. Almost all of Marx's references to Kant are to the Second Critique; his work contained almost no explicit references to the First Critique. *The German Ideology* criticises Kant's emphasis on the goodness of the will by stating that it reflected the backward state of the material conditions of Germany at the time. See Marx and Engels 1976a, pp. 193–5. That Marx was highly critical of Kant did not, however, mean he was not influenced by his idea of treating oneself and others as ends in themselves. By his own acknowledgement, Marx was a Kantian before he became a Hegelian. For Kant's second formulation of the categorical imperative, see Kant 1996a, p. 80: 'So act that you use humanity, whether in your own person or in the person of any other, always at the same time as an end, never merely as means'. See also Kant 1996b, p. 473: 'For a human being can never be treated merely as a means to the purposes of another to be put among the objects of rights to things: his innate personality protects him from this'.

74. Marx 1975o, p. 154.

75. Marx 1975o, p. 164.

basis Marx contrasts *political* emancipation with *human* emancipation. With *political* emancipation, civil society is 'freed' from the state, but at the price of turning political life into a mere means for the satisfaction of private, selfish interests. Although political emancipation is 'a big step forward'[76] in relation to the despotic world of medieval absolutism, it produces an 'upside-down' world in which 'the aim appears as the means, while the means appear as the aim'. Human emancipation, in contrast, *transcends* the bifurcation of civil society and the state – it is the not-yet-realised realm in which individuals treat themselves and their fellow humanity as ends in themselves, never only as a means.[77]

What Marx draws from his critique of modern politics and Hegel's *Philosophy of Right* is the need to transform the *human relations* that compel individuals to subordinate themselves to products of their own creation. He states this principle as: '*All* emancipation is a *reduction* of the human world and relationships to *man himself*'.[78]

Given Marx's sharp critique of modern society in the 1843 *Critique* and 'On the Jewish Question', it is tempting to ask what he envisages as the alternative to its 'abstract' and inverted conditions. While Marx does not directly address the question, several points seem to be implied by his analysis. One, the individualistic and atomised nature of civil society needs to be changed so as to accord with the communal nature of humanity. Two, the separation of the state from the citizenry must be overcome – not only through the development of representative institutions but also by the transformation of egotistical civil society. Three, political and social power should not be monopolised by particular interests at the expense of the general interests of the mass of citizenry, as is the case with modern bureaucracy. Four, a genuine 'mediation' between a transformed civil society and the state is needed – as against the false forms of mediation suggested by Hegel's limited discussion of representative institutions.

Other interpretations of the implications of Marx's *Critique* for envisaging an alternative are possible, and the above is by no means an exhaustive list.[79]

---

76. Marx 1975o, p. 155.

77. Although Marx never uses, as far as I am aware, Kant's formulation 'the kingdom of ends', he does write: 'Hence law withdraws into the background in the face of man's life as a life of freedom'. See Marx 1975f, p. 162.

78. Marx 1875o, p. 168. Emphases are in the original. It is left unclear as of this point in Marx's writings whether human emancipation would require *the abolition of the state per se* as well as the abolition of the separation of the state from civil society. As I will attempt to show, in his later writings Marx does explicitly call for the abolition of the state.

79. See Leopold 2007, pp. 248–51, for an alternative list of possibilities. Although I concur with many of Leopold's points, he underemphasises the extent to which Marx's 1843 *Critique* suggests the need for a radical transformation of civil society.

However, we need to be especially cautious about drawing inferences about Marx's view of an alternative from the 1843 *Critique*. This is not only because it does not explicitly address alternatives. Most of all, it is because it was composed *prior* to Marx's full break with capitalism. The *Critique* never so much as mentions either the proletariat or socialism and communism.

Instead, it states, 'Democracy is the solved *riddle* of all constitutions'.[80] He will later use a similar phrase in his *Economic and Philosophical Manuscripts* of 1844 – except that he will there refer to *communism* as the 'solved riddle'.[81] The *Critique* also states, 'Only democracy, therefore, is the true unity of the general and the particular'.[82] Although Marx will remain a firm defender of democracy for the rest of his life, he writes very differently in 'On the Jewish Question' (written only a few months later) in distinguishing political from human emancipation. Political democracy, he argues, does not end the separation of man from man; instead, it elevates the particular *over* the general. 'It makes every man see in other men not the *realisation* of his own freedom, but the *barrier* to it'.[83] Marx therefore speaks of the need to 'suppress' the 'prerequisite' of civil society by 'declaring the revolution to be *permanent*'.[84] By the time of his 1843–4 essays in the *Deutsch-Französischer Jahrbücher*, Marx realises that a *thoroughgoing* social transformation is needed in order for society to become expressive of humanity's 'species-being' – its capacity for free, conscious, *purposeful* activity.[85]

There may be a philosophical basis to the political limitations in the 1843 *Critique*, in that, in some passages, Marx seems to remain under the spell of young-Hegelian assumptions – even while trying to become free from them. At one point, in objecting to Hegel for positing 'self-knowing and self-willing mind' as the subject, he says he prefers that '*actual mind* [be] the starting

---

80. Marx 1975k, p. 29.
81. In 1844 he writes, 'Communism is the riddle of history solved, and it knows itself to be this solution'. See Marx 1975r, pp. 296–7.
82. Marx 1975k, p. 30. According to Michael Löwy, 'The word "democracy" had for Marx a specific meaning: abolition of the separation between the social and the political, the universal and the particular'. This does not change the fact that there is a significant difference between Marx's 1843 *Critique* and his *Economic and Philosophical Manuscripts* of 1844, in that by the time of the latter he spoke in terms of communism, and not only democracy, as the expression of this abolition. Löwy himself contends that in the 1843 *Critique* Marx remains 'ideologically confused'. See Löwy 2005, pp. 41–5.
83. Marx 1975o, p. 163.
84. Marx 1975o, p. 156.
85. Although the concept of 'species-being' is central to the *Economic and Philosophical Manuscripts* of 1844, it first makes its appearance in 'On the Jewish Question'. The latter essay, as well as his 'Contribution to the Critique of Hegel's *Philosophy of Right*. Introduction', were written at the end of 1843 and appeared in the *Deutsch-Französische Jahrbücher* in early 1844.

point'.[86] This seems some ways from his later emphasis on stressing *the material conditions of society* as the starting point.

Despite these limitations, the 1843 *Critique* marks a crucial moment in Marx's evolution, since through his study of Hegel's *Philosophy of Right* he has come to a much richer understanding of the contradictions and defects of modern political reality. As a result, he now turns to ponder the *future*, in asking what kind of society can overcome these defects. He is not at all sure of the answer. As he writes to Arnold Ruge upon completing the *Critique*, 'Not only has a state of general anarchy set in among the reformers, but everyone will have to admit to himself that he has no exact idea of what the future ought to be'.[87] So how is one to proceed? Marx reiterates his preoccupation with discerning the ideal from within the real. He writes, 'Constructing the future and settling everything for all times is not our concern'. He does not want to 'dogmatically anticipate' the new world. Instead, he wants 'to find the new world through criticism of the old one'.[88] He says the task is to 'develop new principles for the world out of the world's own principles'. He wants to 'merely show the world what it is really fighting for, and consciousness is something that it *has* to acquire, even if it does not want to'.[89]

That Marx is reiterating some of the same concerns expressed in his dissertation, only now mediated by a much richer understanding of the defects of contemporary politics, is shown by his 'Contribution to the Critique of Hegel's *Philosophy of Right*. Introduction'.[90] The ideal towards which we must strive, Marx contends, is to unmask and transcend 'human self-estrangement' in the 'unholy forms' of existing society. This cannot be achieved without a *philosophy* based on 'the *categorical imperative* to *overthrow all relations* in which man is a debased, enslaved, forsaken, despicable being'.[91] At the same time, 'revolutions require a *passive* element, a *material* basis...It is not enough for thought to strive for realization, reality must also strive towards thought'.[92] Marx is clearly reaching for an element *within* reality that can realise the ideal – without putting aside the need to philosophically elucidate the

---

86. Marx 1975k, p. 17.
87. Marx, 1975m, p. 142.
88. Ibid.
89. Marx 1975m, p. 144.
90. This should not be confused with the 1843 *Critique*, of which this was intended to serve as the Introduction. The former was never completed, however, and Marx published the 'Introduction' in the same issue of the *Deutsch-Französischer Jahrbücher* that contained 'On the Jewish Question'.
91. Marx 1975p, p. 182. Emphasis is by Marx in the original.
92. Marx 1975p, p. 183.

ideal. For this reason he takes issue with two 'parties' – the 'practical political party', which turns to reality at the expense of philosophy, and the 'party of philosophy', which turns away from reality. Marx is reiterating, on a higher level, his critique of 'the party of the concept' and 'the party of reality' that he took issue with in his dissertation.[93]

So what is the element within reality that is capable of realising his philosophical ideals? None other than 'a class of civil society which is not of civil society, an estate which is the dissolution of all estates, a sphere which has a universal character by its universal suffering and claims no *particular right*' – the *proletariat*.[94] Hence, 'as philosophy finds its material weapons in the proletariat, so the proletariat finds its spiritual weapons in philosophy'. With his discovery of the proletariat as the revolutionary class, Marx has resolved – or so he thinks – the problematic that preoccupied him for years concerning the need to overcome the diremption of philosophy and reality. 'Philosophy cannot be made a reality without the abolition of the proletariat, and the proletariat cannot be abolished without philosophy being made a reality'.[95]

It is important to note that Marx's discovery of the proletariat as the revolutionary class *precedes* his study of 'economic matters', which began later in 1844. His conception of the proletariat was part of an effort to resolve a *philosophical* problematic.[96] Now that he has fully broken from capitalist society, he will utilise the concepts he had developed in his work of 1842–3 – such as subject-predicate inversion, treating oneself and others as ends in themselves, and the need to transform the *human relations* between individuals – as he turns to explore the *economic* conditions of modern existence.

---

93. See Marx 1975d, p. 86.
94. Marx 1975p, p. 186. Marx's wording here closely follows Emmanuel Sieyès's phrases in discussing the third estate in *Qu'est-ce que le tiers état?*, published in 1789 on the eve of the French Revolution: 'What is the third estate? Everything. – What was it until now in the political respect? Nothing. – What is it striving for? To be something'.
95. Marx 1975p, p. 187.
96. This is not to suggest that Marx's discovery of the proletariat was *purely* a product of philosophical reasoning, let alone a 'literary myth', as some have argued. Upon moving to Paris in November 1843, Marx for the first time directly meets with French workers and groups of German communists, whose membership consisted overwhelmingly of proletarians. Marx's 'discovery' of the proletariat in the 'Introduction' was affected by those experiences. As he later wrote to Feuerbach, 'You would have to attend one of these meetings of the French workers to appreciate the pure freshness, the nobility which burst forth from these toil-worn men'. See Marx 1975l, p. 355.

Marx's critique of economics and philosophy, 1843–4

Marx follows his 1842–3 criticisms of politics and philosophy with a wide-ranging critique of economics and philosophy, beginning in 1844. He plunges into an extensive study of economic literature, taking voluminous notes on Smith, Ricardo, Say, MacCulloch, James Mill, Friedrich List, Frédéric Skarbek and many others.[97] He also makes direct contact with secret societies of self-proclaimed 'materialist communists', in April or May 1844. These groups were distinguished from the utopian socialists in emphasising the need to abolish private property in the means of production through a social revolution. Unlike most of the utopian-socialist groupings, they were largely composed of proletarians.[98]

As Marx comes to a deeper understanding of the nature of capitalism, he becomes more specific about what he sees as its problems. Of foremost importance in this regard are his attitudes towards private property and the market. In an early writing that has often been overlooked in the critical literature on Marx – his 1844 'Comments on James Mill, *Éléments de l'économie politique*' – he sharply attacks the market, exchange-relations, and money, seeing in them 'the social act which man's activity is alienated from itself'.[99] He finds commerce and trade to be an '*estranged* form of social intercourse'.[100] The problem that he has with commerce is that, 'the mediating process between men engaged in exchange is not a social or human process, not *human relationship*: it is *the abstract relationship* of private property to private property, and the expression of this *abstract* relationship is *value*, whose actual existence as value constitutes *money*'.[101]

Exchange represents an object-object relation, in which the subject has little or no say. *Chance* and *accident* rules in relations of exchange, not the deliberate

---

97. See Marx 1981d, pp. 301–591 for his excerpt-notebooks on economics from 1844.

98. It is important to note that Marx never joined any utopian tendencies and groupings, although he did work with the League of the Just, which he joined when it became the Communist League in 1847. It was founded in 1836. In 1840 other groups of communists arose, such as the Society of Egalitarian Workers and the Revolutionary Communist Society. The membership of these groups was almost exclusively working-class, though most were artisans and not industrial workers. In light of this actual history, the claim that the idea of socialism and communism was introduced to the workers 'from outside' by radical intellectuals like Marx – a notion famously propagated by V.I. Lenin in *What Is to Be Done* – is especially specious. For more on this period, see Löwy 2005, pp. 59–85.

99. Marx 1975q, p. 212.

100. Marx 1975q, p. 217.

101. Marx 1975q, pp. 212–13.

acts of human-beings.[102] Whereas, in precapitalist societies, people oppress *people*, in capitalism *things* oppress people. 'What was the domination of person over person is now the general domination of the thing over the person, of the product over the producer'.[103] Marx is measuring market- and exchange-relations against the normative principle, as he expressed in 1843, that '*all* emancipation is a reduction of the human world and relationships to *man himself*'.

Marx's objection to exchange-relations and the market is clearly stated. What is not so clear from the Mill excerpts is *why* exchange-relations take on an alienated form. Is it because of the nature of exchange as such? Or is it because of the social relations that they are the expression of?

Marx provides a possible answer when he writes, 'The relationship of exchange being presupposed, *labour* becomes *directly labour to earn a living*'.[104] The meaning of this phrase is not transparent, since Marx must have known that exchange-relations long precede the emergence of wage-labour. He mentions that, with 'primitive' exchange-relations prior to a developed division of labour, what enters the market is only the labourer's surplus-product. Wage-labour cannot become the medium of social reproduction under such a 'primitive form of *alienated* private property'. It is only later, when 'the division of labour, the product, the material of private property, acquires for the individual more and more the significance of an *equivalent*' that universalised market-relations emerge. At *that* point, '[T]he individual, no longer exchanges only his *surplus*, and the object of his production can become simply a *matter of indifference* to him, so he too no longer exchanges his product for something directly *needed* by him. The equivalent now comes into existence as an equivalent in *money*, which is now the immediate result of labour to gain a living and the *medium* of exchange'.[105]

It therefore appears that it is not exchange as such that is the problem, but conditions in which exchange becomes *depersonalised*. No longer is one person exchanging a surplus-product with another who has his own to exchange. Now *all* products, regardless of their material content and the needs that they may fulfil, are treated as expressions of an abstract equivalent – money. *Generalised* commodity-exchange therefore leads to wage-labour. Marx sees this as an *adverse* development, since 'The complete domination of the estranged

---

102. Ibid. Marx makes the same point in his critical excerpt-notes on Ricardo and Say, written at about the same time. See Marx 1981b, pp. 392–427.
103. Marx 1975q, p. 221.
104. Marx 1975q, p. 219.
105. Marx 1975q, p. 221.

thing *over* man has become evident in *money*, which is completely indifferent…to the personality of the property owner'.[106]

In issuing this criticism, Marx introduces a new concept – *alienated labour*. He refers to it as 'labour to earn a living'. Alienated labour reaches its 'highest peak', he writes, when 'he who *buys* the product is not himself a producer, but gives in exchange what someone else has produced'.[107] He does not say much more about alienated labour at this point, instead returning to the problems of exchange. It is therefore left unclear as to whether alienated labour *produces* alienated exchange-relations or whether it *results* from generalised commodity-exchange. Marx has not yet clarified the *relation* between alienated labour on the one hand and the market and private property on the other.

At the end of the piece he suddenly writes, 'Let us suppose that we had carried out production as human beings'. In this way, he ventures for the first time into a discussion of a postcapitalist society, writing: (1) 'In my *production* I would have objectified my *individuality*, its *specific character*'[108] – that is, alienated labour would no longer exist. 'I would now *enjoy* my activity as well as its products, since the products would express the specific character of my individuality. (2) In doing so I would have the satisfaction of meeting another person's need through the objectification of my activity. (3) I would have been the mediator between you and the species – and so I would see the other person not as a hostile competitor but as a necessary complement to myself. (4) 'In the individual expression of my life I would have directly created your expression of your life' – that is, the separation of private from general interests would be overcome. 'Our products would be so many mirrors in which we saw reflected our essential nature' – *because* 'my work would be a free manifestation of life, as would yours.'[109]

Curiously, it is only in discussing this vision of a new society that Marx indicates that the limitations of the market and exchange *result* from alienated labour. However, since the discussion here of alienated labour is very brief and in the context of a lengthy critique of exchange-relations, it is possible to read the Mill excerpts as suggesting that his main object of criticism is the 'arbitrary' or 'irrational' character of the market.[110] How a major part of the piece is read largely hinges on determining exactly when Marx composed

---

106. Ibid.
107. Marx 1975q, pp. 219–20. Marx here clearly identifies wage-labour with alienated labour – a theme that he will further develop in his later work.
108. Marx 1975q, p. 227.
109. Marx 1975q, p. 228.
110. This is how Allan Megill reads the Mill excerpts. I will respond to this below.

the Mill excerpts. If he did so *before* writing the *Economic and Philosophical Manuscripts* of 1844, it would indicate that there was an evolution of his thinking in which the question of alienated labour took on new importance. If he did so *after* writing the 1844 *Manuscripts*, it could indicate that he considered the critique of market- and exchange-relations as of equal or even greater importance than alienated labour. Although there is no scholarly consensus as to the exact dating of the respective manuscripts, it appears from the most recent research that the Mill excerpts *precede* the 1844 *Manuscripts*.[111]

The *Economic and Philosophical Manuscripts* of 1844 are the most famous of Marx's early works. To see how they mark a further development of the project that he embarked upon from his earliest writings, it is important to grasp the *philosophical* underpinning of his critique of political economy as well as the *economic* ramifications of his critique of Hegelian philosophy. The two sides have not always achieved sufficient attention. To take one prominent example, although Hal Draper devotes considerable attention to Marx's work of the 1840s in his multi-volume *Marx's Theory of Revolution*, he pays scant attention to the Hegelian inheritance, scornfully dismissing it as something Marx 'sloughed off' as he clarified his new world-view.[112] At the other extreme, Michel Henry provides a close reading of Marx's debt to Hegel in *Marx: A Philosophy of Human Reality* while passing over its implications for the critique of political economy.[113] I will seek to show that Marx's encounter with Hegel – as well as the concepts elaborated by him *prior* to his break with capitalism – had a direct impact on his understanding of capital as well as his conception of the alternative to it.

In the 1844 *Manuscripts*, Marx follows the classical-political economists in defining capital as congealed labour. However, he introduces the important additional argument that capital is not the congealment of *any* kind of labour. It is congealed *abstract* or alienated labour. As he writes in the Second Manuscript, capital is the expression of 'a *special* sort of work [which is] *indifferent* to its content, of complete being-for-self, of abstraction from all other being'.[114] Although Marx has not yet developed his concept of the dual character of labour – the split between abstract and concrete labour – which will become so central to *Capital* (and which he defines as his unique contribution

---

111. See Rojahn 1985, pp. 647–63. He writes, 'As for the *exzertpe* from Ricardo's and Mill's books, there is no clear evidence of when exactly they were made…It is however beyond doubt that Marx *read* Mill's book before writing the Third Manuscript' of the 1844 *Manuscripts*. For the shorter version of this argument, see Rojahn 2002, p. 38.

112. See Draper 1977, p. 94.

113. See Henry 1983.

114. Marx 1975r, p. 286.

to the critique of political economy), it is noteworthy that in 1844 he already defines capital as congealed abstract labour. As he writes in the First Manuscript, 'The *proletarian*... lives purely by labour, and by a one-sided, abstract labour... What in the evolution of mankind is the meaning of this reduction of the greater part of mankind to abstract labour?... Political economy considers labour in the abstract as a thing, labour as a commodity... Capital is *stored up labour*'.[115]

The worker is forced to live 'purely by labour' in becoming an instrument of production – a mere appendage to a machine. He writes, 'The machine accommodates itself to the weakness of the human being in order to make the human being into a machine'.[116] The workers' activity is reduced to an 'abstract mechanical movement'. What makes this development possible is the separation of labour from the objective conditions of production. By tearing the labourers from their connection to their 'natural workshop' of the land, capitalism denies workers a direct connection to the means of production. The workers 'own' nothing but their capacity to labour[117] and are compelled to sell it to individual property-owners. Private interest prevails over the general interest in the form of private ownership of the production-process. As noted earlier, Marx views the predominance of the former over the latter as a violation of the communal or social nature of humanity. He therefore aligns himself with the main demand of the socialist and communist movements of his time – the abolition of private property.[118]

However, Marx brings a distinctive perspective to demands to transform property-relations by arguing that the abolition of private property does not necessarily lead to the abolition of capital. To liberate the worker, he argues, it is necessary to go deeper than the property-relation and deal with 'the direct relation of the worker and production'.

In doing so, we discover that in the production-process 'labour itself becomes an object'.[119] Labour, as a subjective activity, becomes *thingified*,

---

115. Marx 1975r, pp. 241, 244, 247.
116. Marx 1975r, p. 308.
117. In the 1844 *Manuscripts*, Marx does not yet distinguish between labour and labour-power. I will discuss the ramifications of this crucial distinction in the chapter dealing with Marx's *Capital*.
118. The identification of communism with the abolition of private property has a lineage that long predates the modern era. The 'materialist communists' first emerged around 1840 and distinguished between private ownership of goods (which they did not oppose) and private ownership of the means of production. The 'materialist communists' – who included such figures as Dézamy, Pillot, Gray, and Charavay – should not be confused with the *utopian socialists* (who included Cabet, Owen, Fourier and Saint-Simon), some of whom tended not to make this distinction.
119. Marx 1975r, p. 272.

reified. It is not hard to notice the separation or alienation of the product from the producer on the basis of the principles enunciated by the classical-political economists, since they argued that labour is the source of all value. It stands to reason, once this premise is accepted, that the workers receive less value in the forms of wages and benefits than is contained in the value of their products. However, classical-political economy *conceals* what Marx considers to be the more important problem – the separation or alienation of labour *from its own activity*. When we directly examine what happens to the worker in the process of production, we see that his own activity 'is turned against him, [becomes] independent of him'.[120] Marx is now applying his critique of subject-predicate inversion to the labour-process. The very activity of the subject becomes the predicate – a thing apart that dominates and controls the *real* subject.

Marx also makes a critique of existing society for treating labour as a mere *means* to an end, instead of as an end in itself. As he puts it, 'In the wage of labour, the labour does not appear as an end in itself but as the servant of the wage'.[121] The products of labour are likewise not treated as ends in themselves, but only as means to satisfy egotistical need.

Although Marx *begins* his criticism by showing that workers are alienated from the product of their labour, he takes great pains to show that the source of this problem lies in the alienated character of labour itself. By reducing labour to a mere *means* to earn a living in which all joy and satisfaction is banished, the workers no longer feel at home in their own labour. This necessitates the existence of an alien-class which extracts *forced* labour from the worker. Only then does it become possible for the product of labour to become alienated from the worker. For this reason, Marx writes, 'The relationship of the worker to labour creates the relation of it to the capitalist (or whatever one chooses to call the master of labour)'.[122] He concludes: '*Private property* is thus the result, the necessary consequence of *alienated labour*, of the external relation of the workers to nature and to himself...though private property appears to be the reason, the cause of alienated labour, it is rather its consequence, just as the gods are *originally* not the cause but the effect of man's intellectual confusion'.[123]

Marx thinks he is onto something important here; he explicitly says it 'sheds light on various hitherto unresolved conflicts'.[124] The inattentive reader may pass over the fact that it resolves a conflict with which Marx himself has been

---

120. Marx 1975r, p. 275.
121. Marx 1975, p. 280.
122. Marx 1975r, p. 279.
123. Ibid.
124. Marx 1975r, p. 280.

struggling. As we saw from the 'Comments on James Mill', Marx initially focuses his critique of capitalism on the existence of private property and relations of exchange. For this reason, his first encounter with Proudhon's work – which held that 'property is theft' – was highly positive. He now takes a very different view. Classical-political economy, he notes, 'starts from labour as the real soul of production' and yet never directly analyses the relation of the worker and production. Instead, it 'gives' everything to its defence of private property. However, 'when one speaks of private property, one thinks of dealing with something external to man'.[125] Property is, after all, the *product* of human activity. Classical-political economy reverses matters, by presenting the predicate – property-relations – as the determining factor while ignoring the alienated nature of the workers' activity. Marx now realises that Proudhon fails to break from this inversion. 'Proudhon has decided in favor of labour against private property'[126] since he opposes private property. However, he does not recognise that capitalism's property-relations are themselves a product of 'the contradiction of *estranged labour* with itself'.[127] Much like the classical-political economists, Proudhon is 'dealing with something external to man'.

Marx, on the other hand, sees the need to go much further. As noted earlier, in 'On the Jewish Question' Marx wrote, 'All emancipation is a *reduction,* of the human world and relationships to *man himself.*'[128] He reaches this view through a critique of religion. In contrast to Bruno Bauer and the Hegelian Left, Marx does not see religion as the cause of secular distress; he rather sees secular distress as the cause of religion. He proceeds to try to comprehend the reasons for secular distress. As he comes into contact with socialist and communist currents and engages in a serious study of political economy in 1844, he sees that the existence of private property is a major reason for such distress. However, since private property is an objectified *product* of human activity, the critique of private property does not satisfy the requirement of *reducing* all emancipation to 'relationships to man himself'. The critique of private property still deals with what is 'external to man'. Marx's normative principle of *human* emancipation – which he reiterates in 1844 as 'man's relation to himself only becomes for him *objective* and *actual* through his relation to the other man'[129] – drives him to look deeper than the property-relation. This takes him to his theory of alienated labour. As he puts it, 'When one

---

125. Marx 1975r, p. 281.
126. Marx 1975r, p. 280.
127. Marx 1975r, p. 281.
128. Marx 1975o, p. 168.
129. Marx 1975r, p. 278.

speaks of labour, one is directly dealing with man himself. This new formulation of the question already contains its solution'.[130]

How does it contain its solution? It follows from the analysis that, while private property must be abolished – since it separates workers from the conditions of production – that alone does not get to the heart of the problem. The heart of the problem is abolishing capital itself, by ending the estrangement in the very activity of labouring. *We have reached the conceptual pivot of what Marx sees as the alternative to capitalism.*

Marx comes to this conclusion by proceeding *phenomenologically*. As noted earlier, the 'Comments on James Mill' *begins* by taking issue with the most obvious, *phenomenal* manifestations of distress in capitalist society: the inequalities generated by private property and the market. As he deepens his critique of capitalism on the basis of the normative principles projected in his early writings, he emphasises the essential determinants responsible for private property and the market. By the end of the 1844 *Manuscripts*, he has reached a self-clarification that was not yet evident in his earlier writings.[131] Marx's process of coming to terms with the alienation of labour is a vivid self-confirmation of his statement that 'the transcendence of self-estrangement follows the same course of self-estrangement'.[132]

Now that Marx has penetrated into the root of the problem of capitalism, he becomes more specific about the postcapitalist society he is searching for. Wages, he writes, are a form of private property, since they are paid to the worker on the basis of the capitalist's ownership of the products of labour. He has shown that private property is not the cause but the consequence of alienated labour. It follows that equality of wages – as proposed by many utopian socialists – fails to address the issue of alienated labour. In fact, Marx writes, 'the *equality of wages*, as demanded by Proudhon, only transforms the relationship of the present-day worker to his labour into the relationship of all men to labour. Society is then conceived as an abstract capitalist'.[133] This is, in many respects, a remarkable passage, for it anticipates the defects of many of the social experiments that will be carried out (ironically enough) in Marx's name in the twentieth century.

---

130. Marx 1975r, p. 281.

131. On these grounds, I differ from Rojahn's assessment: 'The comments by which Marx interrupted his *exzertpe* from Mill's *Elements* surpass in clarity most of the expositions given in the First, Second, and Third Manuscripts'. See Rojahn 2002, p. 45.

132. Marx 1975r, p. 294. In this sense, it is worth keeping in mind the statement from Marx's doctoral dissertation that serves as the epigraph of this chapter. What Marx often presents as knowledge of the outer world can be read as a self-knowledge that he has obtained from his relation to it.

133. Marx 1975r, p. 280.

Two points are worth noting from this. First, wages, like property, are *results* of human activity. They are made *necessary* by the existence of alienated labour. To ignore alienated labour while altering wage- and property-relations through the elimination of private capitalists does not undermine the necessity for a ruling class to impose forced labour on the workers. *Society has a whole* now becomes the 'abstract capitalist'. One form of oppression is ended by instituting an ever-more egregious form of oppression. Second, if everyone is paid the same wage, labour becomes treated as a uniform abstraction. Treating labour as an abstraction, however, is precisely the problem with alienated labour. Proudhon reduces property to 'labour': but he has failed to notice that this is precisely what capitalism does by treating 'labour' as a producer of value irrespective of the labourer's actual *human* characteristics.[134] In the name of 'liberation', Proudhon is fulfilling the central mission of capitalism – to reduce labouring activity to an undifferentiated sameness by failing to take issue with the dominance of abstract labour.

Since Marx's 1844 critique of Proudhon represents the first time that he has distinguished his understanding of a postcapitalist society from that of a fellow-socialist, we need to look more closely at the issue. Although it may not be obvious from a first reading, the concepts that Marx employs in his critique are largely drawn from Hegel's dialectic. Marx's expression that capital is the expression of 'a special sort of work [which is] indifferent to its content, of complete being-for-self, of abstraction from all other being', indicates that he is utilising Hegelian categories to describe capital. Capital, as self-expanding value, is 'indifferent' to otherness, be it of nature or human sensuousness, which it seeks to subsume under its self-movement; yet, at the same time, capital must take on a material, externalised form. Hegel presents a similar dynamic in discussing 'being-for-self' in the *Science of Logic*:

> We say that something is for itself in so far as it transcends otherness, its connection and community with other, has repelled them and made abstraction from them...Being for self is the polemical, negative attitude towards the limiting other, and through this negation of the latter is a reflectedness-into-self, although along with this return of consciousness into itself and the ideality of the object, the reality of the object is also still preserved, in that it is at the same time known as an external existence.[135]

---

134. See Marx 1975r, p. 291: 'Under the semblance of recognizing man, the political economy whose principle is labour rather carries to its logical conclusion the denial of man.' Marx will later write that Proudhon makes a critique of political economy from the standpoint of political economy.

135. Hegel 1979a, p. 158.

Marx's employment of Hegelian categories to delineate the logic of capital will take on even greater significance in the *Grundrisse* and *Capital*. Yet this does not mean that Hegel was important to Marx only insofar as he helps reveal the nature of capital. Hegel's dialectic also had an impact on Marx's conception of what is needed to *transcend* capital.

This is seen especially from his critical appropriation of Hegel's dialectic of negativity 'as the moving and creating principle' in the 1844 *Manuscripts*. In Hegel, all movement proceeds through the power of negativity, the negation of obstacles to the subject's self-development. The actual transcendence of these obstacles is reached not through the negation of their immediate and external forms of appearance (which Hegel calls first negation), but through 'the negation of the negation'. In the 'negation of the negation', the power of negativity gets turned back upon the self, upon the internal as well as external barriers to self-movement. The negation of the negation, or *absolute negativity*, posits from itself the *positive*, the transcendence of alienation. For Hegel, second negativity 'is the innermost and most objective moment of life and spirit, by virtue of which a subject is personal and free'.[136] As he wrote in the *Science of Logic*, 'But in all this, care must be taken to distinguish between the *first* negation as negation *in general*, and the second negation, the negation of the negation: the latter is concrete, absolute negativity, just as the former on the contrary is only *abstract* negativity'.[137]

Marx enters into a direct engagement with Hegel's concept of negativity in the final part of the Third Manuscript, the 'Critique of the Hegelian Dialectic'. He focuses on the concluding chapter of the *Phenomenology of Spirit*, 'Absolute Knowledge', as well as the *Encyclopedia of Philosophical Sciences*. The chapter on 'Absolute Knowledge' contains Hegel's fullest discussion of self-movement through self-reflected negativity, and Marx believes that he has found within it the merits as well as demerits of Hegel's philosophical system as a whole. The significance that Marx accords the chapter on 'Absolute Knowledge' is indicated by the fact that he devotes himself to a more direct and detailed investigation of this than any other single chapter of Hegel's writings.[138]

In his 'Critique of the Hegelian Dialectic', Marx is first of all scathingly critical of what he finds in Hegel's chapter on 'Absolute Knowledge', which

---

136. Hegel 1979a, p. 830.
137. Hegel 1979a, pp. 115–16.
138. This is true both of Marx's early writings on Hegel and his writings and commentaries on Hegel as a whole. Although the 1843 *Contribution to the Critique of Hegel's Philosophy of Right* is lengthier than the 1844 'Critique of the Hegelian Dialectic', Marx does not provide as detailed an analysis of a specific chapter in the former as he does for 'Absolute Knowledge' in the latter.

represents a summation of the stages of consciousness traversed in the *Phe-nomenology* as a whole. He argues that the chapter shows that the *structure* of the *Phenomenology* is fatally flawed because the *subject* of the dialectical move-ment is disembodied self-consciousness, instead of living men and women. Marx writes, 'For Hegel the human being – *man* – equals *self-consciousness*'.[139]

This *dehumanisation of the Idea* has critical ramifications for Hegel's philo-sophical system as a whole. Since Hegel presents the subject as disembodied thought, the externalisation (or alienation) of the subject's creative capacities is treated as mere objects of thought. Or, as Marx puts it, 'the products of men appear as the products of the abstract spirit'.[140] And since externalised objects are mere thought-forms, Hegel poses the transcendence of externalisation or alienation as the return of thought to itself – 'Absolute Knowledge' – and not as return of *humanity* to itself.

In sum, the *structure* of Hegel's philosophical system *inverts* the relation of subject and predicate. Marx contends that, even when the *Phenomenology* brilliantly illuminates the nature of *real* phenomena – such as civil society, the family, and the state – it does so by treating them as emanations of the Idea. What Marx had earlier pinpointed as the central flaw in the *Philosophy of Right* – *the inversion of subject and predicate* – is now seen by him as the Achilles heel of Hegel's entire philosophy. Marx is here clearly relying heavily on Feuer-bach's *The Essence of Christianity*, the work in which Feuerbach made much of Hegel's inversion of subject and predicate.[141]

It is important to recognise, however, that by inversion Marx is *not* refer-ring to Hegel's prioritisation of 'idealism' over 'materialism'. Marx's critique of the *Phenomenology* no more counterposes 'materialism' to Hegel's 'ideal-ism' than does his earlier analysis of the *Philosophy of Right*.[142] As he did ear-lier, Marx *credits* Hegel for his *realistic* insight into actual *material* conditions. This is especially the case when it comes to the concept of *labour*. Marx writes that the 'outstanding achievement' of Hegel's *Phenomenology* 'and of its final outcome' – a direct reference to the chapter on 'Absolute Knowledge' – is its treatment of labour: 'Hegel conceives the self-creation of man as a process, con-ceives objectification as loss of the object, as alienation and as transcendence

---

139. Marx 1975r, p. 334.
140. Marx 1975r, p. 332.
141. The fact that Marx is influenced at this point by Feuerbach's critique of inversion does not mean that he follows all aspects of it; nor, as I noted earlier, does it mean that Marx derives the critique of this Hegelian inversion from Feuerbach.
142. When he poses his own positive alternative to the defects that he finds in Hegel, Marx argues for a *unity* of idealism and materialism: 'Here we see how con-sistent naturalism or humanism is distinct from both idealism and materialism, and constitutes at the same time the unifying truth of both'. See Marx 1975r, p. 336.

of this alienation; that he grasps the essence of *labour* and comprehends objective man – true, because real man – as the outcome of man's *own labour*'.[143]

Marx adds, 'The only labour which Hegel knows and recognizes is *abstractly mental* labour'.[144] This is often taken to mean that Marx is accusing Hegel of dealing only with intellectual labour, not the corporeal labour of the actual process of production.[145] On these grounds, they argue that Marx is counterposing a 'materialist' conception of labour to Hegel's 'idealism'. However, a careful examination of the text raises serious questions about this interpretation. First, it is hard to imagine that Marx would have so superficial an understanding of Hegel as not to realise that the *Phenomenology* discusses labour in *concrete* terms in numerous places – such as in the famous master-slave dialectic. Second, the above interpretation fails to account for Marx's view that the *Phenomenology* gives a *real* account of human relations – labour among them.

So why does Marx write that Hegel recognises only abstractly mental labour? Nicholas Lobkowicz, who takes issue with many traditional readings of Marx's critique of Hegel in *Theory and Practice: History of a Concept from Aristotle to Marx*, helps supply us with the answer:

> In short, Marx does not accuse Hegel of having treated labour as if it were a thought activity. Rather, he accuses him of having in the *Phenomenology* described human history in terms of a dialectic of consciousness, not in terms of [a] dialectic of labour. When he says that the only labour which Hegel recognizes is abstract mental labour, he has in mind the structure of the *Phenomenology* and in fact of Hegel's whole [philosophy], not the passages on labour in the *Phenomenology* and other writings by Hegel. For

---

143. Marx 1975r, pp. 332–3. Marx's discussion here renders implausible Paolucci's (2007, p. 107) claim, 'In sum, Marx rejected Kant's a priori speculative philosophy, Hegel's mystical idealist dialectic...Hegel and Kant failed because their philosophies were not empirically rooted'. As numerous studies have shown, Hegel was a most studious observer of empirical realities as well as of such disciplines as political economy. His idealism, as is the case with many in the idealist tradition, resides in his conception of the *relation* between ideas and empirical reality, not in a failure to deal with the latter.

144. Marx 1975r, p. 333.

145. This interpretation especially characterises C.J. Arthur's work. He writes, 'The first thing that should give us pause is that immediately after this praise Marx qualifies it by complaining that "the only labour Hegel knows and recognizes is *abstract mental* labour". The servant's labour is clearly *material*, so this remark shows that not only has Marx not drawn on that analysis, but he has actually *forgotten* all about it and done Hegel a minor injustice!' It is hard to imagine that Marx could have 'forgotten' that Hegel deals with non-mental labour throughout the *Phenomenology* – especially given that he directly refers to passages where he does so in the 'Critique of the Hegelian Dialectic' (see Marx 1975r, p. 331). Moreover, Arthur – like many others before and after him – is conflating Hegel's discussion of specific manifestations of labour with the *structure* of his philosophical system as a whole. See Arthur 1983, pp. 67–75.

what Marx wants to say is that Hegel's description of the movement of self-consciousness is an adulterated description of the historical movement of labouring humanity.[146]

According to this reading, Hegel sees labour as the creative self-expression of human creativity unfolding through the dialectical process of externalisation and the transcendence of externalisation. Marx was greatly indebted to Hegel for this insight. However, Marx recognises that, by structuring his system upon the notion of a disembodied subject, Hegel lacked access to a vantage-point from which to envisage the actual transcendence of *alienated* labour in capitalist society. Like the classical-political economists, he failed to distinguish between labour as a transhistorical, creative expression of humanity's 'species-being' and labour as the perverse reduction of such activity to an absolute abstraction – value-production. In sum, Marx accuses Hegel of seeing only the positive and not the negative side of labour.[147] By conflating *alienated* labour and 'labour', Hegel uncritically accommodates himself to the peculiar social form of labour in capitalism.

As a result, his philosophical system becomes the expression of alienation itself. As Lobkowicz succinctly puts it:

> Marx claims that the very fact that Hegel translates the real dialectic of labouring humanity into a dialectic of mentally labouring self-consciousness is itself a reflection of alienated labour…Hegel's description of history as a movement of mentally labouring self-consciousness is nothing but 'the self-objectification…of the alienated mind of the world within its self-alienation'.[148]

Once again, the problem is not that Hegel fails to grasp reality. *The problem is that he grasps reality all too well.* By inverting the relation of subject and predicate, Hegel has provided a philosophical expression of 'the general estrange-

---

146. Lobkowicz 1967, p. 322.

147. Marx may have altered his view of Hegel on this issue had he access to Hegel's early writings, which were not published until after his death. Hegel's *First Philosophy of Spirit* (1803/04) discusses labour in terms that are strikingly similar to Marx: 'But in the same ratio that the number produced rises, the value of labour falls; the labour becomes that much deader, it becomes machine work, the skill of the single labourer is infinitely limited.' See Hegel 1979b, p. 248. Greater attentiveness to Hegel's *Philosophy of Spirit* as published in 1817 might also have led Marx to rethink his claim that Hegel sees only the positive side of labour. Hegel writes, 'The labour which thus becomes more abstract tends on the one hand by its uniformity to make labour easier and to increase production – on another to limit each person to a single kind of technical skill, and thus produce more unconditional dependence on the social system'. See Hegel 1978, pp. 257–8.

148. Lobkowicz 1967, p. 343.

ment of the human being and therefore also of human thought'. Hegel has 'brought these together and presented them as moments of the abstraction-process'.[149] In doing so the *Phenomenology* provides the philosophical expression of the very realities that Marx is determined to criticise.

Understanding the reason why Marx accuses Hegel of knowing 'only abstractly mental labour' is of critical importance in pinpointing exactly what he objects to in Hegel. The *inversion* that Marx objects to is *not* that Hegel gets things upside-down by dealing with mental instead of material entities. *He objects to the way in which Hegel inverts the relation of subject and predicate, regardless of whether he is dealing with mental or material entities.* Raya Dunayevskaya argues, 'Deeply rooted as Marx's concept of Alienated Labour is in Hegel's theory of alienation, Marx's analysis is no simple inversion (much less a Feuerbachian inversion) of dealing with labour when Hegel was dealing only with Consciousness'.[150] For all of its critical defects, Hegel's *Phenomenology*, Marx contends, nevertheless grasps, in an 'estranged' form, the 'essence of *labour*' and 'objective man'.[151]

We are now in a position to discern the similarities as well as differences between Marx's 1843 critique of Hegel's *Philosophy of Right* and his 1844 critique of Hegel's *Phenomenology of Spirit* and *Encyclopedia of the Philosophical Sciences*. Marx turns to a critique of the *Philosophy of Right* in the midst of an intense engagement with *political* reality, as part of his effort to discern the limitations of existing political formations. He finds that the *Philosophy of Right* provides the philosophical expression of these limitations. In 1844, he turns to a critique of the *Phenomenology of Spirit* in the midst of an intense engagement with *economic* reality, as part of his effort to discern the limits of existing economic formations. He finds that the *Phenomenology* provides the philosophical expression of these limitations. In posing the subject of dialectical movement as disembodied self-consciousness, the 'gallery of images' and entities analysed in the *Phenomenology* are treated as mere thought-forms. Since actual entities are treated as emanations of the Idea, Hegel adopts an *uncritical* attitude towards them. Hegel's *Logic*, Marx writes, is 'the money of the spirit' – 'its essence which has grown totally indifferent to real determinateness'.[152] Hegel's philosophical system therefore expresses, Marx argues, the very economic process of abstraction that is at the core of capitalism.

---

149. Marx 1975r, p. 343.
150. See Dunayevskaya 2003, p. 52.
151. Marx 1975r, p. 333.
152. Marx 1975r, p. 330. Marx's 'Notes on G.W.F. Hegel, *Phenomenology of Spirit*', written around the same time, also links Hegel's *Logic* to the 'money' of the spirit. For a translation of this document, see the Appendix.

However, there is also a critical *difference* between Marx's attitude towards the *Philosophy of Right* and the *Phenomenology of Spirit*. Although Marx credits the *Philosophy of Right* with expressing the alienated nature of modern politics, he never suggests that it intimates the transcendence of such realities. It is a very different question when it comes to the *Phenomenology*. Instead of completely rejecting the concept of self-movement through second negativity, Marx argues that it contains a key-insight: namely, that the transcendence of alienation is reached as a result of a movement through *second* negativity. Marx sees in this an 'estranged insight' that points to an alternative to capitalism – *'positive* humanism, beginning from itself'.[153]

Marx appropriates Hegel's discussion of the dialectic of negativity in the *Phenomenology* and *Encyclopedia* by arguing that the first negation is the abolition of private property. Yet this negation by no means ensures liberation; on the contrary, 'this type of abolition of private property is…only a retrogression, a sham universality'. He calls it 'the *abstract* negation of the entire world of culture and civilization'.[154] This 'vulgar communist' negation of private property must itself be negated in order to reach liberation. Whether this type of communism is 'democratic or despotic' makes little difference: it is defective because it is infected with its opposite in focusing exclusively on the question of property. To abolish capital the negation of private property must itself be negated. Only then would there arise 'positive Humanism, beginning from itself'. For this reason, Marx calls genuine communism (which he equates to 'a thoroughgoing Naturalism or Humanism') 'the position as the negation of the negation'.[155]

It is on this issue of the negation of the negation that Marx parts company with Feuerbach, who rejected the concept *tout court* as a mystical abstraction that has no bearing on reality. Marx writes:

> Feuerbach thus conceives the negation of the negation *only* as the contradiction of philosophy with itself – as the philosophy which affirms Theology (the transcendent, etc.) after having denied it…But because Hegel has conceived

---

153. This crucial difference between Marx's critique of the *Philosophy of Right* and the *Phenomenology of Spirit* helps explain why he felt the need to return to a close textual engagement with Hegel in 1844, after issuing such a sharp criticism of him in 1843. Despite the importance of his critique of the *Philosophy of Right*, it is circumscribed by the limits of its subject-matter – Hegel's political theory, which does not intimate a transcendence of capitalist alienation. Marx returns to 'settle accounts' with Hegel in 1844 because the *Phenomenology* discloses something that is not found in the *Philosophy of Right* – an intimation, 'estranged' as it is, of the transcendence of alienation through double negation.
154. Marx 1975r, p. 295.
155. Marx 1975r, p. 306.

the negation of the negation from the point of view of the positive relation inherent in it, to that extent he has discovered, though only as an *abstract, logical,* and *speculative* expression, the movement of history...[156]

Marx then writes, 'It is now time to formulate the positive aspects of the Hegelian dialectic within the realm of estrangement'. What he praises is nothing less than *Hegel's concept of the transcendence*[157] *of alienation through second negativity*:

> *Supersession* as an objective movement of *retracting* the alienation *into self*. This is the insight, expressed within the estrangement, concerning the *appropriation* of the objective essence through the supersession of its estrangement: it is the estranged insight into the real objectification of man, into the *real appropriation* of his objective essence through the annihilation of the *estranged* character of the objective world...[158]

Marx contends that the transcendence of alienation in Hegel represents the mere return of *thought* to itself because Hegel treats the subject of the dialectic as disembodied self-consciousness. However, Marx holds that when this defect is corrected by treating 'real corporeal *man*'[159] as the subject of the dialectic, this same concept of the transcendence of alienation through double negation expresses the path to *freedom* – which he refers to as the 'return of man from religion, family, state, etc., to his *human*, i.e., *social* existence'.[160]

Marx's intense focus on Hegel's concept of 'the negation of the negation' is also evident in his Excerpt-Notes on the chapter 'Absolute Knowledge', composed around the same time as the 1844 'Critique'. Although Hegel actually never explicitly mentions the term 'negation of the negation' in the chapter on 'Absolute Knowledge', Marx singles it out as a conceptual determinant underpinning that chapter and the *Phenomenology of Spirit* as a whole. He summarises the chapter on 'Absolute Knowledge' as follows:

> Being, Essence, Concept; Universality. Particularity. Individuality. Position. Negation. Negation of the Negation; simple, differentiated, transcended opposition. Immediacy. Mediation. Self-transcending mediation. Being in itself. Externalisation. Return to itself from externalization. In-itself. For-itself. In-and-for-itself. Unity. Differentiation. Self-differentiation.

---

156. Marx 1975r, p. 329.
157. *Aufhebung* is sometimes translated as 'sublation' instead of 'transcendence'. In either case, it refers to a state in which something is both 'negated' and 'preserved' in the sense of 'raised to a higher level'.
158. Marx 1975r, p. 341.
159. Marx 1975r, p. 336.
160. Marx 1975r, p. 297.

Identity. Negation. Negativity. Logic. Nature. Spirit. Pure Consciousness. Consciousness. Self-Consciousness. Concept. Judgment. Syllogism.[161]

Most critically of all, Marx's intense focus on Hegel's concept of self-movement through second negativity leads him to posit a vision of a new society that surpasses the limitations of other radicals on the scene at the time. This is especially seen in his discussion of man/woman relations. Taking off from an insight voiced by Fourier, he argues that 'In this relationship, therefore, is *sensuously manifested*, reduced to an observable *fact*, the extent to which the human essence has become nature to man, or to which nature to him has become the human essence of man. From this relationship one can therefore judge man's whole level of development.'[162] He quickly moves beyond Fourier's position, however, by attacking the idea of the communal possession of women. He contends that 'this idea of *the community of women gives away the secret* of this as yet completely crude and thoughtless communism.'[163] Marx says the 'crude communist' attempt to replace private ownership of women by the patriarchal family with their collective ownership by a community does posit a 'negation' of traditional social formations. But it is a mere 'abstract negation'[164] because it fails to liberate women from being *owned*, from being treated as sexual *objects*. In Hegelian dialectics, 'abstract negation' corresponds to the first negation. First negativity remains dependent on its object of critique, since the negation of the other fails to free itself from its presuppositions. The initial negation of private property, whether in the factory or the family, remains dependent on its object of critique insofar as it presupposes that *having* is more important than *being*. It merely replaces private ownership with collective ownership. Just as in the labour-process 'the category of the worker is not done away with, but extended to all men', so in the man/woman relation the domination of women is not abolished, but becomes extended to all women. *In subjecting the crude communists to critique for favouring the community of women, Marx is specifying the shortcomings of stopping short of the negation of the negation.* Genuine communism for Marx does not consist of the mere abolition of private property in either the sphere of material production or sexual reproduction. Genuine communism represents the negation of that very negation. The latter is *concrete* or *absolute* negativity. For this reason he concludes this section of the 1844 *Manuscripts* by writing that genuine 'communism is the position as the negation of the negation'.[165]

---

161. See the Appendix, below, p. 217.
162. Marx 1975r, pp. 295–6.
163. Marx 1975r, p. 294.
164. Marx 1975r, p. 295.
165. Marx 1975r, p. 306.

Through his critical appropriation of the concept of self-movement through absolute negativity, Marx's 1844 *Manuscripts* projects a truly new and revolutionary world-conception, one which takes him far from the positions held by other socialists and communists of the time.[166] He sees the process of revolutionary transformation not as a singular act, as the negation of private property and political overthrow of the bourgeoisie, necessary as that is, but as a consistently self-critical *social* revolution, that is, as a process of *permanent* revolution. Crude communism – the abolition of private property – is only the first negation. It is a necessary but insufficient step towards liberation. To achieve 'positive humanism, beginning from itself' much more is needed – the negation of the negation. Unlike Feuerbach, who rejects Hegel on the grounds that he posits positivity as a result of a logical movement, the movement through negation and double negation, Marx finds in this very movement an 'estranged' insight into how 'positive humanism' – a world free from alienation – actually comes into being. While Marx is highly critical of the way in which Hegel presents the dialectic of negativity, he appropriates Hegel's concept of self-movement through absolute negativity when it comes to projecting his own conception of the future.[167]

---

166. Many have overlooked the fact that in the very work in which Marx praises Feuerbach the most – his 1844 'Critique of the Hegelian Dialectic' – is where he parts company with him, precisely on the issue of Feuerbach's wholesale rejection of Hegel's concept of the transcendence of alienation through the negation of the negation. A striking illustration of this is Patrick Murray's sometimes-valuable *Marx's Theory of Scientific Knowledge*. Murray places great emphasis on Marx's critique of Hegel's *Logic* for representing 'the money of the spirit'; however, he does not so much as mention the passages in which Marx *praises* Hegel's concept of the transcendence or supersession of alienation. Although he mentions in passing Marx's 'humanism', he fails to connect it to Marx's critical appropriation of Hegel's concept of the negation of the negation. This tendency to emphasise Marx's debt to Hegel as being limited to the concept of externalisation or alienation has a lengthy history in Marx scholarship. Especially influential along these lines is Georg Lukács's *The Young Hegel*, which contends that *Entäusserung* is the 'central philosophical concept' of both Hegel's *Phenomenology* and Marx's appropriation of Hegel's dialectic. See Lukács 1976, pp. 537–68. Lukács likewise fails to single out Marx's praise of Hegel's discussion of the supersession of alienation. For a detailed criticism of Lukács' position, see Hudis 1989. I am suggesting in this work that the reluctance of many commentators to recognise that Marx critically appropriates Hegel's conception of the transcendence of alienation through second negativity appears to be connected to the fact that they refrain from entering into a discussion of Marx's conception of the *alternative* to capitalism.

167. Stathis Kouvelakis therefore makes a highly questionable assertion when he writes, 'As for the philosophy that culminates in the Hegelian system, it is merely the reflexive consciousness of this alienation, a purely speculative, formal and abstract transcendence of the limits alienation imposes'. This one-sided reading overlooks the fact that Marx sees a *positive* dimension within Hegel's 'speculative' concept of transcendence that he appropriates for his own understanding of the kind of society that must replace capitalism. See Kouvelakis 2003, p. 168.

Marx goes so far as to write, 'Communism is the necessary form and dynamic principle of the immediate future, but communism as such is not the goal of human development, the form of human society'.[168] But if communism is only the *immediate* but not *ultimate* goal, what is Marx really striving for? It appears that it is what he calls 'a totality of human manifestations of life'.[169] He refers to a new society as one that 'produces man in this entire richness of his being – produces the *rich* man *profoundly endowed with all the senses* – as its enduring reality'.[170] This is far beyond what he calls 'crude communism', which like capitalism reduces human sensuousness to *one* sense – the sense of *having*. Yet it is not clear that Marx considers even genuine communism or 'positive humanism' as the *end* or *goal* of human development, in that manifesting a totality of latent and acquired sensuous abilities is *an endless process of becoming*. Perhaps it was not without good reason Marx spoke of continuing the revolution 'in permanence'.

Marx peers into the future in the 1844 *Manuscripts* in asking what would happen when we 'Assume man to be man, and his relationship to the world to be a human world'. When that is achieved there *would* be exchange – but an exchange of 'love only for love, trust only for trust, etc.'. If one wants to enjoy any manifestation of life, be it art or anything else, one would need to develop a *sense* for it. Simply obtaining *things* in lieu of such attunement leaves one impoverished. 'Every one of your relations to man and to nature must be a *specific expression*, corresponding to the object of your will, of your *real individual life*'[171] – which is another way of saying that '*All* emancipation is a *reduction* of the human world and relationships to *man himself*'.[172]

It can be argued that much of what Marx is discussing about the future is vague and indeterminate. He surely provides little or no discussion of the institutional forms[173] that might help promote a totality of manifestations of life. Yet it would be a mistake to interrupt the apparently ethereal character of much of Marx's discussion to mean that he was either unclear about the kind

---

168. Marx 1975r, p. 306.
169. Marx 1975r, p. 299.
170. Marx 1975r, p. 302.
171. Marx 1975r, p. 326.
172. Marx 1975o, p. 168.
173. The closest Marx comes in 1844 to discussing institutional forms of a new society is in his discussion of landed property in the First Manuscript, where he argues against both monopolisation of land and dividing up the land into small private holdings. He advocates an 'association' of producers that 'shares the economic advantage of large-scale landed property' as well as 'the original tendency' towards equality. At this point, he does not mention nationalisation or state-ownership of the land. See Marx 1975r, p. 268.

of society that he wanted or that he saw no need to envisage the nature of an alternative to capital at all. He writes in the 1844 *Manuscripts*,

> In order to abolish the *idea* of private property, the *idea* of communism is quite sufficient. It takes *actual* communist action to abolish actual private property. History will lead to it; and this movement, which *in theory* we already know to be a self-transcending movement, will constitute in actual fact a very rough and protracted process. But we must regard it as a real advance to have at the outset gained a consciousness of the limited character as well as of the *goal* of this historical movement – and a consciousness that reaches out beyond it.[174]

Far from refraining from any discussion about the future, Marx is here reflecting on the future on two levels. One is the idea of communism – the *immediate* principle of the future – that has as its task the elimination of private property and alienated labour. The other is a realisation of the idea of freedom that is much more open-ended and harder to define or even give a name to, since it involves the return of humanity to itself as a sensuous being exhibiting a totality of manifestations of life. Marx considers it a 'real advance' to be able to say this much about the future. We now need to see how he will further specify this when faced with an array of specific social tendencies and problems.

Discerning the ideal within the real, 1845–8

Upon completing the 1844 *Manuscripts*, Marx becomes directly involved in workers' movements and writes a series of works to further clarify his break from capitalism and the need to replace it with a totally new kind of society, culminating in his famous *Communist Manifesto*.[175] His writings of 1845–7 contain especially rich reflections about the alternative to capitalism. The central issue that concerns him is summed up in a passage in *The German Ideology*: 'Individuals always proceeded, and always proceed, from themselves. Their relations are the relations of their real life process. How does it happen that their relations assume an independent existence over against them? And that the forces of their own life become superior to them?'[176]

---

174. Marx 1975r, p. 313.
175. The *Manifesto* was written in late December 1847 and first published (in London, in the German original) in February 1848. It was written primarily by Marx, though Marx and Engels were listed as co-authors. Engels had originally been commissioned by the Communist League to write it, but Marx considerably revised his initial draft, entitled 'Principles of Communism', in the *Manifesto* itself.
176. Marx and Engels 1976a, p. 93.

Marx is specifying the inversion of subject and predicate as the defining feature of modern social existence, in that the relations formed by individuals become a 'person apart' that governs their lives without their consent. His primary criticism of contemporary thinkers is that they fall prey to this inversion. In *The Holy Family*, he makes a critique of Bruno Bauer and other young Hegelians for presenting 'truth as an automaton that proves itself'. For them, '*history*, like *truth*, becomes a person apart, a metaphysical subject of which the real human individuals are mere bearers'.[177] He writes in reply: '*History* does *nothing*, it "possesses *no* immense wealth," it "wages *no* battles". It is *man*, real, living man who does all that, who possesses and fights: "history" is not, as it were, a person apart, using man as a means to achieve its own aims; history is *nothing but* the activity of man pursuing his aims'.[178] On these grounds, he rejects the view that history unfolds in necessarily-progressive stages. He pours scorn upon Bauer's contention that socialists and communists endorse unilinear theories of progressive improvement. Marx insists that the very opposite is the case, since figures like Fourier considered 'progress' to be no more than an 'abstract phrase'. Marx writes, 'In spite of the pretensions of "*Progress*", continual *retrogressions* and *circular movements* occur . . . the category, "*Progress*" is completely empty and abstract'.[179] Holding that history is destined to proceed along fixed 'progressive' lines assumes that we are helpless victims (or beneficiaries) of what we ourselves create.

On the same grounds, he attacks those who pose 'society' as a quasi-autonomous force. *The German Ideology* states, 'Society is abstracted from these individuals, it is made independent, it relapses into a savagery of its own, and the individuals suffer as a *result* of their relapse'.[180] Marx is further developing his understanding of the relation between civil society and the state that he first formulated in his critique of Hegel's *Philosophy of Right*. He attacks the notion that the state holds together civil society. On the contrary, it is civil society that holds together the state.[181] This is in keeping with his view that the state is

---

177. Engels and Marx 1975, p. 79. Although the vast bulk of *The Holy Family* was written by Marx, with only a very short section written by Engels, as a sign of appreciation Marx insisted on including Engels's name before his own on the title page.

178. Engels and Marx, p. 93.

179. Engels and Marx, p. 83. Marx's view of progress appears to be in accord with what a number of scholars contend is Hegel's position as well. H.S. Harris writes, 'There is nothing in [Hegel's] logical theory to warrant the belief that the motion of consciousness must always be progressive. Every position of consciousness contains the earlier positions in a sublated form, and every position is a stable circle that can maintain itself against criticism. Thus stability is "natural" and regression is just as possible as progress'. See Harris 1995, p. 107.

180. Marx and Engels 1976a, p. 464.

181. See especially the discussion of this is in Engels and Marx 1975, pp. 120–2.

an edifice created by mutually-interacting individuals, instead of being some autonomous force that shapes civil society of its own accord. Marx is not satisfied, however, with simply pointing out the logical priority of civil society over the state. He wants to know why the state *appears* to have priority over civil society. The answer lies in the limits of civil society itself. He asks,

> How is it that personal interests always develop, against the will of the individuals, into class interests, into common interests which acquire independent existence in relation to the individual persons, and in their independence assume the form of *general* interests? ... How is it that in this process of private interests acquiring independent existence as class interests the personal behavior of the individual is bound to be objectified, estranged, and at the same time exists as a power independent of man and without him?[182]

His answer is that 'definite modes of production' arise that *compel* civil society to take the form of incompatible relations between private and general interests. The *abstraction* of individual from general interests makes *necessary* a state that externally mediates the relation between these mutually-antagonistic forces. The state, a product of human activity, now takes on a life of its own and governs the behaviour of individuals behind their backs – *because* of the limitations of civil society. He therefore argues in the 'Theses on Feuerbach', 'The standpoint of the old materialism is civil society; that of the new is human society, or social humanity'.[183]

'Social humanity' is not, however, a 'person apart' that externally imposes its will upon individuals. It is, rather, a condition in which individuals freely relate to themselves and each other on the basis of their self-activity.[184] Marx refers to this in the 1844 *Manuscripts* as: 'Above all we must avoid again postulating "society" as an abstraction *vis-à-vis* the individual. The individual is the *social being*'. Marx is not trying to *wall* humanity into the 'social'; he rather seeks a mutual *compatibility* between individual and general interests.[185]

Yet exactly how does the *present* mode of production *compel* civil society to assume an abstract form? The answer is the social division of labour. By forcing individuals to adhere to a social division of labour, individuals become

---

182. Marx and Engels 1976a, p. 245.
183. Marx 1976a, p. 5. Marx also contends that civil society is the standpoint of classical-political economy, a tendency that he strongly opposes.
184. Marx writes in *The Holy Family*, 'Society behaves just as exclusively as the state, only in a more polite form; it does not throw you out, but it makes it so uncomfortable for you that you go out of your own free will'. See Engels and Marx 1975, p. 96.
185. For a searing criticism of twentieth-century 'socialism', which 'walls man into his socialness', see Kosik 1976.

radically *separated* from one other. This separation takes on a *fixed* form, regardless of their actual talents and abilities. Society becomes an abstraction that governs the lives of individuals, instead of the other way around: 'As long as man remains in naturally evolved society, that is, as long as the cleavage exists between the particular and the common interest, so long, therefore, as activity is not voluntary, but naturally, divided, man's own deed becomes an alien power opposed to him, which enslaves him instead of being controlled by him.'[186]

We have reached the acme of subject-predicate inversion. Marx is now supplying a historical, *materialist* explanation for the inversion that he objected to so strongly in his analyses of Hegel's *Philosophy of Right* and *Phenomenology of Spirit*.

How is this inversion to be overcome? By abolishing the social division of labour. Once individuals are allowed to *freely* pursue a variety of talents and tasks as befits their particular nature, instead of having their role 'fixed' by some pre-ordained social power 'above' them, a new society would exist. He famously describes such a society as follows: '[I]n communist society, where nobody has one exclusive sphere of activity but each can become accomplished in any branch he wishes, society regulates the general production and thus makes it possible for me to do one thing today and another tomorrow, to hunt in the morning, fish in the afternoon, rear cattle in the evening, criticize after dinner, just as I have a mind, without every becoming a hunter, fisherman, shepherd, or critic.'[187]

Marx clearly has some notion of a postcapitalist society. Yet he remains wary as of this point about saying much more about it. Instead, he writes, 'It is not a question of what this or that proletarian, or even the whole proletariat, at the moment *regards* as its aim. It is a question of *what the proletariat is*, and what, according to this *being*, it will historically be compelled to do'.[188]

Marx's reticence about indulging in detailed speculation about the future society – in place of what the proletariat itself *is* and is compelled to *do* – is closely connected to his opposition to the subject-predicate inversion. Posing a vision of the new society *for* the proletariat, or *irrespective* of what it *is*, amounts to foisting a product of intelligence or imagination upon the actual subject of history. Much of what Marx has criticised in capitalism in his early writings centres on the tendency to foist the products of human development upon the subject, irrespective of its own needs and desires. Why would he now

---

186. Marx and Engels 1976a, p. 47.
187. Ibid. Note that Marx does not mention to the *state* as regulating the general production, but rather *society*.
188. Engels and Marx 1975, p. 37.

favour promoting a vision of the new society irrespective of the proletariat's needs and desires? Furthermore, a major theme that Marx has emphasised since his doctoral dissertation (if not earlier) has been the need to discern the ideal from within the real. Indulging in speculation about the future, irrespective of the subjective force that can realise the ideal, amounts to a violation of one of Marx's primary normative standpoints.

Early in 1845, not long after composing *The Holy Family*, Marx develops a new concept that represents a further expression of his effort to discern the forms of the future from within the contours of the present. In his 'Draft of an Article on Friedrich List's Book *Das Nationale System der politischen Ökonomie*', he poses the development of modern industry as providing the material conditions for a postcapitalist society. He writes of 'the power which industry has without knowing or willing it and which destroys it and creates the basis for a human existence'.[189] This power is in the proletariat, which is produced by modern industry. Utilising a metaphor he will later employ in *Capital* and other writings, the proletariat is the 'human kernel' contained within the 'shell' of industry that will burst forth from its further development. Industry, the product of human activity, takes on a life of its own and becomes the subjective force of capitalist society. Although Marx opposes this inversion, he now sees in it the seeds of *an inversion of the inversion*, since the point will one day be reached when the product of industry – the workers – will step forth as the real subject, as the 'bearers of human development'. History in the modern era takes on a life of its own and operates behind the backs of its participants; but in doing so, it brings forth the subjective force that can dissolve this upside-down world. Genuine history will at that point finally *begin*.

The German Ideology further develops this by emphasising the development of the productive forces as the pre-condition for communism. The productive forces include technology, scientific knowledge, and the overall level of industry. The most important productive force is the proletariat, which is generated by all three. Any effort to create a communist society without the development of these productive forces, he argues, would ensure that communism remains a local and transient phenomenon. 'The proletariat can thus exist only *world-historically*, just as communism, its activity, can only have a "world-historical" existence'.[190] Marx rejected any conception that socialism or communism could be created in a single isolated country or group of countries.

---

189. Marx 1975s, p. 282.
190. Marx and Engels 1976a, p. 49.

What will help bring communism into being, Marx suggests, is capitalism's drive to subject all human relations to value-production through the creation of a world-market. Capitalism's inherent drive for global expansion contains within itself the material conditions for its dissolution. He concludes, 'Communism is for us not a *state of affairs* which is to be established, an ideal to which reality [will] have to adjust itself. We call communism the *real* movement which abolishes the present state of things'.[191]

This does not mean, however, that *consciousness* of a future communist society is unnecessary. He argues that 'communist consciousness' on a *mass-scale* is needed because 'an alteration of men on a mass scale is necessary'. It is needed not just to overthrow the bourgeoisie, but in order for a revolution to 'succeed in ridding itself of all the muck of the ages and become fitted to found society anew'.[192] If society itself brings about the millennium in quasi-automatic fashion, it remains a 'person apart' insofar as the social individual is concerned. The 'perverse' inversion of subject and predicate that characterises capitalism remains in place, and with it, the 'muck of the ages'. This inversion can only be inverted through the *conscious* intervention of a *human* subject that strives to reorganise social relations from top to bottom. Marx has not departed from, but rather has made more concrete, his insistence (expressed in a letter to Ruge) of 1843 that 'consciousness is something that [humanity] *has* to acquire, even if it does not want to'.[193]

It may appear that there is a tension or contradiction between these two sides of formulating the issue. On the one hand, communism is a state of affairs that will emerge immanently from the contradictions of capitalism; yet, on the other hand, it remains necessary to develop an awareness of a future communist society in order for a revolution to succeed in radically altering human relations. However, on closer examination, there is no tension or contradiction in Marx's position at all. He consistently holds throughout his life that revolutionary consciousness spontaneously emerges from the oppressed in response to an array of specific material conditions. He does not hold that such consciousness is brought 'to' the masses 'from without' – in direct contrast to Lassalle, Kautsky and Lenin, who held the contrary position.[194] At the same time, Marx does not equate the *consciousness* that emerges from the oppressed with revolutionary *theory*. The latter does not emerge spontaneously from the masses, but from hard conceptual labour on the part of theoreticians. Revolutionary theory needs to elicit and build upon mass

---

191. Ibid.
192. Marx and Engels 1976a, p. 53.
193. Marx 1975m, p. 144.
194. For more on this, see Hudis 1998.

consciousness, but it is not reducible to it. If it were no different than mass-consciousness, it would be impossible for Marx, or anyone else for that matter, to explain the *objectivity* of their *subjective* role as theoreticians. In other words, while the class- and socialist consciousness that spontaneously emerges from the masses is of critical importance, it is not the full equivalent of a *philosophy of revolution* that helps disclose the complex forms and dynamics of capitalism as well as the alternative to it. On these grounds, Marx holds that the immanent rhythm of reality will prepare the way for an alternative; yet he does not appear to assume that its emergence is for that reason guaranteed.[195] *Hard* and *continuous* theoretical and philosophical labour that is rooted in, but not reducible to, the consciousness of the oppressed, is needed to help bring forth a conceptual alternative. Marx, therefore, feels that nothing prohibits him from directly discussing the distinguishing feature of a postcapitalist society even as he warns against engaging in idle speculation about the nature of such a state of affairs:

> Communism differs from all previous movements in that it overturns the basis of all earlier relations of production and intercourse, and for the first time consciously treats all naturally evolved premises as the creations of hitherto existing men...Its organization is, therefore, essentially economic, the material production of the conditions of this unity; it turns existing conditions into conditions of unity. The reality which communism creates is precisely the true basis for rendering it impossible that anything should exist independently of individuals, in so far as reality is nevertheless only a product of the preceding intercourse of individuals.[196]

Marx is here defining the new society that he is striving for on the basis of a critique of subject-predicate inversion and on the basis of the normative principle that '*All* emancipation is a *reduction* of the human world and relationships to *man himself*'.[197]

He further specifies additional aspects of a postcapitalist society in his writings of 1845–7. He argues that in such a society the proletariat does not become the ruling class, since there are neither classes nor a proletariat. The proletariat simply ceases to exist: 'When the proletariat is victorious, it by

---

195. The same is true, of course, when it comes to obtaining a proper understanding of capital and capitalism. Many people realise on their own initiative that capitalism is an unfair and exploitative system; but that is not the same as composing a work such as Marx's *Capital*, which aims to grasp capital's 'law of motion' by penetrating its mystifying, albeit *necessarily*-mystifying, forms of appearance. Simply agreeing on the need to *develop* an alternative does not by itself *constitute* one.

196. Marx and Engels 1976a, p. 81.

197. Marx 1975o, p. 168.

no means becomes the absolute side of society, for it is victorious only by abolishing itself and its opposite. Then the proletariat disappears'.[198] He also writes that since 'the communist revolution is directed against the hitherto existing mode of activity' it 'does away with *labour*'.[199] Marx does not suggest that laboring-activity literally comes to an end, but that 'the whole opposition between work and enjoyment disappears'.[200] 'Labour' as an activity distinct from the enjoyment of a wealth of sensuous possibilities no longer mediates social interaction and reproduction. Labour in this sense is *abolished*.

Along these lines, he further develops the emphasis of the 1844 *Manuscripts* on developing 'a totality of manifestations of life' as a defining feature of the new society. He now speaks of the 'development of a totality of desires', arguing that individuals become fixated on a small number of desires when society prevents them from pursuing a wide range of them. Marx thinks it is an 'absurdity' to presume that one can satisfy one passion or desire 'apart from all others'. When one passion is pursued at the expense of a multiplicity of desires, the passion becomes interminable; it 'assumes an abstract, isolated character' and confronts the individual as 'an alien power'.[201] He reiterates his earlier critique of the interminable desire to *have*, which becomes overwhelming in capitalism.

Partly on these grounds, the *Communist Manifesto* notes that 'buying and selling' – the market – disappears in a communist society. Yet he reserves his harshest words for the market in labour-power: 'Communism does not deprive man of the power to appropriate the products of society; all that it does is to deprive him of the power to subjugate the labour of others by means of such appropriation'.[202]

In the *Manifesto*, Marx also writes that 'the theory of the Communists may be summed up in the single sentence: Abolition of private property'.[203] It may seem that Marx has muted, if not moved away from, his perspective of 1844, in that the abolition of private property here seems to be posed not just as a mediatory stage, but as the ultimate goal. However, this would be too facile a reading. Marx focuses on the need to negate private property because it is the most *immediate* expression of the power of bourgeois society over the worker. Through the bourgeois property-relation, the workers are forced to sell themselves for a wage to the owners of capital, who appropriate the products of

---

198. Engels and Marx 1975, p. 36.
199. Marx and Engels 1976a, p. 52.
200. Marx and Engels 1976a, p. 218.
201. Marx and Engels 1976a, p. 262.
202. Marx and Engels 1976b, p. 500.
203. Marx and Engels 1976b, p. 498.

their productive activity. Without the abolition of this property-relation, the economic and political domination of the bourgeoisie remains unchallenged. However, this does not mean that Marx has forgotten about, or is downplaying, alienated labour. Though the phrase 'alienated labour' does not appear in the *Manifesto*, it does single out the need to uproot the *conditions* of labour. Right before citing the need to abolish private property, it states:

> Owing to the extensive use of machinery and to the division of labour, the work of the proletarians has lost all individual character, and, consequently, all charm for the workman. He becomes an appendage of the machine, and it is only the most simple, most monotonous and most easily acquired knack, that is required of him.... In proportion, therefore, as the repulsiveness of the work increases, the wage decreases.[204]

In another passage reminiscent of the language found in the 1844 *Manuscripts*, he writes, 'In bourgeois society capital is independent and has individuality, while the living person is dependent and has no individuality'.[205] He goes on to say that the abolition of this condition is the essence of proletarian revolution: 'The proletarians cannot become masters of the productive forces of society, except by abolishing their own previous mode of appropriation, and thereby also every other previous mode of appropriation'.[206] Only *after* writing this does he state:

> The distinguishing feature of Communism is not the abolition of property generally, but the abolition of bourgeois property. But modern bourgeois private property is the final and most complete expression of the system of producing and appropriating products that is based on class antagonisms, on the exploitation of the many by the few. In this sense, the theory of the Communists may be summed up in the single sentence: Abolition of private property.[207]

It is important not to read the *Manifesto* selectively, by skipping over the phrase 'in this sense' in the last sentence and the word 'but' in the previous one. That Marx did not alter his view of the relation between alienated labour and private property between 1844 and 1847 is further confirmed by what he writes in an article written at around the same time as the *Manifesto*: '[P]*rivate property*, for instance, is not a simple relation or even an abstract concept, a principle, but consists in the totality of the *bourgeois* relations of

204. Marx and Engels 1976b, pp. 490–1.
205. Marx and Engels 1976b, p. 499.
206. Marx and Engels 1976b, p. 495.
207. Marx and Engels 1976b, p. 498.

production...a change in, or even the abolition of, these relations can only follow from a change in these classes and their relationships with each other, and a change in the relationship of classes is a historical change, a product of social activity as a whole'.[208]

Most importantly, Marx emphasises the need to address the goals of a new society, in the section of the *Manifesto* dealing with 'the relation of communists to the proletarians as a whole'. He singles out the distinctive contributions of communists as: (1) internationalism instead of nationalism; and (2) 'always and everywhere [they] represent the interests of the movement as a whole'. He then states that the communists put forth 'the ultimate general results of the proletarian movement'.[209] This raises an important issue: if the defining role of the communist party is to understand and transmit the 'ultimate results' of the struggle, how can Marx, who is authoring the *Communist Manifesto*, claim not to have some idea of those results? Moreover, the *Manifesto* begins by stating, 'It is high time that communists should openly...publish their views'.[210] And it concludes by stating, 'The Communists fight for the attainment of the immediate aims, for the enforcement of the momentary interests of the working class; but in the movement of the present, they also represent and take care of the future of that movement'.[211]

It therefore appears that Marx is not opposed to addressing the ultimate goal of a new society. What is at issue is *how* to go about doing so. Marx opposes any tendency to project a vision of a postcapitalist society that comes out of the theoretician's own head, independent of the actual struggles of the proletariat. But that does not mean that he opposes projecting a conception of the ultimate goal that is based on 'the actual struggles springing from existing class struggles'.[212] It is important not to conflate these two points. Marx opposes utopian socialists for projecting a view of the future that comes out of their heads rather than from the actual struggles of the real subject – the proletariat. Although many of the utopians were familiar with Feuerbach's critique of subject-predicate inversion, Marx's position seems to be that they fall into this very same inversion on another level by posing the results of

---

208. Marx 1976c, p. 337.
209. Marx and Engels 1976b, p. 497. This discussion should not be confused with the end of Section II of the *Manifesto*, which discusses the immediate goals of the communist movement – such as the centralisation of credit, communications, factories, and instruments of production 'in the hands of the state'. Marx is here not discussing socialism or communism, but a political transitional form immediately following the working classes' seizure of political power. In discussing the ultimate goals of the communists in the *Manifesto*, Marx makes no reference to the state.
210. Marx and Engels 1976b, p. 481.
211. Marx and Engels 1976b, p. 518.
212. Marx and Engels 1976b, p. 498.

their thinking as the subject of history. Thus, Marx's criticism of subject-predicate inversion not only underlies his critique of bourgeois society as well as of Hegel's philosophy, it also underlines his understanding of how to bring to consciousness the ultimate goals that he believes are worth living and dying for.

Evaluating the young Marx's concept of a postcapitalist society

This discussion by the young Marx indicates that his approach to articulating an alternative to existing society centres on viewing the ideal as immanent within the real. He therefore opposes any effort to introduce a speculative discussion of the future, irrespective of actual material conditions and forces of liberation. That does not mean, however, that Marx opposes positing any conception of an alternative at all. His main concern is with the *manner* of projecting an alternative, not whether or not to do so.

I have also so far shown that Marx came to view such phenomena as private property, alienated labour, and the separation of civil society and the state as problematic because of a set of normative concerns that he brought to bear upon his study of capitalism. Without these normative concerns, his critique of capitalism would hardly have been possible. This raises the question of how Marx's normative standpoint affected his view of the market. A study by Allan Megill – *The Burden of Reason (Why Marx Rejected Politics and the Market)* – raises important questions about this issue. Megill contends that Marx was not so much a 'materialist' as a *rationalist* who privileged universality, necessity, and predictability in his approach to historical phenomena. Like Hegel, he 'aimed to discover underlying logical essences that, he claimed, could not be discovered merely by generalizing from empirical data'.[213] He therefore finds the claim that Marx was a 'materialist' as constituting a superficial and one-sided reading of his work. Marx did not privilege matter over consciousness; on the contrary, Megill argues, Marx raised consciousness or reason to a veritable universal in emphasising how it is *embedded* in historical phenomena. Megill writes,

> Marx was profoundly influenced by a Hegelian conception of rationality, in which logic equates to ontology and in which ontology thus equates to mind, or spirit, thinking. Hegel's ontologization of logic resonated in Marx's work throughout the whole of his intellectual career. It is thus an egregious error to think that Marx can be adequately characterized as a

---

213. Megill 2002, p. 3.

materialist, at least as the term *materialist* is normally used...Hegel and
Marx, like many other nineteenth century thinkers, adhered to the notion
of embedded rationality.[214]

Notions of embedded rationality involve a privileging of universality, necessity, and predictivity. 'Chance' becomes the enemy of a theory based on a
notion of embedded rationality. Megill argues that Marx's adherence to this
notion explains his hostility to the market. Market-relations are defined by
chance and irregularity. Marx did not oppose the market, Megill argues,
because of any authoritarian tendencies on his part. He opposed the market
because it 'is not, and cannot be, subsumed under laws'[215] that are universal, necessary, and predictable. For Megill, this is Marx's gravest error. His
uncritical acceptance of the notion of embedded rationality – a theme that
appears in his work from as early as his very first writings, in 1837 – inexorably led Marx, he argues, to assume an unrealistically negative attitude
towards any form of the market.

Megill makes a powerful case that the interpretation of Marx as a 'materialist' fails to do justice to the nuances of his thought. As I have shown above,
Marx did not subject Hegel to critique simply for being an 'idealist'. Marx
writes, 'Hegel often gives a real presentation, embracing the thing itself,
within the speculative presentation'.[216] And, although Marx often calls himself a materialist after 1844, he criticises the 'one-sided' and 'abstract' materialism of the British empiricists as well as that of Feuerbach.[217] Most important
of all, in the 1844 *Manuscripts*, he explicitly affirms the unity of idealism and
materialism in spelling out his own philosophical world-view.

Megill is also correct in saying that Marx opposes market- and exchange-
relations in his early writings, even if the critique therein does not serve (as
I have argued above) as the crux of his critique of capitalism. He finds the
market to be *irrational*, in that prices are determined by arbitrary vacillations
of supply and demand, instead of by the human relations of person to person.
As Marx writes in *The Holy Family*, 'Value is determined at the beginning in
an apparently rational way, by the cost of production of an object and by
its social usefulness. Later it turns out that value is determined quite fortuitously and that it need not to bear any relation to either the cost of production or social usefulness.'[218] Marx is highly critical of arbitrary and fortuitous

---

214. Megill 2002, pp. 8, 9.
215. Megill 2002, p. 173.
216. Engels and Marx 1975, p. 61.
217. In the *Theses on Feuerbach*, he criticised 'contemplative materialism' and praised
idealism for developing 'the active side of history'. See Marx 1976a, p. 6.
218. Engels and Marx 1975, p. 32.

social relations such as the market because they represent 'relations [which] become independent of individuals' and become 'subordinated to general class relations'.[219] The market, as Marx sees it, is a product of the social division of labour – which is what produces the very separation of individual and general interests that he finds so offensive in capitalism.

There is also no question that Marx was committed to a notion of embedded rationality. As I have shown, Marx contends that reality must embody a 'rationality' that can enable the idea of freedom to be ultimately *realised*. If reality lacks such rationality, even the most noble and inspired efforts at social change would prove quixotic. However, the critical issue is, what is the agent or subject *within* reality that embodies reason? What is the 'internal principle' that guides reality towards the idea of freedom? Megill argues that, for Marx, the internal principle is *human* intelligence as expressed in *scientific* knowledge. He writes, 'The driving force of history is clearly *thought* – more specifically, it is the dimension of thought that is concerned with mastering nature with a view to satisfying human beings' needs'. This driving force is 'intellectual labour', labour that 'involves the application of knowledge to the productive process'.[220] It propels history towards the idea of freedom by developing the forces of production, which ultimately bring forth the social revolution against capitalism.

Despite Megill's close engagement with the writings of the young Marx (his book only goes up to 1846), there are many problems with his claim that Marx poses the intentional agent as science and technology. He writes, 'Marx's commitment to natural science, and to naturalism, was in place by 1844 at the latest'.[221] He refers specifically to Marx's embrace of 'naturalism' in the concluding essay of his *Economic and Philosophical Manuscripts* of 1844, where Marx writes: 'Here we see how consistent naturalism or humanism is distinct from both idealism and materialism, and constitutes at the same time the unifying truth of both. We see also how only naturalism is capable of comprehending the action of world history'.[222] Megill takes this to mean that for Marx, 'history…needs to be understood in the light of an understanding of nature – and that means, in the light of natural science'.[223] He fails to mention, however, that the passage does not equate naturalism to 'natural science'. Instead, it equates naturalism to *humanism*. In spelling out this 'positive humanism', Marx speaks of humanity as 'a suffering, conditioned, and

---

219. Marx and Engels 1976a, p. 438.
220. Megill 2002, p. 2.
221. Megill 2002, p. 13.
222. Marx 1975r, p. 336.
223. Megill 2002, p. 13.

limited creature'. As Megill acknowledges on several occasions, rationalism and 'natural science' – at least as traditionally understood in the modern Western tradition – tend to neglect feelings, suffering, and passions in favour of universality, necessity, and predictability. However, by equating naturalism to *humanism*, by which Marx means a philosophy that grasps 'actual corporeal humanity' in all its sensuousness, his reference to 'naturalism' emphasises not some predetermined pattern of predictability and certainty, but that which is particular, contingent, and unpredictable.

Megill also fails to mention one of the most important statements in the 1844 *Manuscripts* – 'to have one basis for science and another for life is *a priori* a lie'.[224] This is not an isolated statement. Much of Marx's work consists of an affirmation of contingency and sensuousness, as against the abstractive and objectivist standpoint of modern science. He opposed capitalism because it is based on a system of *abstract* labour, in which *having* predominates over *being*. Capitalism's *necessarily* abstractive character, Marx argues, prevents us from seeing that 'man is not merely a natural being: he is a *human* natural being. That is to say, he is a being for himself... Neither nature objectively nor nature subjectively is directly given in a form adequate to the *human* being'.[225] He opposes the one-sidedness of natural science, even while acknowledging its contributions, because it prioritises universality, necessity and predictability at the *expense* of human 'sensuousness' – its contingency and *suffering*. Instead of running away from such contingency, Marx *affirms* it: 'To be sensuous is to *suffer*'.[226]

If Marx were the hyper-rationalist that Megill claims, it would be hard to see how he could make such comments. Since the emphasis on contingency and 'actual sensuousness' is a major theme throughout his early work, from the doctoral dissertation to *The German Ideology*, this can hardly be considered a theoretical inconsistency or an exception from his overall perspective. In fact, one can draw the exact opposite conclusion that Megill does on the basis of these and related passages. I would therefore argue that Marx opposed capitalism because it forecloses the possibility of contingency and spontaneous development by positing *abstract labour* as the universal medium of social interaction and reproduction.

Moreover, Marx presents the intentional agent for social transformation as neither 'science' nor even human intelligence, but instead the proletariat. This is in keeping with his criticism of subject-object inversion. Science and human

---

224. Marx 1975r, p. 303.
225. Marx 1975r, p. 337.
226. Ibid.

intelligence are products of subjective human interaction that, under specific social conditions, take on a life of their own and control the actions of the producers. Marx could not pose science as the intentional agent at the same time as maintaining his criticism of subject-predicate inversion – a criticism, as I have shown, that permeates all of his early writings.[227]

Megill's claim also makes it hard to understand the persistence of Marx's critique of Hegel. Marx attacks Hegel for posing disembodied thought as the *subject*, instead of 'actual, corporeal man', Marx does not view actual corporeal man as a mere *embodiment* of abstract rational categories. He views actual corporeal man as the *generator* of such categories. When he speaks of the proletariat being a 'bearer' of philosophy, he refers not to what he considers Hegel's dehumanised philosophy of consciousness but to 'positive humanism, beginning from itself'. Why would Marx spend so much time on a critique of Hegel for claiming to comprehend contingent phenomena prior to their actual empirical analysis if he was the hyper-rationalist that Megill claims he was?

Of particular interest in this regard is that, in the 'Critique of the Hegelian Dialectic', Marx takes issue with the very last sentence of Hegel's *Phenomenology*, which states that without the unity of history and its 'philosophical comprehension' found in 'Absolute Knowledge', all would be 'lifeless, solitary and alone [*ohne den er das leblose Einsame wäre*]'.[228] Marx contends on the contrary, 'a being which is neither an object itself, nor has an object...outside it...would exist solitary and alone'.[229] A being can be considered *alive* only if it does *not* embrace all of existence, only if objects and other people exist on *their own* terms, *independent* of that being. Marx emphasises the irreducibly contingent and limited character of human existence, in contrast to what he sees as Hegel's excessive rationalism. He criticises Hegel's deification of reason insofar as it turns actual people into expressions of cognitive

---

227. This critical stance towards science was largely overlooked among Marx's 'orthodox' followers, as especially seen in the huge influence that the thought of Ferdinand Lassalle exerted among the first generation of post-Marx Marxists. Lassalle's argument that the vehicle of 'science' was not the proletariat, but rather the radicalised bourgeois intelligentsia, proved enormously influential in the organisational theories of Karl Kautsky and V.I. Lenin in particular. See Dunayevskaya 2000, p. 77: 'Lassalle suffered from the illusion of the age: that science is "classless". Such an attitude made it natural for him to think that he represented "science and the worker", for science was surely incorporated in the intellectual, the leader. Marx, on the other hand, rejected this "puerile stuff".'

228. Hegel 2008, p. 531.

229. Marx 1975r, p. 337.

categories abstracted from real life.[230] *It is to counter this defect in Hegel that Marx calls himself a humanist.*

At the same time, Marx's critique of Hegel and his embrace of 'positive humanism, beginning from itself' also emphasise the crucial importance of *natural* existence. Marx denies that nature can be completely subsumed by human subjective activity. Human activity is an extension and part of nature. Humanity goes *beyond* nature insofar as its capacity for conscious, purposeful activity enables it to create social existence. 'Human nature' is the capacity to go beyond physical nature in creating an artificial environment. Human activity therefore contains the potential of overcoming natural necessity. However, this does not mean that nature can ever become an irrelevant or totally subordinate moment in our existence, since humanity is both a 'natural being' and 'a being for himself'.[231] Marx rejects any perspective that totally dissolves nature into human subjective activity on the grounds that 'a being which is neither an object itself, nor has an object…outside it…would exist solitary and alone'.[232] This has crucial implications for conceiving of a postcapitalist society. Since humanity is a 'natural being', even as it is a 'being for himself',[233] nature must not be viewed in terms of an exteriority to be annulled. An irreducible gap exists between human praxis and the natural world, no matter how much humanity strives to overcome it, and this gap needs to be accepted and celebrated. Capitalism denies this, since it reduces everything – including the natural world – to *having* and *consumption*. Natural limits are ignored for the sake of gratifying one human need at the expense of all others. By treating nature as a person apart that is to be possessed, consumed, and destroyed for the sake of augmenting value, capitalism indeed leaves us with a world that is 'lifeless, solitary, and alone'.

Marx, therefore, does not project an abstract humanism that ignores natural limits and realities. In insisting that nature cannot be separated from human nature, he is implying that one cannot be degraded for the sake of the other. This is because humanity, like all natural beings, 'has its nature outside itself'.[234] I belong not just to me, and not just to the objects that I claim belong to me, for

---

230. That Marx sharply criticises the conclusion of Hegel's *Phenomenology*, and especially his concept of 'Absolute Knowledge' in 1844 does not mean that it is his last word on the subject. As Dunayevskaya argues, Marx returns to Hegel's Absolutes in the course of working on *Capital*, in delineating the 'absolute law of capitalist accumulation'. See Dunayevskaya 2002 and 2003 for an appreciative re-reading of the conclusion of Hegel's *Phenomenology* in light of the realities of the twentieth century.
231. Marx 1975r, p. 337.
232. Ibid.
233. Ibid.
234. Ibid.

I also belong to the objective, natural world. Sensuous beings like ourselves are bound to suffer, since to be sensuous is to 'have sensuous objects outside oneself'. But this 'suffering' is not the suffering of exploitation, discrimination, and alienation. It is the 'suffering' involved in accepting and celebrating the fact that, like all natural beings, we too are limited and contingent.

While Marx does not explicitly spell out his comments on nature in terms of what he envisages for life after capitalism, they stand at quite a distance from the rationalist scientism that Megill ascribes to him. Megill's reading of Marx makes it difficult to understand why he poses *naturalism* and *humanism* as *interchangeable* terms. On the other hand, thinking out the ramifications of their interchangeability is a crucial part of developing an ecological critique of capitalism that affirms and respects natural limits.

Marx's emphasis on the inseparability of 'naturalism' and 'humanism' also speaks to a criticism often made of his early writings – namely, that he held a perfectionist view of human nature. Leszek Kolakowski argues in his major study of Marxism that Marx envisages a postcapitalist society as 'a society of perfect unity, in which all human aspirations would be fulfilled, and all values reconciled'.[235] Kolakowski views this radical utopianism as a major defect, since it led 'Marxist' régimes of the twentieth century to attempt to forcefully impose a degree of social transformation that was impossible to actualise. However, we again need to keep in mind that Marx's emphasis on contingency and sensuousness leads him to write, 'to be sensuous is to *suffer*'. The phrase appears several times in the 1844 *Manuscripts*. Humanity, he contends, as a sensuous being is a *limited* being, and a limited being is a *suffering* being. Marx does not explicitly say *why* suffering is an inevitable part of the human condition, but it appears related to our ability to envisage the transgression of finite limits that our sensuous existence prevents us from actualising. In any case, Marx's emphasis on achieving a 'totality of manifestations of life' does not imply a life free of pain, contradiction, and suffering. It only implies a life in which we are able to come to terms with such afflictions, once we are no longer alienated from ourselves.

If Marx did not oppose the market because he privileged scientific necessity and predictability above all else, why then did he criticise it? The answer is that the market does not meet the three normative criteria by which he measures reality in his early writings. These three normative criteria, which I have discussed above, are opposition to subject-predicate inversion, opposition to treating oneself and others as mere means to an end, and Marx's view that '*all* emancipation is a *reduction* of the human world and relationships to

---

235. Kolakowski 1978, p. 523.

man himself'. The market controls the fate of the producer by setting prices in a way that has little or nothing to do with their actual value or the subjective activity by which the products are created. The products come to dominate the producer. The producer's activity becomes a mere means to serve the product, rather than *vice versa* – *because* the nature of the activity that creates the product in the first place becomes a mere means to an end, instead of an end in itself. The market is characterised – at least once there is *generalised commodity-exchange* – by depersonalised object-object relations, instead of *human* relations.

It needs to be emphasised, however, that the critique of the market is not the *pons asini* of Marx's critique of capitalism. Marx sees the market, like private property, as the *result* of alienated labour, not its cause. Moreover, his early writings contain far more discussion of private property than the market; his comments about the latter are far from extensive or systematic. In contrast to how Marx was understood by much of twentieth-century 'Marxism', our exploration indicates that his real object of critique was not the market or private property, but rather the social relations that underpin them.

Chapter Two

The Conception of a Postcapitalist Society in the Drafts of *Capital*

The 'first draft' of *Capital: The Poverty of Philosophy* (1847)

The process by which Marx composed his greatest theoretical work, *Capital*, is long and complicated. As early as 1845, Marx had sketched out plans to write a two-volume work on economics that he provisionally entitled *A Critique of Politics and Political Economy*. After he temporarily put aside this work, in order to concentrate on polemical writings like *The Holy Family* and *The German Ideology*, he returned to a direct study of economics in the late 1840s. However, the first volume of what became *Capital* was not completed until 1867, after Marx made numerous changes to both the form and content of his projected book. Marx composed a considerable number of drafts of *Capital* in the two decades preceding its publication in 1867, and they have been the subject of prolonged and detailed examination and debate by a large number of scholars and researchers on Marx's work over the past several decades.[1]

Most commentators on Marx have seen the *Grundrisse*, composed in 1857–8, as the first draft of *Capital*. There are grounds for considering that Marx's initial conceptual outline of what later became *Capital* began much earlier, however, in 1847 with his

---

1. See especially Rosdolsky 1968, Uchida 1988, Heinrich 1989, Dussel 2000, Bidet 2009, Musto (ed.) 2008, Fineschi 2009, and Bellofiore and Fineschi (eds.) 2009.

The Poverty of Philosophy and the associated manuscript on 'Wages'. These were composed in a period when Marx, having completed his criticism of the young Hegelians, felt the need to present to the public a positive exposition of his economic theories. Near the end of his life (in 1880) he wrote that *The Poverty of Philosophy* 'contains the seeds of the theory developed after twenty years' work in *Capital*'.[2] A considerable number of critical concepts that became central to *Capital* – such as surplus-value (although the phrase itself does not explicitly appear in *The Poverty of Philosophy*), the relation between production and distribution, the 'reserve-army of labour', the distribution of the elements of production, and the distinction between actual labour-time and socially-necessary labour-time – first appear in his writings of 1847.

For this reason, I will follow the approach taken by Samuel Hollander's recent study of Marx's economic theory,[3] by considering *The Poverty of Philosophy* and related manuscripts composed in 1847 as the 'first draft' of what became *Capital*. The *Grundrisse* will be treated as the second draft, and the manuscript of 1861–3 as the third.[4]

The Poverty of Philosophy (1847) represents Marx's first published work on economics and marked a crucial step in the two-decades long process that led to the publication of his greatest work, *Capital*. Marx had, of course, written extensively on political economy prior to *The Poverty of Philosophy*, as seen in his *Economic and Philosophical Manuscripts* of 1844 and *The German Ideology*. However, neither of these was published until long after his death. Moreover, a number of crucial concepts that later became central to *Capital* and that are not found in either the 1844 *Manuscripts* or the *German Ideology* make their first appearance in *The Poverty of Philosophy*.[5]

The purpose of *The Poverty of Philosophy* was to take issue with Pierre-Joseph Proudhon's *The Philosophy of Poverty* (1846), which sought to apply the insights of David Ricardo's economic theory in developing a criticism of the inequities of modern capitalism. Proudhon, as Marx shows, was a rather schematic and eclectic thinker whose arguments are not always internally coherent. Never-

---

2. See Marx 1989g, p. 326. This first appeared as a letter to *L'Egalité* of 7 April 1880. Marx also writes that *The Poverty of Philosophy* 'might thus serve as an introduction to the study of *Capital*'.

3. See Hollander 2008, pp. 194–5.

4. Marx also composed what can be considered a fourth draft of *Capital*, in 1863–5. Except for its sixth chapter, 'Results of the Immediate Process of Production', it has not been found.

5. *The Poverty of Philosophy* was written and published in French, and a German edition did not appear until after Marx's death, in 1885. The book was not republished in Marx's lifetime, although several chapters did appear in serialised form in several socialist publications between 1872 and 1875. Marx had also studied the political economists, first in French, as seen in *MEGA*² IV/3.

theless, Proudhon consistently counterposed the 'rationality' of Ricardo's principle of the determination of value[6] by labour-time to capitalism's 'irrational' and disorganised process of exchange. Proudhon argued that because labour is the source of all value, the costs of production represent 'constituted value' – the relative amount of labour-time that it takes to produce a given commodity. This principle of value-determination, he argued, is hidden and distorted by the exchange-process, in which workers are paid on the basis of a portion of the *price* of the commodity, instead of upon the *value* of their labour. Proudhon therefore proposed altering the exchange-relations of capitalism by paying workers a 'fair' equivalent of the value of their labour in the form of labour-tokens or time-chits. Workers would be paid not in money – which Proudhon saw as a wholly arbitrary and unnatural phenomenon – but, instead, in tokens or vouchers that express the amount of time the labourer works in a given period. These tokens would then be exchanged for an equivalent of goods and services produced in the same amount of time (or which have the same 'value').

Marx is scathingly critical of Proudhon's position, on the grounds that it utilises the central principle of capitalist production – the determination of value by labour-time – as the defining feature of a 'just' or non-capitalist society. Whereas Proudhon holds that the inequities of capitalism result from an inadequate or incomplete application of the determination of value by labour-time, Marx holds that this is the very *basis* of its inequalities: 'It will think it very naïve that M. Proudhon should give as a "revolutionary theory of the future" what Ricardo expounded scientifically as the theory of present-day society, of bourgeois society, and that he should thus take for the solution of the antimony between utility and exchange value what Ricardo and his school presented long before him as the scientific formula of one single side of this antimony, that of *exchange value*'.[7]

Ricardo, Marx notes, 'shows us the real movement of bourgeois production, which constitutes value'. Proudhon leaves 'this real movement out of account' and seeks the 'reorganization of the world on a would-be new formula, which formula is no more than the theoretical expression of the real movement which exists and which is so well described by Ricardo'. Hence, 'Ricardo takes present-day society as his starting point to demonstrate to us

---

6. In *The Poverty and Philosophy* (1847), the *Grundrisse* (1858), the *Contribution to the Critique of Political Economy* (1859), and the 1861–3 draft of *Capital* Marx uses the terms 'value' and 'exchange-value' more or less interchangeably. It is not until the second German edition of Volume I of *Capital* in 1872 that he explicitly distinguishes between them by referring to exchange-value as the value-form or form of appearance of value. This will be discussed further in Chapter Three, below.

7. Marx 1976b, p. 121.

how it constitutes value – M. Proudhon takes constituted value as his starting point to constitute a new world with the aid of this value'.[8]

In sum, Marx vigorously objects to applying categories that are specific to capitalism – such as the determination of value by labour-time – to conceptualising the kind of society that should replace it.

Nowhere in the text does Marx suggest that Proudhon erred by discussing a future organisation of society *per se*. Instead, he takes issue with the *content* of Proudhon's discussion – that he conceives of a future society drawn from the basis of principles of capitalism. *The Poverty of Philosophy* indicates that Marx is not averse to discussing the future, since his differences with Proudhon's understanding of a future non-capitalist society grounds his entire critique. Moreover, the book also contains a detailed critique of English socialists (such as John Bray) for importing, along similar lines as Proudhon, categories specific to bourgeois society into his envisagement of a 'socialist' alternative.

Bray had written several influential works in the 1830s arguing for 'equitable labour exchange bazaars'. A number of these were set up by utopian socialists in the 1830s in order to organise commodity-exchange without a capitalist intermediary. Marx writes of Bray, 'In a purified individual exchange, freed from all the elements of antagonism he finds in it, he sees an *"egalitarian"* relation which he would like to see society adopt'.[9] Marx argues that almost all the early English socialists – Thomas Hodgskin, William Thompson, T.R. Edmunds, as well as Bray – 'have, at different periods, proposed the equalitarian application of the Ricardian theory'.[10] He will further develop his criticism of such positions throughout his two decades of work on *Capital*.

Why was Marx opposed to the 'egalitarian' application of Ricardo's theory? The main reason is that it rests upon a fundamental theoretical error – the conflation of actual labour-time with socially-necessary labour-time. Marx agrees with Ricardo that labour is the source of all value. However, he does not agree that value expresses the *actual number of hours* of labour performed by the worker. If value were based on the actual hours of labour, commodities that take longer to produce would have a greater value. Since capitalism is based on augmenting value, that would mean that capitalists would try to get workers to work slower rather than faster. This is, of course, clearly not the case. The reason, Marx argues, is that 'Value is never constituted all alone. It is constituted, not by the time needed to produce it all alone, but in relation to the quota of each and every other product which can be created in the

---

8. Marx 1976b, pp. 123–4.
9. Marx 1976b, p. 144.
10. Marx 1976b, p. 138.

same time'.[11] Value is not determined by the actual amount of time employed to create a commodity; it is determined by the *average* amount of *necessary* labour-time needed to create it. If a worker in Detroit assembles an automobile in 24 hours while one in South Korea assembles a similar model in only 16 hours, the extra eight hours of labour performed by the worker in Detroit creates no value. 'What determines value is not the time taken to produce a thing, but the *minimum* time it could possibly be produced in, and this minimum is ascertained by competition'.[12]

In other words, the value of the commodity is not determined by actual labour-time but by simple or equalised labour-time. Labour is equalised, or reduced to an abstract equivalent, through the 'subordination of man to machine or by the extreme division of labour'. Marx writes of how 'The pendulum of the clock has become as accurate a measure of the relative activity of two workers as it is of the speed of two locomotives'.[13] As competition reveals the minimum-amount of labour-time necessary, on average, to create a given commodity, the workers are forced to produce the commodity in that time unit, irrespective of their human needs or bodily capacities. Their labour-time takes the form of an abstract equivalent. This abstract equivalent is the source and substance of value. In capitalism, 'Time is everything, man is nothing; he is, at most, time's carcass. Quality no longer matters. Quantity decides everything; hour for hour, day by day'.[14]

The value of the commodity is therefore determined by labour-time only to the extent that labour has been subsumed by an abstract, alienating activity. The formula adopted by Proudhon and the English socialists – the determination of value of labour-time – cannot serve as the basis of a new society, because it is the principle that governs the alienation of the labourer. Marx argues, 'It is upon this equality, already realised in automatic labour, that M. Proudhon wields his smoothing-plane of "equalisation", which he means to establish universally in "time to come"!'[15]

Of course, Proudhon, like the English socialists, opposed the exploitation of labour. They viewed themselves as champions of the workers, and, in a sense, they were since they wanted them to obtain a 'fair' share of social wealth. Yet, in failing to distinguish between actual labour-time and socially-necessary labour-time, they ended up defining the new society on the basis of

---

11. Marx 1976b, p. 147.
12. Marx 1976b, p. 136. It is important to note that this social average is *ascertained* by competition, not *created* by it. Marx sees competitive pressures as a function of the drive to augment value, instead of vice-versa.
13. Marx 1976b, p. 127.
14. Ibid.
15. Ibid.

the cardinal principle of capitalism. Marx concludes, 'After all, the determination of value by labour time – the formula M. Proudhon gives us as the regenerating formula of the future – is therefore merely the scientific expression of the economic relations of present-day society, as was clearly and precisely demonstrated by Ricardo long before M. Proudhon'.[16] Ideas have their own logic, independent of the intentions and political agendas that may inspire them.

Marx also shows that Proudhon confuses the value of the commodity with the value of labour. To Proudhon, the value of the commodity is equivalent to the value of labour that creates it. On these grounds, he argues that there is no reason why workers should not receive the same value in wages (computed in labour-tokens or time-chits) as the value of the product. The exchange-relation should be equalised by eliminating the class of capitalists, usurers, and middlemen that make off with a portion of the workers' value. Marx shows that such calls for equal exchange are based on an erroneous conflation of the value of labour with the value of the commodity: 'It is going against economic facts to determine the relative value of commodities by the value of labour. It is moving in a vicious circle, it is to determine relative value by a relative value which itself needs to be determined'.[17]

In sum, instead of opposing the 'equalisation' that has living labour become dominated by an abstraction, Proudhon dominated by an abstraction, Proudhon endorses it as a principle of equality. He accepts the equalisation of labour as a given in order to derive from it a principle of equal exchange. He has overlooked the contradictions inherent in capitalist production while seeking a modification in the form and mechanism of exchange-relations.

For Marx, in contrast, the problem of capitalism is not that it distributes value in an unequal manner in contradistinction to the principle of equalisation involved in its system of production. Instead, Marx argues that the problem of capitalism, and the reason for its unequal forms of exchange, is the *equalising* tendencies of value-production itself. All labour in capitalism is dominated by an abstraction, labour in general, as a result of the 'collisions between the worker and the employer who sought at all costs to depreciate the workers' specialized ability'.[18] The unequal distribution of wealth, Marx contends, is a consequence of a *class*-relationship in which concrete labour is governed by an equal standard – simple, general labour. There is no value-production without the 'equalisation' of labour – without living labour being dominated by a uniform abstraction. Proudhon's position is 'accepting the

---

16. Marx 1976b, p. 138.
17. Marx 1976b, p. 128.
18. Marx 1976b, p. 188.

present state of affairs; it is, in short, making an apology… for a society without understanding it'.[19]

Here, in Marx's first public discussion of his economic theory, he not only directly discusses the nature of a postcapitalist society; in doing so, he makes it clear that value-production is incompatible with socialism.

There is, however, an important difference between Proudhon's position and those of the English utopian socialists, even though their theoretical views rest on similar premises. While Proudhon embraces payment according to labour-time as the governing principle of 'socialism', Marx writes that Bray 'proposes merely measures which he thinks good for a period of transition between existing society and a community regime'.[20] Does Marx therefore endorse an alteration of exchange-relations based on paying workers the value of their labour as a transitional form that could lead to a new society? A close reading of *The Poverty of Philosophy* suggests that the answer is in the negative. Marx does not think that production-relations can be altered by tinkering with the form in which products are exchanged; instead, he argues that alterations in the form of exchange follow from the transformation of relations of production: 'In general, the form of exchange of products corresponds to the form of production. Change the latter, and the former will change in consequence'.[21] Moreover, he indicates that maintaining an exchange of equivalents based on value-production undermines the effort to effect a fundamental transformation in production-relations. He writes, 'Thus, if all the members of society are supposed to be immediate workers, the exchange of equal quantities or hours of labour is possible only on condition that the number of hours to be spent on material production is agreed on beforehand. But such an agreement negates individual exchange'.[22]

Marx is here envisaging a situation in which a social average that operates behind the workers' backs – socially-necessary labour-time – no longer dictates the amount of time that the worker must spend producing a given product. Instead, the amount of time will be 'agreed on beforehand' by the associated producers. Material production is now determined by the producers' conscious decisions, instead of by the autonomous force of value-production. Such a situation 'negates individual exchange' in that products are not exchanged based on the amount of labour-time embodied in them. Marx appears to be unequivocal on this point: 'Either you want the correct proportions of past centuries with present-day means of production, in which

---

19. Marx 1976b, p. 134.
20. Marx 1976b, p. 142.
21. Marx 1976b, p. 143.
22. Ibid.

case you are both reactionary and utopian. Or you want progress without anarchy: in which case, in order to preserve the productive forces, you must abandon individual exchange'.[23]

Hence, although Marx notes that Bray upholds the principle of the determination of value by labour-time as a *transitional* form *to* a new society rather than the governing principle of socialism itself, he remains sharply critical of Bray's perspective. He is especially critical of Bray for proposing a national savings-bank, established by the government, to regulate the distribution of labour-tokens or time-chits. Marx terms this 'the golden chain by which the government holds a large part of the working class. The workers themselves thus give into the hands of their enemies the weapons to preserve the existing organization of society which subjugates them'.[24] He sums up his critique thusly:

> Mr. Bray does not see that this egalitarian relation, this *corrective ideal* that he would like to apply to the world, is itself nothing but the reflection of the actual world; and that therefore it is totally impossible to reconstitute society on the basis of what is merely an embellished shadow of it. In proportion as this shadow takes on substance again, we perceive that this substance, far from being the transfiguration dreamt of, is the actual body of the existing society.[25]

There is, therefore – at least for Marx – no room for a 'transition' to socialism based on the governing principles of the old society. He conceives of a sharper break between capitalism and the transition to socialism than that advocated by its neo-Ricardian socialist critics. The manner in which he further develops this argument emerges as one of the central themes in his subsequent drafts of what will eventually become Volume I of *Capital*.

The 'second draft' of *Capital*: the *Grundrisse* (1858)

The *Grundrisse*, Marx's first book-length draft of *Capital*[26] (although it can be considered the 'second draft' in light of his writings of 1847), is a remark-

---

23. Marx 1976b, p. 138.

24. Marx 1976d, p. 427. The manuscript on 'Wages', written in December 1847, is part of his studies associated with his initial efforts to work out a critique of political economy and is closely connected with the content of *The Poverty of Philosophy*.

25. Marx 1976b, p. 144.

26. Marx did not provide a title for the work; it was entitled the *Grundrisse* or 'rough draft' by its editors. Different as it is from *Capital* in many respects, it covers the subject-matter that is contained in all three volumes of what eventually became *Capital*.

able work of over eight hundred pages that contains a wealth of important philosophical insights. Written in 1857–8 but not published until 1939, it has sparked numerous re-examinations and reconsiderations of Marx's contribution as a whole since it became widely available in the 1970s.[27]

What is especially striking about the *Grundrisse* is its wealth of discussion of the alternative to capitalism. Indeed, it can be argued that no single work of Marx discusses a future postcapitalist society as directly or as comprehensively.

One reason for this is that the *Grundrisse* begins with a lengthy criticism of the concept of a postcapitalist society promoted by French and English socialists of the time, Proudhon especially. The latter's sway over the labour and socialist movements had not receded by 1857–8; instead, in many respects, his ideas had become more influential than ever. Marx was gravely concerned about this and devoted considerable space in the *Grundrisse* to distinguishing Proudhon's concept of a new society from his own. As Marx moves on to deal with other issues in the rest of the work – such as the difference between indirectly and directly social labour, the contradiction between necessary and surplus labour-time, and the phases that characterise human development – he discusses the contours of a postcapitalist society to an extent not found in many of his other works.

At the same time, much of the *Grundrisse's* critique of Proudhon and other socialists returns to, and further develops, the points Marx had earlier formulated in 1847 in *The Poverty of Philosophy*. Marx begins the first chapter of the *Grundrisse*,[28] which deals with money, with a critique of Louis Alfred Darimon, a leading French follower of Proudhon who advocated a reform of the banking system through the creation of a currency based on denominations of labour-time. Marx writes,

---

27. Parts of the *Grundrisse*, such as the fragment 'Bastiat and Carey' and its 'Introduction', were published in 1902–4 in *Die Neue Zeit*, edited by Karl Kautsky. However, the work did not appear in full until 1939–41, when the Marx-Engels-Lenin Institute in Moscow published it in two volumes, in German. Very few copies of this edition ever reached the Western world and the work was not widely known until the 1960s. The first full English translation appeared in 1973. See Marx 1973. I am here making use of the more recent translation published in the late 1980s and early 1990s, contained in Volumes 28 and 29 of the *Marx-Engels Collected Works*.

28. Aside from the 'Introduction' and the fragment on 'Bastiat and Carey' (which deals with the historical specificity of capitalism in the USA), the original manuscript contains only two chapters, with no subheadings or divisions into parts. 'The Chapter on Money' is about 150 pages long, while 'The Chapter on Capital' comes to over 650 pages. Marx referred to the 'shapelessness' of the manuscript in his correspondence.

> The general question is: is it possible to revolutionize the existing relations
> of production and the corresponding relations of distribution by means of
> changes in the instrument of circulation – changes in the organization of
> circulation? A further question: can such a transformation of circulation be
> accomplished without touching the existing relations of production and the
> social relations based on them?[29]

Darimon, like Proudhon and many of the English socialists of the time,
thought that it was possible to 'revolutionise' relations of production through
an alteration of the medium of exchange. Why, Darimon asks, do capitalists
accumulate so much wealth, given that labour is the source of all value?
The reason, he argues, is the 'irrational' nature of the medium of exchange,
money, which alters and distorts the determination of value by labour-
time. Commodities are not sold at their value but, instead, at their *price*, as
denominated in money. The 'unregulated' nature of the medium of circulation, contends Darimon, is the lever that enables capitalists to 'unfairly' pay
workers less than the value of their labour. He argues that if commodities
were *directly* sold at their 'true value', according to the actual amount of
labour-time that it takes to produce them – instead of *indirectly* through the
medium of money – the very existence of the capitalist would become superfluous. Hence, altering the medium of circulation would abolish class-society.
To achieve this, Darimon proposed creating a national bank to regulate the
medium of circulation by replacing money with gold-tokens representing
the amount of labour-time that workers perform in producing a given set
of commodities.[30]

Marx engages in a lengthy and complex criticism of Darimon's position.
Much of it is based on his understanding of 'the inner connection between the
relations of production, distribution, and circulation',[31] as spelled out in the
'Introduction' to the *Grundrisse*. He there takes issue with such political economists as John Stuart Mill for viewing relations of production as governed by
'eternal natural laws independent of history'.[32] Mill's view that production-
relations adhere to eternal natural laws led him to argue that the proper object
of political economy, which deals with specific historical formations, is the
sphere of *distribution*. Marx objects to this on the grounds that 'The struc-

---

29. Marx 1986a, p. 60.
30. Darimon's proposal is somewhat different from that of the English socialists
whom Marx also addresses in his critique, in that the latter propose *paper*-tokens
or vouchers representing actual labour-time whereas Darimon prefers gold labour-
tokens. As Marx sees it, however, both positions rest upon the same fundamental
(and mistaken) set of premises.
31. Marx 1986a, p. 61.
32. Marx 1986a, p. 25.

ture of distribution is entirely determined by the structure of production'.[33] He develops this by directly employing the central Hegelian categories of Universal, Particular, and Individual.[34] Production, he writes, is the determinant category of capitalist society and therefore represents the Hegelian concept of the *Universal*. Consumption – without which production cannot be realised – corresponds to the Hegelian category of the *Individual*. Production and consumption are opposites and non-identical, but one cannot exist without the other: they co-exist in a state of negative self-relation. Distribution and exchange is the medium by which the Universal is individualised; it corresponds to the Hegelian concept of the *Particular*. 'Production, distribution and exchange, and consumption thus form a proper syllogism'.[35] Distribution or exchange is not an independent sphere in its own right. It does not govern, it is governed; it does not determine, it is determined; it is a mediatory moment between production and consumption.[36] This serves as the *philosophical* basis of his criticism of Darimon's *economic* theories.

Marx contends that Darimon's error lies in advocating a change in the *form* of wage-labour, instead of calling for the abolition of wage-labour itself. He wants to change the manner in which labour is *remunerated*, while leaving its commodification intact, since workers are to be paid in a labour-voucher, instead of in money. *Yet this retains the need for a universal equivalent with which labour can be bought and sold.*

In passages that recall his earlier discussion in *The Poverty of Philosophy*, Marx contends that Darimon dethrones money from its special role as universal equivalent by proposing that the quantity of labour-time assume that particular role. This is like saying 'Let the Papacy remain, but make everyone Pope. Do away with money by turning every commodity into money and endowing it with the specific properties of money'.[37] In the name of getting rid of the prevailing universal equivalent, money, every product of labour (as computed in labour-time) gets placed in the position of serving as the universal equivalent. *This completely overlooks what allows a universal equivalent to exist in the first place.* One product of labour can be exchanged for all products of labour only if labour itself is dominated by an abstraction, subsumed by an abstract universal – abstract labour. Darimon and Proudhon's plan for the

---

33. Marx 1986a, p. 32.
34. See Hegel 1979a, pp. 664–704.
35. Marx 1986a, p. 27.
36. Another way to state this is to say that production and consumption represent a unity of opposites mediated by way of distribution and exchange. As Marx puts it, 'This identity of production and consumption amounts to Spinoza's proposition: *determinatio est negatio'*. See Marx 1986a, p. 28.
37. Marx 1986a, p. 65.

reform of money not only fails to transform relations of production in which labour is dominated by an abstraction, but it pushes matters further in that very direction by bestowing universal equivalency upon all commodities.

Marx is not simply arguing that their approach would fail to *improve* matters. He indicates that it would actually make matters *worse*. He first asks if it is worthwhile to tinker with the form of money or the market 'without abolishing the production relation itself which is expressed in the category of money; and whether it is not then necessarily a self-defeating effort to overcome the essential conditions of relationship by effecting a formal modification within it'.[38] Marx suggests this would be a waste of time, since it would create an even greater despotism than what exists under traditional market-capitalism: 'The inconveniences resulting from the existence of a special instrument of exchange, of a special and yet general equivalent, are bound to reproduce themselves (if in different ways) in every form' – even if it may 'entail fewer inconveniences than another'.[39]

Ironically, what Marx here subjects to critique is a striking anticipation of what passed for 'Marxism' in many 'socialist' and 'communist' régimes of the twentieth century. Such régimes eliminated private property and the 'free market' by bringing the process of distribution and circulation under the control of the state. But they did little or nothing to transform *production-relations*. Concrete labour was still reduced to a monotonous, routinised activity through the dominance of abstract labour. Abstract labour continued to serve as the substance of value. Marx's discussion in the *Grundrisse* suggests that a planned economy – so long as there is no fundamental change in relations of production – may avoid some of the inconveniences of traditional market-capitalism, but the problems end up becoming reproduced on another level. For instance, instead of a surplus of products that cannot be consumed (which characterises traditional capitalism), there is a shortage of products that cannot be produced (which characterised statist 'socialism'). Imbalances between production and consumption are bound to show up, one way or another, so long as the relations of production are not transformed, precisely because value-production rests on a non-identity or non-equivalence between production and consumption. Marx puts the matter as follows: 'The money system in its present form can be completely regulated – all the evils deplored by Darimon abolished – without the abandonment of the present social basis: indeed, while its contradictions, its antagonisms, the conflict of classes, etc. actually reach a higher degree'.[40]

---

38. Marx 1986a, p. 61.
39. Marx 1986a, p. 65.
40. Marx 1986a, p. 71.

One reason that Darimon and Proudhon objected so strenuously to money as the medium of exchange is that gold and silver tend to appreciate in value relative to other commodities in periods of economic crisis. Since the wealthier classes tend to possess greater amount of precious metals and money than workers, the former's income tends to rise even as the latter falls. Organising exchange through a national banking system based on labour-vouchers, Darimon claimed, would put an end to such inequities. Marx counters that he overlooks the other side of the issue – namely, that gold and silver tend to *depreciate* relative to other commodities in periods of economic *growth*. Marx does not deny that prices of commodities wildly fluctuate in periods of economic growth and crisis, and often to the detriment of the workers. Yet he does not agree with Darimon's proposed solution. Does he have a solution of his own to offer? I would argue that he does. He writes,

> Formulated in this way, the riddle would have solved itself at once: abolish the rise and fall in prices. That means, do away with prices. That, in turn, means abolishing exchange value, which, in its turn, requires the abolition of the system of exchange corresponding to the bourgeois organization of society. This last entails the problem of revolutionizing bourgeois society economically. Then it would have become evident from the start that the evils of bourgeois society cannot be remedied by banal 'transformations' or the establishment of a rational 'money system'.[41]

Marx here endorses efforts to eliminate the deleterious impact of price-fluctuations on the agents of production. He explicitly refers to the 'abolition' of prices and exchange-value.

But why does he so sharply criticise the Proudhonists for proposing alterations in the sphere of exchange? The reason is that the abolition of prices and exchange-value presupposes a revolutionary transformation of the underlying relations of production. What Marx means by 'revolutionizing bourgeois society economically' is a radical transformation of *production*-relations that would create correspondingly new relations of *distribution*. He argues that taking the contrary approach, by focusing first of all on transforming exchange-relations, not only leaves production-relations intact but also fails to resolve the problems of exchange that so concern the Proudhonists in the first place.

Marx illustrates this by further developing the distinction posed in *The Poverty of Philosophy* between actual labour-time and socially-necessary labour-time. He argues, 'Not the labour time incorporated in [previous] output, but

---

41. Marx 1986a, p. 72.

the currently necessary labour time determines value'.[42] Proudhon and his followers conflate the two. As a result, they fail to see that their 'solution' – reorganising exchange-relations to conform to the determination of value by labour-time – would do nothing to correct the deleterious impact of the depreciation of the medium of exchange. Marx writes, 'According to the general economic law that production costs fall continually, that living labour becomes more and more productive, and that the labour time objectified in products therefore continually depreciates, constant depreciation would be the inevitable fate of this gold labour money'.[43]

Darimon sees only the *appreciation* of gold and silver during an economic crisis. Yet Darimon does not realise that his labour-money will tend to *depreciate* in value, since the average amount of labour-time necessary to produce a given commodity tends to fall. The labour-tokens are bound to depreciate as the mode of production undergoes innovation under the pressure of competition. In the long run, workers would have less ability to 'buy back' the value of their product than in a traditional monetary economy. Marx notes that this situation would in no way be altered if workers were paid in *paper*-vouchers (as advocated by many English and French socialists of the time), instead of in gold or silver labour-money: 'The labour time embodied in the paper itself would be of as little account as the paper value of banknotes. The one would simply be a representative of labour hours, as the other is of gold or silver'.[44]

Marx shows that all of these efforts to address social problems by tinkering with the form of remuneration or exchange rest on the illusion that the distinction between value and price is arbitrary and unnecessary. The French – and many English – socialists considered value to be real and necessary, since it is determined by the quantity of labour-time spent in producing an object. They considered price to be fictive and unnecessary, since it is determined by the whim of supply and demand. They therefore wanted to replace commodity-prices with labour-tokens that express the 'real' value of the product.

Marx counters that price cannot be treated as a mere nominal expression of value. Value *must* diverge from price because the value of the commodity is not determined by the actual number of hours engaged in producing the commodity, but only by the *average* amount of time that is *socially necessary* for doing so.[45] This average is established behind the backs of the producers

---

42. Marx 1986a, p. 73.
43. Ibid.
44. Ibid.
45. See Marx 1986a, p. 75: '*Price*, therefore, differs from *value*, not only as the nominal differs from the real; not only by its denomination in gold and silver; but also in that the latter appears as the law of the movements to which the former is subject. But they

and is never *directly* observed or even known by them. Hence, commodities never sell at their value; they sell at prices that are above or below their value. It cannot be otherwise in a society in which the value of the product is established *behind the backs of the producers*, independent of their conscious activity. Marx writes, 'The market value equates itself to the real value by means of constant fluctuations, not by an equation with real value as some third thing, but precisely through continual inequality of itself (not, as Hegel would say, by abstract identity, but by a continual negation of the negation, i.e., of itself as the negation of the real value)'.[46]

Marx finds much that is irrational in price-formation under capitalism, since prices are not determined by the conscious decisions of the agents of production. *But this is because value-production is itself inherently irrational* insofar as the value of the commodity is not determined by the conscious decisions by the agents of production. To leave production-relations intact while attempting to eliminate the 'irrationality' of price-formation on the market is inherently self-defeating, since it assumes away the very irrationality of value-production of which it is the expression.

The essence of Marx's critique centres on the non-equivalence of actual labour-time and socially-necessary labour-time, on the one hand, and the non-equivalence of value and price, on the other. *Taken together, both indicate that the labour-vouchers proposed by Darimon and Proudhon are in principle non-convertible.* Marx writes, 'The labour-time ticket, which represents the *average labour-time*, would never correspond to the *actual labour-time*, and never be convertible into it'.[47] Since socially-necessary labour-time is a constantly shifting magnitude, the amount of value embodied in the commodity would never be the same as the nominal 'value' (or price) of the product expressed in the labour-token. It is, of course, possible to consciously *assign* a given value to a labour-voucher based on the number of hours of labour-time that it expresses. However, the 'value' of that voucher will never coincide with the actual value of the commodity, which is determined by the *average* amount of time *necessary* to produce it – an average that cannot be consciously assigned since it undergoes constant change and variation.[48] The labour-token would

---

are always distinct and never coincide, or only quite fortuitously and exceptionally. The price of the commodities always stands above or below their value'.

46. Marx 1986a, p. 75.

47. Marx 1986a, pp. 76–7. Emphases in the original.

48. Such efforts to consciously plan out the 'value' of the commodity characterised the command-economies of the Soviet Union and Maoist China. That their state-capitalist economic plans, no matter how elaborate, failed to overcome the discrepancies between the *nominal* and *real* value of the commodity was reflected in the

never command the same 'value' as the *actual* value of the commodity; in fact, the value of the former would depreciate in comparison with the latter. Hence, the labour-tokens would be non-equivalent or non-convertible. But without such convertibility, the labour-token could not function as a medium of exchange – which is the entire reason for proposing them in the first place! Marx concludes,

> *Because price does not equal value, the element determining value, labour time, cannot be the element in which prices are expressed. For labour time would have to express itself at once as the determining and the non-determining element, as the equivalent and the non-equivalent of itself.* Because labour time as a measure of value only exists ideally, it cannot serve as the material for the comparison of prices.[49]

On these grounds, he contends,

> Just as it is impossible to abolish complications and contradictions arising from the existence of money alongside specific commodities by changing the form of money…[I]t is likewise impossible to abolish money itself, so long as exchange value remains the social form of products. It is essential to understand this clearly, so as not to set oneself impossible tasks, and to know the limits within which monetary reform and changes in circulation can remodel the relations of production and the social relations based upon them.[50]

So far it may seem that Marx's critique is primarily *negative*, in that he emphasises his opposition to the Proudhonist conception of how to organise a post-capitalist society. Does his critique posit or at least imply an alternative to capitalism? I will argue that as he further develops his discussion, a positive vision of the future does begin to emerge – especially as he goes deeper into the reasons *why* the labour-vouchers advocated by the Proudhonists are non-convertible.

Later, at the end of the 'Chapter on Money', Marx notes that 'this particular labour time cannot be directly exchanged for every other particular labour time; its general exchangeability must first be mediated, it must

---

widespread existence of a black market in goods and services. Where planning is, in principle, incapable of 'rationally' allocating resources through the calculation of commodity-values on the basis of political or other non-economic factors, the market will continue to manifest itself, in however distorted or non-traditional a form. This can also be seen as a major reason why virtually all of the state-command economies eventually found it necessary to reconcile theory with reality by openly embracing market-capitalism, in one or another variant.

49. Marx 1986a, p. 77.
50. Marx 1986a, p. 83.

acquire an objective form distinct from itself, if it is to acquire this general exchangeability'.[51] Labour-time cannot be *directly* exchanged for labour-time because labour is *indirectly* social so long as capitalist production-relations prevail. We have already seen a reason for this in the distinction between actual labour-time and socially-necessary labour-time: the former expresses a specific number of hours of labour engaged in by a worker, while the latter expresses a social average that operates irrespective of that worker. Hence, the value of the product is not determined directly by the particular acts of the producers, but indirectly, through a social average of many acts of labour among an array of individuals.

What does it mean to say that labour is indirectly social under capitalism? The abstract, undifferentiated, and indirect character of labour in societies governed by value-production reaches its full expression in *money*. Money, as the universal equivalent, connects one individual's labour and product of labour to someone else's. The social connection between individuals is established through the mediation of exchange. Yet this social relation is *indirect* since one individual is connected to another through an *abstraction* – a universal equivalent. Under capitalism, individuals are *socially* connected through the *indirect* medium of money because the production-relation that exchange is based upon is itself indirect. As Marx puts it, money 'can possess a social character only because the individuals have alienated their own social relationship in the form of an object'.[52]

This is why 'this particular labour time cannot be directly exchanged for every other particular labour time'. The advocates of the labour-voucher assume that value-production is compatible with *direct* social relations, since a given unit of labour-time is (presumably) directly exchangeable for an equivalent product created in the same amount of time. Indeed, Proudhon and his followers assume that the determination of value by labour-time is the condition for a truly 'rational' and *direct* system of commodity-exchange. *But their position becomes implausible as soon as it is recognised that value-production is anything but directly social.* Proudhon wants to eliminate the indirect character of exchange by harmonising relations of exchange with value-production, social relations of production that are themselves indirect.

In the course of elaborating upon this difference between directly and indirectly social labour – the first time in his writings that he has made this distinction – Marx enters into a discussion of what he sees as the content of a new society. He writes,

---

51. Marx 1986a, p. 107.
52. Marx 1986a, p. 97.

Now if this assumption is made, the general character of labour would not be given to it only by exchange; its assumed communal character would determine participation in the products. The communal character of production would from the outset make the product into a communal, general one. The exchange initially occurring in production, which would not be an exchange of exchange values but of activities determined by communal needs and communal purposes, would include from the beginning the individual's participation in the communal world of products...labour would be *posited* as general labour prior to exchange, i.e., the exchange of products would not in any way be the *medium* mediating the participation of the individual in general production. Mediation of course has to take place.[53]

This is a remarkable passage that is worth close analysis. First, Marx acknowledges that labour would have a 'general' character in a new society. However, its generality would be radically different from what exists in capitalism, where discrete acts of individual labour become connected to one another (or are made general) through the act of commodity-exchange. In contrast, labour becomes general in the new society *prior* to the exchange of products, on the basis of the 'the communal character of production' itself. The community distributes the elements of production according to the individuals' needs, instead of being governed by social forms that operate independently of their deliberation. Labour is general insofar as the community directly decides the manner and form of production. Marx is not referring here to the existence of small, isolated communities that operate in a world dominated by value-production. As noted above, Marx never adhered to the notion that socialism was possible in one country, let alone in one locale.[54] He is pointing, instead, to a communal network of associations in which value-production has been superseded on a systemic level. *Labour is therefore directly social, not indirectly social.* Second, Marx acknowledges that exchange *of some sort* would exist in a new society. However, exchange would be radically different from what prevails in capitalism, which is governed by the exchange of *commodities*. Instead of being based on exchange-values, prices, or markets,

---

53. Marx 1986a, p. 108.
54. Considerable confusion continues to characterise contemporary discussions of 'socialism' when it comes to this issue. The proclamation of a 'Bolivarian road to socialism', for instance, as advanced by Hugo Chávez in Venezuela, does not, obviously, provide a reason to designate the society itself as socialist – regardless of the amount of national industry and resources that are brought under the direct control of the government. This is not to suggest that nationalisation of foreign-owned industry and property is not an important and progressive measure. It is to suggest that it is insufficient to characterise that society as socialist or even as moving towards socialism.

distribution would be governed by an exchange of *activities* that are 'determined by communal needs and communal purposes'. The latter determines the exchange of *activities*, instead of being determined by the exchange of products that operate independently of it. Third, Marx acknowledges that social mediation would exist in a new society. However, mediation would be radically different from that under capitalism, where it has an abstract character, since 'mediation takes place through the exchange of commodities, through exchange value' and money. In socialism, in contrast, 'the presupposition is itself mediated, i.e., communal production, community as the basis of production, is assumed. The labour of the individual is from the outset taken as [directly] social labour'.[55]

Marx's distinction between indirectly and directly social labour is central to his evolving concept of a postcapitalist society – not only in the *Grundrisse* but also (as I will attempt to show) in much of his later work. He contends that in capitalism the 'social character of production is *established* only *post festum* by the elevation of the products into exchange values and the exchange of these exchange values', whereas in socialism, 'The *social character of labour is presupposed*, and participation in the world of products, in consumption, is not mediated by exchange between mutually independent labourers of products of labour. It is mediated by social production within which the individual carries on his activity'.[56] Marx is envisaging a totally new kind of social mediation, one that is *direct*, instead of *indirect*, *sensuous*, instead of *abstract*: 'For the fact is that labour on the basis of exchange values presupposes that neither the labour of the individual nor his product is *directly* general, but that it acquires this form only through *objective* mediation by means of a form of money distinct from it'.[57] In sum, a society is governed by exchange-value only insofar as the sociality of labour is established not through itself, but through an objective form independent of itself. Such a society is an *alienated* one, since (as Marx showed from as early as his writings of 1843–4), the domination of individuals by objective forms of their own making is precisely what is most problematic and indeed *perverse* about capitalism.

Marx proceeds to go deeper into what he means by directly social 'communal production' by addressing the role of *time* in a new society. He writes, 'Ultimately, all economy is a matter of economy of time'.[58] All societies strive to reduce the amount of time spent on producing and reproducing the necessities of life. No society is more successful at doing so than capitalism, in which

---

55. Marx 1986a, p. 108.
56. Marx 1986a, pp. 108–9.
57. Marx 1986a, p. 109.
58. Ibid.

production-relations *force* individual units of labour to conform to the average amount of time necessary to produce a given commodity. Since this compulsion issues from within the production-process, instead of from a political authority which lords over it from outside, capitalism is far more effective at generating efficiencies of time than were precapitalist modes of production.[59] Marx repeatedly refers to this as capitalism's 'civilising mission'. He says this because the development and *satisfaction* of the individual ultimately depends upon the saving of time so that life can be freed up for pursuits other than engaging in material production.

But how does the economisation of time relate to a new society governed by 'communal production'? Marx indicates that it becomes just as important as in capitalism, although it exists in a different form and for a different purpose:

> If we presuppose communal production, the time factor naturally remains essential. The less time society requires to produce corn, livestock, etc., the more time it wins for other production, material or spiritual... Economy of time, as well as the planned distribution of labour time over the various branches of production, therefore, remains the first economic law if communal production is taken as the basis. *It becomes a law even to a much higher degree.* However, this is essentially different from the measurement of exchange values (of labours or products of labour) by labour time.[60]

Marx does not detail exactly *how* the economisation of time operates in a society governed by communal production; the text mentions no single mechanism or lever for accomplishing this. However, in light of his earlier writings, we can surmise that he sees the motivation for the economisation of time in a new society as resting upon the effort to achieve what he called in 1844 a 'totality of manifestations of life'. When society is freed from the narrow drive to augment value as an end in itself, it can turn its attention to supplying the multiplicity of needs and wants that are integral to the social individual. Instead of being consumed by *having* and possessing, individuals can now focus upon what is given short shrift in societies governed by value-

---

59. This applies most of all to sectors of the capitalist economy that directly feel the pressure to organise themselves according to the social average of labour-time because they are subject to competitive pressures. Where competition is restricted or eliminated due to social or political factors, such efficiencies of time will generally not be as forthcoming. One of the arguments by capitalists for privatisation, free trade and globalisation is to extend such efficiencies of time into all sectors of the capitalist economy. The current drive in the USA and Europe to privatise public-sector employment can be seen as one reflection of this.

60. Marx 1986a, p. 109; my emphases.

production – their *being*, their manifold sensuous and intellectual needs, whether 'material or spiritual'. The more people get in touch with their *universality of needs*, the greater the incentive to economise time, to reduce the amount of hours engaged in material production, so that such multiple needs (such as cultural, social, or intellectual enjoyment) can be pursued and satisfied. In a word, whereas in capitalism the incentive to economise time is provided by an abstract standard, exchange-value,[61] in socialism it is provided by the concrete sensuous needs of the individuals themselves. The drive to economise time no longer comes from *outside* the individuals, from value's need to grow big with value, but from *within*, from the quest to manifest the totality of the individuals' intellectual, sensuous, and spiritual capabilities.

Marx further spells out his concept of a postcapitalist society in the *Grundrisse* by outlining the three broad stages of human history. The first stage, which characterises precapitalist societies, is based on *personal dependence*; labour is directly social but *unfree*. Social relations dominate and control the individual. The individual is *personally* dependent on the lord or king, vizir or pharaoh. In such societies 'human productivity develops only to a limited extent and at isolated points'.[62] Satisfaction is obtained on the basis of a narrow and relatively under-developed, patriarchal standpoint. The second stage, which characterises capitalism, is 'personal independence based upon dependence mediated by things'; labour is now indirectly social. In capitalism, individuals are *formally* 'free' but they are *actually* dominated not only *things* but also by an abstraction, *value* – both of which are products of their own creation. Dead labour, in the form of capital, dominates living labour. The social power of the individual develops in accordance with exchange-value and money; subjective powers are now expressed in an *objective* form. Individuals are subsumed *under* social production, even as the personal bonds that connect them are broken up and dissolved: 'Their production is not *directly* social, not the offspring of association distributing labour within itself'.[63] *Dissatisfaction* is obtained on the basis of a broad and relatively developed standpoint. However, this 'second stage' creates the conditions for the

---

61. Marx had earlier argued in the *Economic and Philosophical Manuscripts* of 1844 that societies dominated by exchange-value *narrow* and *constrict* many needs, at the same time as they conflate and exaggerate other ones. Whereas the need for having, owning, and consuming is amplified by capitalism, the need for caring, sharing and loving is not. A major issue that concerns Marx in the *Grundrisse* is the extent to which capitalism's 'civilising mission' of achieving greater economisation of time comes at the expense of hollowing out the richness of the human personality. I will return to this, below.

62. Marx 1986a, p. 95.

63. Marx 1986a, pp. 95–6.

third stage, postcapitalist society. Marx refers to this stage as follows: 'Free individuality, based on the universal development of the individuals and the subordination of their communal, social productivity, which is their social possession'.[64] Labour is now both directly social and *free*.

Remarkably, Marx does not here use the word socialism or communism to describe a postcapitalist society. He instead refers to it as 'free individuality'. In fact, most of Marx's references to 'socialism' in the *Grundrisse* are *critical* references to the standpoint of Darimon, Proudhon, and the English neo-Ricardian radicals. The word 'communism' appears even more rarely. Marx appears to be trying to distinguish himself from other opponents of capitalism by further clarifying his understanding of the alternative to it. The 'free individuality' that defines the third stage is a very different kind of individuality than that found in capitalism, since it is based upon the '*universal* development of individuals'. What predominates is 'the free exchange of individuals who are associated on the basis of common appropriation and control of the means of production'.[65] Marx is suggesting that capitalism *narrows* our individuality in that every aspect of life is reduced to one and only one sense: the sense of *having* or *possession*. The wealth and multi-dimensionality of the individual's needs and desires are narrowed down and hollowed out in capitalism, where augmenting value – as expressed most of all in obtaining money – is considered the greatest good. In contrast, in a socialist or postcapitalist society the *universal* needs of the individual determine social development.

Marx sharply distinguishes this third stage of history from precapitalist formations, in that society and/or the community no longer *dominate* the individual. Relations of personal dependence are transcended. *The individual now becomes the social entity.*[66] He also sharply distinguishes the realm of free individuality from the second stage – capitalism – because individuals are no longer cut off from connection or communion with one another but, instead, relate to each other on the basis of their mutually-acknowledged *universal* needs and capabilities.

Marx elaborates upon this by writing that in capitalism, 'The individuals are subsumed under social production, which exists outside them as their fate; but social production is not subsumed under the individuals who manage it as their common wealth'.[67] In capitalism individuals are subsumed by social production insofar as relations of production and exchange take on a life of their own and confront the individual as a hostile force. Marx denies

---

64. Marx 1986a, p. 95.
65. Marx 1986a, p. 96.
66. Marx 1975r, p. 299.
67. Marx 1986a, p. 96.

that capitalist society respects the freedom of the individual; instead, it dominates and controls individuals under social relations of their own making. *Therein lies the perversity of capitalism.* It is therefore quite pointless to speak of a new society as one in which the freedom of individuals is overcome by subjecting them to the control of social relations *because this is exactly what governs the social relations of capitalism.*

To use Karel Kosik's phrase, Marx does not envisage a new society as one in which the individual is 'walled in' by society.[68] He argues that this is what occurs under capitalism. He conceives of the new society as the realm of *free* individuality.

But what about capitalism's 'civilising mission'? Marx does not leave aside the *contributions* of capitalism as he envisages a new society. He notes that 'the dissolution of all products and activities into exchange values presuppose both the dissolution of all established personal (historical) relations of dependence in production, and the all-round dependence of producers upon one another'.[69] Capitalism gives rise to the *idea* of free individuality even as it subsumes individuals under social relations of their own making. Value-production acts as the great *dissolver* of firm and fixed social relations, allowing individuals for the first time to conceive of themselves as self-determining subjects. Hence, the 'free individuality' that Marx conceives of as defining the third stage 'presupposes precisely the production on the basis of exchange value, which, along with the universality of the estrangement of individuals from others, now also produces the universality and generality of all their relations and abilities'.[70] The achievement of a new society based on 'free individuality' depends on the formation of new needs and capabilities generated by capitalist relations of production and exchange. Without the generation of such new needs and capacities, a new society would lack the incentivising principle for economising on labour-time. Largely for this reason, Marx repeatedly argues in the *Grundrisse* that the third stage of human history arises from the 'material and spiritual conditions'[71] created by capitalism itself.[72]

---

68. See Kosik 1976.
69. Marx 1986a, p. 93.
70. Marx 1986a, p. 99.
71. See Marx 1987a, p. 133: 'It is precisely the production process of capital that gives rise to the material and spiritual conditions for the negation of wage-labour and capital'. See also Marx 1986a, pp. 98, 337: 'The beauty and greatness lies precisely in this spontaneously evolved connection, in this material and spiritual exchange' and 'the expansion of the range of needs, the differentiation of production, and the exploration and exchange of all natural and spiritual powers'.
72. This should not be confused with the claim, which became predominant among the Marxists of the Second International and among many others in the twentieth century, that *every country in the world* therefore must first undergo capitalism before it

He sums this up in writing, 'It is equally certain that individuals cannot subordinate their own social connections to themselves before they have created them.'[73] It makes a huge difference as to whether the effort to create a postcapitalist society arises from the womb of social relations already in existence, or whether it must, instead, create such relations *sui generis*. It is impossible to create a new society from scratch. Marx clearly rejects the notion that a new society can be constructed by turning one's back on history. The 'universally developed individuals' that characterise the stage that follows capitalism are themselves a product of prior stages of historical development.

Largely for this reason, the *Grundrisse* contains a considerable amount of historical analysis of the development of capitalism as well as of precapitalist forms of production. The latter range from discussions of the economic and social formations in the ancient Greco-Roman world to communal forms of labour and land-tenure that characterised precapitalist societies in India, Russia, and China. The section on 'Precapitalist Economic Formations' is one of the most famous and widely-discussed sections of the *Grundrisse*, and it has given rise to lively debates since it first became widely available (at least in German, Russian and Chinese) in the 1950s.[74] At issue in many of these debates is *why* Marx accorded so much attention to precapitalist formations. Was it part of an effort to extend a 'historical-materialist' analysis of capitalism to a delineation of the forms of social production that have characterised all of human history? Or did Marx have a different aim in mind?

There is no question that Marx was deeply interested in understanding the manner in which capitalist social relations emerged from out of the womb of precapitalist modes of production.[75] At the same time, the *Grundrisse* indicates that Marx was just as interested in how a historical understanding of the emergence of capitalist commodity-production could shed light on a future *postcapitalist* society. He points to this in writing,

---

can be ready for socialism. Marx explicitly argued against that position in his writings on the Russian village-commune in particular at the end of his life. For an exploration of Marx's position on this issue, see Anderson 2010.

73. Marx 1986a, p. 98.

74. For a discussion of how discussions of Marx's analysis of precapitalist formations in the *Grundrisse* were stimulated by the Chinese Revolution of 1949, see Bailey and Llobera (eds.) 1981.

75. It would be incorrect to presume that Marx was mainly concerned with the transition from *feudalism* to capitalism in this section of the *Grundrisse*, since he denied that feudalism characterised social relations in South Asia and China prior to the intervention of European imperialism. Instead, he contended that such societies were characterised by a different mode of production, which he often referred to as 'the so-called Asiatic mode of production'. For more on this, see Marx 1975t as well as Hudis 2004a and Hudis 2010.

On the other hand – and this is much more important for us – our method indicates the points at which historical analysis must be introduced, or at which bourgeois economy as a mere historical form of the production process points beyond itself towards earlier historical modes of production…These indications, together with the correct grasp of the present, then also offer the key to the understanding of the past – a work in its own right, which we hope to be able to undertake as well. This correct approach, moreover, leads to points which indicate the transcendence of the present form of production relations, the movement coming into being, thus *foreshadowing* the future. If, on the other hand, the pre-bourgeois phases appear as *merely historical,* i.e. transcended premises, so [on the other hand] the present conditions of production appear as conditions which *transcend themselves* and thus posit themselves as *historical premises* for a new state of society.[76]

Thus, Marx contends that the analysis of earlier historical forms facilitates the effort to envisage *future* social forms. The social relations of any given society generally appear 'natural' and 'normal' in the eyes of its participants, especially when they have prevailed for a considerable length of time. This proclivity to *naturalise* social relations is no less prevalent among philosophers, as he shows in his comments about John Stuart Mill and others in the 'Introduction' to the *Grundrisse*. One way to challenge this tendency towards naturalisation is through the historical investigation of social formations that *preceded* capitalism. The peculiar and transitory nature of capitalism is brought into focus by elucidating the marks that distinguish its relations of production from precapitalist forms. Thus shaking up this proclivity towards naturalisation, the examination of the past, in turn, creates a conceptual lens with which to discern intimations of the *future*. The antagonistic contradictions of the present historical form are brought into focus through an examination of the past, which makes it possible to see how such contradictions foreshadow their transcendence in a future form of social organisation. In this sense, Marx not only addresses the nature of a possible postcapitalist society when he directly comments on the future; but he also does so in drawing out a contrast between capitalist and precapitalist societies.

This is illuminated in a number of ways in the *Grundrisse's* discussion of precapitalist economic forms. First, Marx argues that while capitalist wage-labour is superior in many respects to slavery in precapitalist societies, wage-labour does not represent a normatively 'free' contractual relation between employers and employees. Wage-labourers are *formally* free insofar as they sell their capacity to labour to a discrete entity, the capitalist, in exchange for

---

76. Marx 1986a, pp. 388–9.

monetary remuneration. The capitalist pays the workers not for the actual amount of time worked, but rather for their potential or *ability* to work.[77] In contrast, slaves are not formally free since the master purchases not their *capacity* to labour but their *actual* labour – their full physical being, the entire *body* of their labour. Therefore, 'labour capacity in its totality appears to the free worker as his own property, one of his own moments, over which he as subject exercises control, and which he maintains in selling it'.[78] Since the wage-labourer appears to act as a self-determining subject insofar as a contractual relationship is established with the capitalist, it *appears* to be a social form that best corresponds to the concept of freedom. For many living in such a system, this condition of formal 'equality' seems to offer the best of all possible worlds. Matters are very different, however, in precapitalist societies, where no slave (or peasant) considers herself the equal of the master since a contractual relation is absent; the master simply *imposes* labour upon the slaves and decides arbitrarily how they shall live. By contrasting such precapitalist forms with capitalism, Marx is able to pinpoint a contradiction *immanent* to wage-labour that it is easy to overlook. In slavery and serfdom, there is no separation between the active *being* of persons and the 'inorganic or objective conditions'[79] of their existence. In capitalism, there *is* such a separation, since 'living labour appears as *alien* vis-à-vis labour capacity whose labour it is, whose life it expresses, for it is surrendered to capital in return for objectified labour, for the product of labour itself'.[80] *Despite appearances, in capitalism, there is no equal exchange of objectified labour (in the form of capital) for living labour.* There is, instead, an exchange of objectified labour for labour-*capacity*. The contractual relation between worker and capitalist rests on *that* basis. In being paid not for their actual labour but only for their capacity to labour, the active being of the workers is *separated* or *alienated* from the objective conditions of existence. 'Labour itself, like its product, is *negated in its form as the labour of the particular, individualized worker*'.[81] Wage-labour is therefore far from being either natural or an expression of *actual* freedom. It is, rather, a peculiar social relation in which the *formal* equality between capitalist and worker rests upon

---

77. The *Grundrisse* is the first work in which Marx makes this all-important discussion between labour and labour-power, or labour-capacity. Tom Rockmore summarises the concept thus: 'What the worker offers is not labour, but labour power required to maintain himself, which he does by objectifying himself in the form of a commodity, or product exchanged for money. In other terms, there is a difference between labour and labour time, and the latter is the quantified form of the power, or the capacity to produce commodities, and, in this way, capital'. See Rockmore 2002, p. 102.

78. Marx 1986a, p. 393.
79. Marx 1986a, p. 413.
80. Marx 1986a, p. 390.
81. Marx 1986a, p. 398.

the *alienation* of labour. It follows that wage-labour will come to an end with the abolition of alienated labour.

Second, Marx shows that, while relations of exchange and commodity-production long preceded capitalism and are found in diverse forms of precapitalist societies, only in capitalism do they *define* and *determine* social reproduction. Relations of exchange, as is the case with exchange-value, exist on the margins of precapitalist society, or in their 'interstices'.[82] The subordination of the producers to relations of exchange that exist outside of their control is historically specific and is not at all 'natural'. *The same is true of the concept of value itself.* He writes,

> The economic concept of value does not occur among the ancients. Value as distinct from *pretium* [price] was a purely legal category, invoked against fraud, etc. The concept of value wholly belongs to the latest political economy, because that concept is the most abstract expression of capital itself and of the production based on it. In the concept of value, the secret of capital is betrayed.[83]

It follows that, just as value-production and exchange-value do not *dominate* society prior to capitalism, they do not do so *after* capitalism.

Third, by focusing on communal forms of association, production and distribution that precede capitalism, Marx shows that the isolated individuality and atomisation that characterise modern capitalism are by no means natural or eternal. The *Grundrisse* contains one of the most extensive treatments of the Germanic, Slavic, and 'Asiatic' communal forms found in any of his writings. He denies that the 'Asiatic' form is a historical aberration. The historical aberration is, instead, the concept of free individuality abstracted from the communal conditions that prevail in modern capitalist societies. The very concept of the atomised and independent individual, he argues, arises and can only arise on the basis of developed social and economic relations, including communal ones. As he puts it, 'Man becomes individualized only through the process of history'.[84] Moreover, he argues that a society dominated by precapitalist communal forms, despite the social backwardness and political despotism that were often associated with them, 'seems very exalted, when set

---

82. See Marx 1986a, p. 155: 'In antiquity, exchange value was not the *nexus rerum*; it appears as such only among the trading nations, but they had only a carrying trade and did not themselves produce. At least production was secondary among Phoenicians, Carthaginians, etc. They could live in the interstices of the ancient world, like the Jews in Poland or in the Middle Ages'.
83. Marx 1987a, pp. 159–60.
84. Marx 1986a, p. 420.

against the modern world, in which production is the end of man, and wealth the end of production'.[85]

This suggests that just as non-communal forms of labour and production did not prevail prior to capitalism, they would not prevail after capitalism. Marx fleshes out this conception by directly addressing the contours of a post-capitalist society, as follows:

> In fact, however, if the narrow bourgeois form is peeled off, what is wealth is not the universality of the individual's needs, capacities, enjoyments, productive forces, etc., produced in universal exchange; what is it if not the full development of human control over the forces of nature – over the forces of so-called Nature, as well as those of his own nature? What is wealth if not the absolute unfolding of man's creative abilities, without any precondition other than the preceding historical development, which makes the totality of this development – i.e., the development of human powers as such, not measured by any *previously given* yardstick – an end-in-itself, through which he does not reproduce himself in any specific character, but produces his totality, and does not seek to remain something he has already become, but is in the absolute movement of becoming?[86]

Although there is much that could be said of this striking passage, what stands out most of all is the distinction Marx makes between material wealth and value-production. In capitalism, material wealth takes the form of value; however, there is no reason for wealth to forever exist in a value-form. *It ceases to do so in Marx's vision of a postcapitalist society.* In a new society, wealth becomes reconfigured from a merely quantitative to a qualitative determinant; instead of expressing the reduction of human sensuousness to the abstraction of value, wealth becomes 'the absolute unfolding of man's creative abilities'.[87] In such a society, material wealth is not, as in capitalism, a mere *means* to the augmentation of value. Instead, wealth – understood as the unfolding of the richness of the human personality – now becomes an end in itself.

Marx is here returning to and deepening the conception he elaborated in 1844, when he wrote: 'It will be seen how in place of the *wealth* and *poverty* of political economy come the rich *human* being and the rich *human* need. The rich human being is simultaneously the human being *in need of* a totality of human manifestations of life – the man in whom his own realization exists as

---

85. Marx 1986a, p. 411.
86. Marx 1986a, pp. 411–12.
87. In a work written shortly after the completion of the *Grundrisse*, Marx quotes favourably the comment of Pierre Le Pesant Boisguillebert: 'True wealth...is the complete enjoyment not only of the necessities of life but also of all the superfluities and of all that can give pleasure to the senses.' See Marx 1987b, p. 295.

an inner necessity, as *need*.[88] For Marx the new society is the realm in which the development of the totality of human powers is its own end. In capitalism, human powers exist to service capital, self-expanding value.[89] The latter serves as the 'yardstick' of social development. In contrast, no 'previously-given' yardstick independent of the individuals' subjective self-activity governs social development in a postcapitalist society.[90]

Capitalism, as Marx was fully aware, constantly creates new needs as the forces of production expand. Such needs, however, are generated in order to service capital's thirst for self-expansion. A new society, on the other hand, is one in which the creation and development of human needs is a *self-sufficient* end.[91] New needs are generated through a 'universal exchange' of humanity's creative capacities and serve no purpose other than to augment those capacities. The generation of such needs is potentially endless; needs are limited only by the capacity to envisage them (their realisation is, of course, a different matter).[92] However, this is not commensurate with the 'bad infinite' of value-production, in which new needs are generated for the sake of endlessly augmenting an abstraction, value. Value, as Marx notes several times in

---

88. Marx 1975r, p. 304.

89. Marx defines capital as 'a sum of values employed for the production of values', and as 'self-reproducing exchange value'. It should be noted that Marx is not satisfied with Smith and Ricardo's definition of capital as congealed or accumulated labour, since that suggests that capital is a transhistorical phenomenon that characterises all modes of production. See Marx 1986a, p. 189.

90. This is especially important when it comes to treating abstract universal labour-time as the yardstick of social development – an issue that will be revisited in more detail in Chapter Four, where I deal with Marx's *Critique of the Gotha Programme*.

91. There are striking similarities between Marx's discussion of activities that are ends-in-themselves and Aristotle's discussion of the self-sufficient end in his *Ethics* and *Politics*. Whereas Marx speaks of human *power* as an end in itself, Aristotle speaks of *energeia* (sometimes translated as energy or power, but more recently rendered as 'being-at-work') as an end in itself: '[A]mong some ways of being-at-work, some are necessary and are chosen for their own sake, it is clear that one ought to place happiness as one of those that are chosen for their own sake and not among those that are for the sake of something else, since happiness stands in need of nothing but is self-sufficient'. See Aristotle 2002, p. 190 [1176b3–7].

92. It is possible to discern a parallel between Marx's understanding of *need* and Emmanuel Levinas's discussion of metaphysical *desire*: 'The metaphysical desire does not rest upon any prior kinship. It is a desire that can not be satisfied...The metaphysical desire has an other intention; it desires beyond everything that can simply complete it. It is like goodness – the Desired does not fulfil it, but deepens it. It is a generosity nourished by the Desired, and thus a relationship that is not the disappearance of distance, not a bringing together, or – to circumscribe more closely the essence of generosity and goodness – a relationship whose positivity comes from remoteness, from separation, for it nourishes itself, one might say, with its hunger.' See Levinas 1969, p. 34.

the *Grundrisse*, appears as the *absolute subject* in capitalism.[93] In contrast, once wealth is freed from its value-integument, a 'multiplicity of needs'[94] is generated for the sake of augmenting a concrete, *sensuous* force – that of the individuals themselves, who step forth as the real, *human* subject. *The actual individual now finally emerges as the absolute subject.* Largely for this reason, Marx writes that an 'absolute movement of becoming'[95] characterises postcapitalist society. Such an 'absolute movement' of *human* capability and creativity, which is thwarted by capitalist value-production, is the basis of the new society.

Throughout the *Grundrisse*, Marx points to a possible transcendence of value-production by emphasising the *dissolution* of social formations. There is hardly any word that appears more often in his work than *dissolution*.[96] He writes, 'Wage labour appears as the dissolution, the destruction of relations in which labour was fixed in all respects of income, content, locality, scope, etc. *Hence as negation of the fixity of labour and its remunerations'.*[97] He adds, 'The dissolution of all products and activities into exchange values presupposes both the dissolution of all established personal (historical) relations of dependence in production, and the all-round dependence of producers upon one another'.[98] And he writes of how capital promotes the '*dissolution* of the relation to the earth – to land or soil – as a natural condition of production'.[99]

Marx's emphasis on dissolution is no less emphatic when it comes to analysing precapitalist economic formations, as the following passage – in which dissolution is mentioned no less than six times – suggests:

---

93. See Marx 1986a, p. 196: 'But the whole of circulation considered in itself consists in the same exchange value, exchange value as subject, positing itself once as commodity and again as money; it is the movement by means of which exchange value posits itself in this dual determination'. See also Marx 1986a, p. 237: 'Value enters as subject'. It should be noted, however, that value is the subject in capitalism only in a *restricted* sense, since (as Marx states) 'it is *labour* which appears confronting capital as subject'. 'Value enters as subject' insofar as labour is employed as a means to augment value, which means that the self-expansion of value is *dependent* on a force or subject that is *other* to itself – living labour. Value is the absolute subject only in a qualified, Hegelian sense – as an absolute that contains its highest opposition within itself.

94. Marx 1986a, p. 451.

95. The formulation recalls Marx's statement in 'Private Property and Communism' that 'communism as such is not the goal of human development, the form of human society'. No particular form of society represents the 'end' of history if it is defined by the satisfaction of human needs and capacities as an end in itself, since needs are interminable. See Marx 1975r, p. 306.

96. The German term is *Auflösung*, which means 'unravelling' but which also carries an implication of a subsequent solution.

97. Marx 1986a, p. 13.

98. Marx 1986a, p. 93.

99. Marx 1986a, p. 421.

Such historical processes of dissolution can take the form of the dissolution of the dependent relationship which binds the worker to the soil and to the lord but which actually presupposes his ownership of the means of subsistence... They can also take the form of the dissolution of these relations of landed property which constitute him as yeoman, as a free working petty landowner or tenant (*colonus*), i.e. as a free peasant. The dissolution of the even more ancient forms of communal property and of real community needs no special mention. Or they can take the form of the dissolution of guild relations... Lastly, they can take the form of the dissolution of various client relationships...[100]

The reason for Marx's repeated emphasis on dissolution is not immediately self-evident. The *Grundrisse* explores a number of social formations that existed for many centuries or even millennia, including the 'Asiatic' mode of production. Surely not all of these formations were forever on the verge of collapsing or dissolving. Why, then, does Marx place so much emphasis on the tendency towards dissolution, even when he is analysing relatively stable social formations?

I would argue that Marx was not interested in writing a history of social or economic *development* as much as detailing the process by which a new, *free* society is compelled to come into being. If Marx were engaged in historical analysis for the purpose of developing an empirical sociology, he would need to give as much weight to tendencies towards stability and equilibrium as to dissolution and decay. Yet Marx does not do so: his historical analyses are decidedly one-sided, insofar as they emphasise the constraints faced by social formations in the face of changing historical circumstances. He does so because his real object of analysis is not so much the past as the future. In tracing out how various formations undergo dissolution, Marx is elucidating the factors immanent in the present that point to a future state of affairs.

Contrary to the claim that Marx focused mainly on the present and secondarily on the past, his emphasis on tendencies towards dissolution in his analyses of both the present and the past indicate that he was most of all concerned about the future. For Marx, however, the future cannot simply be spelled out on the basis of the individual's imagination: it must be traced out through an analysis of *existing* social formations. Marx spells this out in the following passage:

---

100. Marx 1986a, p. 426.

> Within bourgeois society, based as it is upon *exchange value*, relationships of
> exchange and production are generated which are just so many mines to blow
> it to pieces. (A multitude of antagonistic forms of the social entity, whose
> antagonism, however, can never be exploded by a quiet metamorphosis).
> On the other hand, if we did not find latent in society as it is, the material
> conditions of production and the corresponding relationships of exchange
> for a classless society, all attempts to explode it would be quixotic.[101]

Marx locates the specific process by which capitalist social relations create
the conditions for a supersession of value-production in his discussion of
the relation between necessary and surplus labour-time. This represents one
of the most important sections of the *Grundrisse*. Along with its accompany-
ing discussion of the machinery and 'the automaton', it has given rise to a
number of debates in Marxism and Marx scholarship.

For Marx, necessary labour is the amount of labour-time needed to create
enough value to ensure the *subsistence* of the labourer – the time requisite
for enabling the worker to re-enter the labour-process on a renewed basis. It
depends on an assortment of factors, such as the level of a society's material
development, what is specifically required in a given time or place for workers to replenish their labour-power, moral considerations, etc. Surplus-labour
refers to the excess amount of time beyond what it takes to produce the workers' subsistence. This distinction is of great importance, as it serves as the
basis of Marx's concept of *surplus-value*.[102] He argues,

> The great historical aspect of capital is the *creation* of this *surplus labour*,
> superfluous from the point of view of mere use value, of mere subsistence,
> and its historical mission is fulfilled when, on the one hand, needs are
> developed to the point where surplus labour beyond what is necessary has
> itself become a general need and arises from the individual needs themselves;
> and on the other, when, by strict discipline of capital to which successive
> generations have been subjected, general industriousness has been developed
> as the universal asset of the new generation.[103]

Capital spurs the formation of new needs *beyond* what is required for subsistence, as part of spurring the augmentation of value. The lesser the (relative)
amount of value that goes to sustain the worker, the greater the (relative)

101. Marx 1986a, pp. 96–7.
102. To my knowledge, the first time that Marx explicitly used the term 'surplus-
value' was in the *Grundrisse*, in the course of discussing the difference between necessary and surplus-labour. See Marx 1986a, pp. 249–50. The concept is implicit in *The
Poverty of Philosophy*; however, the term 'surplus-value' does not appear there.
103. Marx 1986a, p. 250.

amount of value that accrues to capital. The greater the ratio of surplus-labour relative to necessary labour, the more expansive human needs become – even as they are subjected to capital's dominance. Capital's 'progressive' or 'civilising' mission is to expand the boundaries of human needs. Although this unfolds in an alienating process at the expense of the workers, it creates the possibility of richer and more expansive conditions of life: 'As the ceaseless striving for the general form of wealth, however, capital forces labour beyond the limits of natural need and thus creates the material elements for the development of the rich individuality'.[104]

There are, however, internal barriers to capital's effort to surmount all obstacles to its drive to increase the proportion of surplus-labour relative to necessary labour, since 'The smaller the fractional part already which represents *necessary* labour, the greater the *surplus labour*, the less can any increase in productivity perceptively diminish necessary labour'.[105] Surplus-labour expands so dramatically *vis-à-vis* necessary labour that capital cannot further reduce necessary labour without undermining the only source of value, living labour itself:

> It is the law of capital, as we have seen, to produce surplus, disposable time. It can do this only by setting in motion *necessary labour*, i.e., by entering into exchange with the worker. It is therefore the tendency of capital to produce as much labour as possible, just as it is its tendency to reduce necessary labour to a minimum... It is just as much the tendency of capital to render human labour (relatively) superfluous, as to drive it on without limit.[106]

As Marx sees it, the logic of capital therefore drives capitalism into an ultimately untenable position, by failing to give full employment to its own value-creating substance.

Moreover, as capital renders human labour relatively superfluous, even as the magnitude of capital increases, the rate of profit begins to decline. The decline in the rate of profit, Marx argues, is a manifestation of the increased productivity of labour – that is, capital's effectiveness at increasing surplus-labour relative to necessary labour. Capital can, of course, try to get around this problem. One way is by increasing the length of the working-day, to increase *absolute* surplus-value. Yet there are limits to this since a day only contains 24 hours. Another way is through a 'spatial addition *of more simultaneous working days*'[107] – such as by increasing the size of the labouring populace by

---

104. Marx 1986a, p. 251.
105. Marx 1986a, p. 265.
106. Marx 1986a, p. 326.
107. Ibid.

evicting farmers from the land. At the same time, however, capital's tendency is to 'reduce to a minimum the many simultaneous working days'.[108] As much as capital tries to increase the amount of working-time in order to accrue more value, it is driven, at one and the same time, to reduce the amount of *necessary* working-time. Surplus-labour increases at a faster rate than necessary labour-time, replicating the original problem. There is too much capital relative to living labour.

Capitalist value-production therefore finds itself caught in an insuperable contradiction: 'Capital, in positing surplus labour, equally and simultaneously posits and does not posit necessary labour; it exists only as necessary labour both exists and does not exist'.[109] This very contradiction creates the conditions for a higher form of social organisation, since 'an individual can satisfy his *own* needs only by simultaneously satisfying the needs of, and producing a surplus over and above that for, *another* individual'. Thus, 'it is this very development of wealth which makes it possible to transcend these contradictions'.[110]

Marx concludes, 'Capital posits the *production of wealth* itself and thus the universal development of the productive forces, posits the continual overthrow of its existing presuppositions, as the presuppositions of its reproduction'. Capital is based on conditions that point beyond itself, not despite but because 'the elaboration of the productive forces, of general wealth, etc., knowledge, etc., takes place in such a way that the working individual *alienates* himself'. This serves as 'The basis [of] the possibility of the universal development of the individuals, and their actual development from this basis as constant transcendence of their *barrier*, which is recognised as such, and is not interpreted as a *sacred* limit. The universality of the individual not as an imaginary concept, but the universality of his real and notional relations'.[111]

The development of the material productive forces posits the *possibility* of this transcendence; however, it does not by itself *constitute* it. What constitutes the transcendence of capitalist value-production is a state of existence in which the universality of needs is fulfilled and *actualised*. The very process that limits and impoverishes the workers by reducing their labouring activity to a mere means of increasing the productive forces turns into its opposite, in that this process helps lead to a new sensitivity and understanding of universal needs, connections, enjoyments, and experiences that can realise the wealth of the human personality.

---

108. Marx 1986a, p. 327.
109. Ibid.
110. Marx 1986a, p. 328.
111. Marx 1986a, pp. 465–6.

It appears, therefore, that even when tackling such basic economic categories as the relation between necessary and surplus labour-time, Marx focuses much of his theoretical attention on forms of social existence that could follow capitalism.

This is further elaborated in Marx's discussion of machinery and 'the automaton' in the concluding part of the 'Chapter on Capital'. He argues that the logical trajectory of capitalism is to replace living labour at the point of production with dead labour – machinery and labour-saving technology. His discussion focuses on the ramifications of an ever-increasing productivity of labour. The value of each particular commodity *decreases* with increases in productivity, since the commodity embodies fewer hours of labour-time. Yet by producing greater amounts of commodities in a given unit of time, the total amount of value *increases* considerably. As a result, 'immediate labour and its quantity disappear as the determining principle of production, of the creation of use-values.' Although labour remains 'indispensable' to capitalist production, it 'becomes a subaltern moment in comparison to scientific work, the technological application of the natural sciences'.[112]

It appears, at first sight, that Marx is simply discussing the well-known tendency of capitalism to promote technological innovation. While that is surely his empirical focus, he is not only detailing a major component of how capitalism grows and develops. His attention is also focused on how this phenomenon points to a form of social existence that can *follow* capitalism. He writes, 'Thus capital works to dissolve itself as the form which dominates production'.[113] Since living labour as the source and determinant of value begins to disappear under the impact of technological innovation, the existence of value-production itself is placed in jeopardy – even though the mass of capital grows under its impetus. As the importance of living labour as the source of value begins to recede, the possibility arises of another way of producing use-values – one that is not tied to labour as the universal medium of social reproduction. The very principle that governs the *development* of capitalism – the increased productivity of labour through the use of labour-saving devices – points towards a possible *supersession* of capitalism. Thus, just when capital takes over and dominates living labour to an unprecedented degree, the conditions that ensure the existence of capital begin to dissolve. Marx states that capitalism 'quite unintentionally reduces human labour, the expenditure of human energy, to a minimum. This will be to the advantage of emancipated labour and is the condition for its emancipation'.[114]

---

112. Marx 1987a, p. 86.
113. Ibid.
114. Marx 1987a, p. 87.

Marx argues that the logical trajectory of this substitution of dead labour for living labour is the following:

> Labour no longer appears so much as included in the production process, but rather man relates himself to that process as its overseer and regulator...[the labourer] stands beside the production process, rather than being its main agent. Once this transformation has taken place, it is neither the immediate labour performed by man himself, nor the time for which he works, but the appropriation of his own general productive power, his comprehension of Nature and domination of it by virtue of his being a social entity – in a word, the development of the social individual – that appears as the cornerstone of production and wealth...As soon as labour time in its immediate form ceases to be the great source of wealth, labour time ceases and must cease to be its measure, and therefore exchange value [must cease to be the measure] of use value. The surplus labour of the masses has ceased to be the condition for the development of general wealth, just as the non-labour of a few has ceased to be the condition for the development of the general powers of the human mind. As a result, production based upon exchange value collapses, and the immediate material production process itself is stripped of its form of indigence and antagonism.[115]

Marx is envisaging a situation in which labour ceases to be the measure or medium of social relations. Thus, he denies that labour is the 'cornerstone of production and wealth' in all forms of society. Least of all does he think that labour will serve as the cornerstone of a postcapitalist society. Instead, 'the development of the social individual' in its variety of manifestations – including those not limited to labour or material production – would serve as the cornerstone of wealth. Capitalism prepares the way for this through its proclivity to reduce the relative importance of living labour. This will free up individuals in the new society to pursue talents and capacities that are not restricted to the labour-process. Marx envisages the following: 'Free development of individualities, and hence not the reduction of necessary labour time in order to posit surplus labour, but in general the reduction of necessary labour of society to a minimum, to which then corresponds the artistic, scientific, etc., development of individuals, made possible by the time thus set free and the means produced for all of them'.[116]

These passages clearly highlight Marx's emphasis on how the specific features of a postcapitalist society emerge from within the womb of capital-

---

115. Marx 1987a, p. 91.
116. Ibid.

ism itself. At the same time, his analysis raises some major questions. If living labour 'disappears' or is severely reduced as capitalism fully develops, how is a new society actually going to come into being? Will it arise quasi-automatically, through the development of the capital-relation? Or will it arise consciously, through a revolution by social agents resisting the capital-relation? How is it possible to uproot the capital-relation from within if the role of living labour 'disappears' from the process of producing and reproducing it? Marx does not explicitly address these questions in this section of the *Grundrisse*.[117] It appears that there is somewhat of a discord between objective and subjective factors in his analysis, in that he does not directly indicate how subjective forms of resistance can overcome the objective tendency of capitalist accumulation that he outlines in his analysis.[118]

On these grounds, many objectivist Marxists have argued that the *Grundrisse* indicates that Marx did not place as much emphasis on class-struggle and subjective forms of resistance as has widely been assumed. Moishe Postone sees the *Grundrisse* as the most graphic confirmation that, for Marx, not living but *dead* labour is the emancipatory alternative. Postone is in this regard very much following the lead of Herbert Marcuse, who argued four decades earlier that this section of the *Grundrisse* anticipates contemporary capitalism, insofar as a politicised working class opposed to capital has become largely non-existent.[119]

In contrast to Marcuse, Postone, and other objectivist Marxists, Antonio Negri has argued that the *Grundrisse* is more deeply-rooted in proletarian subjectivity than any of his other major works. He does so by focusing on the sections of the *Grundrisse* in which Marx explicitly connects subjective and objective factors, as when he writes, 'But capital too, cannot confront capital, if it is not confronted by labour, for capital is capital only as non-labour, in this antithetical relation'.[120] Negri also makes much of the section on machinery and 'the automaton' by arguing that its discussion anticipates the emergence of a post-industrial information-economy. As a result of decades of intense proletarian revolt, Negri contends, capitalism has been forced to replace

---

117. Marx does nevertheless note, 'Just as the system of bourgeois society unfolds to us only gradually, so also does its negation of itself, which is its immediate result'. See Marx 1987a, p. 98.

118. Raya Dunayevskaya has argued that the role of subjective resistance tends to be downplayed in the section on machinery, in part because the *Grundrisse* was written during the quiescent 1850s, when the working class was not in motion: 'Thus, as against *Capital's* graphic description of the workers' resistance to the discipline of capital in the process of production itself, the *Grundrisse* still stresses the *material* condition for the solution of conflict and contradictions'. See Dunayevskaya 2003, p. 70.

119. See Marcuse 1964, pp. 22–48.

120. Marx 1986a, p. 218.

living labour with labour-saving devices, thereby making the former so super-fluous that value-production has ceased to govern contemporary capitalism. What Marx's *Grundrisse* posits as occurring *after* capitalism – the transcen-dence of value-production through the elimination of living labour from the production-process – Negri sees as defining the contemporary information-economy. Value-production, he argues, no longer characterises capitalism, which makes it all the easier, in his view, to move towards replacing it with an alternative form of social organisation. The emancipatory project, for Negri, is fundamentally *political* in character, since capitalism has already sublated its economic reliance on value.

While a full analysis and evaluation of these positions cannot be developed here, it is important to exercise caution when it comes to drawing conclusions from the passages in the *Grundrisse* concerning the relation of necessary and surplus labour-time and machinery. While Marx sometimes writes of the 'dis-appearance' of living labour in the production-process, it appears that he is addressing a *tendency* more than an accomplished *result*. This is reinforced by the fact that the 'Chapter on Capital' also emphasises the ways in which the incorporation of labour-saving devices into the production-process can also *increase* the employment of living labour. Marx writes,

> This is striking proof that, under the dominion of capital, the employment
> of machinery does not reduce work, but rather lengthens it. What it reduces
> is necessary labour, not the labour necessary for the capitalist. Since fixed
> capital is devalued as long as it is not employed in production, its growth
> is linked with the tendency to make work *perpetual*.[121]

While capitalism strives to reduce the relative amount of labour-time at the point of production, it also strives to augment value. Capitalism is defined by a complex dynamic, rather than by a unilinear replacement of all workers by machines. The incorporation of new machinery in the production-process necessitates that the value of the constant capital is reproduced with each new cycle of capitalist production, thereby creating an impetus to increase the absolute (if not relative) employment of labour. Marx refers to this pro-cess as follows: 'By striving to reduce labour time to a minimum, while, on the other hand, positing labour time as the sole measure and source of wealth, capital itself is a contradiction-in-progress'.[122] Two contradictory ten-dencies occur side-by-side. On the one hand, capitalism is driven to reduce necessary labour-time to a minimum; on the other hand, capitalism creates

---

121. Marx 1987a, p. 204.
122. Marx 1987a, p. 91.

disposable time by increasing surplus-labour. Marx notes that this contradiction becomes increasingly evident with the development of the productive forces.[123] The reduction of necessary labour-time does not necessarily lead to an absolute reduction of surplus labour-time. Marx writes, '*Hence, the most developed machinery now compels the labourer to work for a much longer time than the savage does, or than the labourer himself did when he was using the simplest, crudest instruments*'.[124]

Marx refers to this contradiction being superseded in a new society, in which necessary labour 'will be measured by the needs of the social individual' while 'the *disposable time* of all will increase'.[125]

Nevertheless, there seems to be a problem here in Marx's argument, for the *Grundrisse's* discussion of capitalism's tendency to eliminate value-creating labour from the production-process does not square easily with the claim that the transcendence of value-production is achieved by a subjective force that is internal to it, *the proletariat*. This is not to suggest that Marx did not believe that such an outcome was conceivable or even inevitable; it rather suggests that such a conclusion does not *dialectically flow* from the contours of the passages under consideration in the *Grundrisse*. No thinker, not even one as great as Marx, is immune to the circumstances in which his or her ideas are composed; and the *Grundrisse* was composed in a quiescent political period in Europe in which the working class was not exactly storming the heavens.

Two important qualifications need to be kept in mind here, however. First, it seems over-hasty to conclude that the *Grundrisse* suggests that the actual elimination of living labour from the production-process will occur under *capitalism*. Marx is delineating a *tendency*, not a finished *result*. Objectivist and subjectivist Marxists appear to have seized on these passages by jumping to conclusions not warranted by the full text. Marx neither infers that value-production would be annulled in capitalism, nor does he suggest that living labour ceases to be a socially-determinative force in it. The transcendence of value-production and labour as the medium governing the social metabolism occur in a new, postcapitalist society, even if the conditions for this future state of existence are readied and prepared in the womb of the old one. Second, Marx seriously revised his discussion of the reduction of living labour from the production-process in *Capital*, in which he ties capitalism's objective movement much more integrally to human forces of resistance than in the *Grundrisse*, which was an unfinished draft that he chose not to publish. He makes a crucial comment that reflects this revised view in Volume III of

123. Marx 1987a, p. 94.
124. Ibid. Emphasis is in the original.
125. Ibid.

Capital (drafted after the *Grundrisse*, in the mid-1860s), writing: 'A develop-ment in the productive forces that would reduce the absolute number of work-ers, and actually enable the whole nation to accomplish its entire production in a shorter period of time, would produce a revolution, since it would put the majority of the population out of action'.[126]

Marx's point is that although capital's tendency is to eliminate living labour, it faces 'characteristic barriers' that prevent this tendency from becom-ing fully realised. One of them is the threat of *social revolution* by *unemployed workers* who are cast aside as capitalism becomes increasingly productive.[127] Capitalism does not meekly surrender to this subjective threat; nor does the threat end capitalism's tendency to replace value-creating labour by machin-ery at the point of production. Instead, capitalism responds to the risk that its actions will 'produce a revolution' by increasing the employment of non-productive workers even as it reduces, absolutely as well as relatively, the number of value-creating productive workers at the point of production. This helps explain the significant growth of a service-economy and a public sector as capitalism develops. Yet, since capitalism is continuously driven to reduce the proportion of living labour to dead labour, over time even the relative over-employment of non-productive workers comes under attack by capital. This is the situation that West faces at the start of the twenty-first century, as seen in the concerted effort to reduce the number as well as the wages and benefits of public-service workers through austerity-measures. Whether such measures will prove counter-productive from the vantage-point of capital, by producing the revolution that Marx speaks of in Volume III of *Capital*, remains a key question.

Finally, Marx takes a step further into a new society at the end of the *Grun-drisse* in addressing whether *play* can replace *labour* after capitalism. He cites Fourier, stating that it was his 'great merit' to have emphasised the need to transform conditions of production, instead of relations of exchange. How-ever, he takes issue with Fourier's view that play can replace labour on the

---

126. Marx 1981a, p. 372. *Capital*, unlike the *Grundrisse*, was written in a period of considerable working-class revolt and organisation in both Europe and the USA, as seen in the American Civil War and the formation of the International Workingmen's Association, in which Marx was a principle leader and activist.

127. In Volume I of *Capital*, Marx also radically revises his discussion of this phe-nomenon, as compared with the *Grundrisse*, in his discussion of 'The Absolute General Law of Capitalist Accumulation'. He there emphasises the formation of a surplus-army of labour – *the unemployed* – as a direct result of the rising organic composition of capital. He discusses this reserve-army of labour as both a stabilising factor for capitalism and as a potentially revolutionary force that can bring the system down. See Marx 1976e, pp. 927–30.

grounds that freely-associated human relations require great discipline and development. Marx conceives of free activity as not only *leisure* but also as *exercise*,[128] writing of the importance of 'material creative and self-objectifying science, with respect to the developed man, whose mind is the repository of the accumulated knowledge of society'.[129] Truly *free* activity, for Marx, consists of *conscious*, purposeful activity, which is an arduous exercise – what Hegel called 'the suffering, the patience, and the labour of the negative'.[130]

Far from downplaying the role of ideas or seeing them as merely epiphenomenal, Marx considers it imperative for a new society to appropriate the 'accumulated knowledge' of previous historical eras. The fully-developed person, who seeks to express a totality of manifestations of life, cannot do without the vast storehouse of accumulated knowledge that human history bequeaths us. A new society is not defined only by its level of material development, but also by the level of human intellect and human spirit.

The 'third draft' of *Capital*, 1861–3

After finishing the *Grundrisse*, Marx published a relatively brief work entitled *A Contribution to the Critique of Political Economy*. Although it marked an effort to publicly present some of his theoretical development of the late 1850s, it is far less comprehensive and sweeping than either the *Grundrisse* or Volume I of *Capital*. Marx was not yet prepared in 1859 to publish the comprehensive study that he had had in mind for some time; therefore, *A Contribution to the Critique of Political Economy* has a more modest scope, containing only two brief chapters – 'The Commodity' and 'Money or Simple Reproduction'. Later, Marx considerably re-worked these chapters for Volume I of *Capital*, first published in 1867. Since many of the points contained in *A Contribution to the Critique of Political Economy* are found in either the *Grundrisse* or *Capital*, it will not be analysed here.

---

128. The parallels with Aristotle's discussion of rational happiness [*eudaimonia*] in his *Ethics* are again striking. Aristotle writes, 'Therefore, happiness does not consist in play, for it would be absurd for our end to be play, and to work hard and undergo troubles all through one's life for the sake of playing. For we choose everything so to speak, for the sake of something else, except happiness, since this is the end. But to be earnest and to labour for the sake of play seems foolish and too childish'. See Aristotle 2002, p. 191 [1176b30–33]. Of course, Marx is talking about what all human-beings are capable of, whereas Aristotle is referring to an aristocratic few.

129. Marx 1987a, p. 97.

130. Hegel 1977, p. 10.

More germane is the work that comes between *A Contribution to the Critique of Political Economy* and Volume I of *Capital* – the 1861–3 draft of *Capital*. This 'third' draft of *Capital*[131] is extremely detailed and comprehensive, consisting of over 2,000 printed pages.[132] A section of the draft, consisting of a lengthy criticism of the works of other economic theorists, was published several decades after Marx's death as a separate work, entitled by its editors *Theories of Surplus Value*.[133] The entire draft has only become available in the past several decades and is just beginning to receive the scholarly attention that it deserves.[134]

The 1861–3 draft contains a number of innovative formulations and concepts that are not explicitly found in Marx's earlier work, the *Grundrisse* included. These include a detailed analysis of the origin and nature of surplus-value, the contradiction between 'living labour' and objectified or 'dead labour', and a preliminary discussion of the *forms* of value as well as the fetishism of commodities. The draft of 1861–3 also represents Marx's first effort to develop a theory of 'average prices', and discussion of the difference between 'market-value' and 'individual value', over-production, and capitalist crisis, all of which later became critically important to Volumes II and III of *Capital*.

The 1861–3 draft also touches on the nature of a postcapitalist society in a number of important ways. However, Marx's discussion of this is not as explicit or detailed as in the *Grundrisse*. One reason for this may be that Marx decided not to directly engage in a critical discussion of the shortcomings of other socialist and communist writers in this work on the grounds that it was more important for him to focus on a critique of the major *bourgeois* economists. He writes, 'In accordance with the plan of my work socialist and com-

---

131. Recall that this is based on my having considered the 1847 *Poverty of Philosophy* as the first 'draft'. Most discussions of the manuscript of 1861–3 consider it as the *second* draft of *Capital*.

132. The English edition of the 1861–3 draft of *Capital* takes up four full volumes of the *Marx-Engels Collected Works* – volumes 30–33.

133. Karl Kautsky published the first German edition of this work in 1905–10, which he extracted from the manuscript of 1861–3 and published as a separate book. The rest of the manuscript remained unpublished and did not appear even in German until the late 1970s and early 1980s. Although Marx originally intended (as of 1863) for what he called the 'history of theory' to be included in the first volume of *Capital*, he changed his mind in the mid-1860s and decided, instead, to relegate this material to a separate 'Book Four' of *Capital*. Since he originally planned that what appeared, after his death, as Volumes II and III of *Capital* to be a single volume comprising 'Book Two' and 'Book Three', *Theories of Surplus Value* should be considered 'Volume IV' of *Capital*. It has never, however, been published in this form, which in part explains its neglect by many commentators on Marx's works. See Marx 1976e, p. 93.

134. See Dussel 1988. A somewhat abbreviated version is available in English in Dussel 2001.

munist writers are entirely excluded from the historical reviews...I therefore exclude such eighteenth-century writers as Brissot, Godwin and the like, and likewise the nineteenth-century socialists and communists'.[135]

At the same time, since most of the socialist and communist writers subject to critique by Marx in other contexts take Ricardo's formulation of the determination of value by labour-time as their conceptual point of departure, Marx's extended criticism of Ricardo in the draft of 1861–3 helps in important ways to understand his view of the alternative to capitalism.

Marx's criticisms of Ricardo and his followers (such as James Mill, John Stuart Mill, Thomas Hodgskin and others) are quite lengthy, totaling over six hundred pages. His main objection is that Ricardo and the post-Ricardians focus exclusively on the *quantitative* side of value, on the *amount* of labour-time embodied in a product, rather than on the *qualitative* side, on the *kind* of labour that creates value. He writes, 'Ricardo starts out from the determination of *the relative values (or exchangeable values) of commodities by "the quantity of labour"*.' However, 'The character of this "labour" is not further explained'.[136] If the value of all commodities is determined by the quantity of labour-time embodied in them, all commodities must contain a common *substance*. Commodities have differing exchange-values insofar as they contain different amounts of this substance. Yet why does living labour, a *subjective* activity, take the *form* of this *substance*? Ricardo and his followers never ask the question because they assume that value is simply a *natural* property of labour. Marx, on the contrary, argues that living labour serves as the substance of value only when labour assumes a specific social *form* – the *dual* form of concrete versus abstract labour. Labour can serve as the substance of value only if it is *alienated* labour. 'But *Ricardo* does not *examine* the form – the peculiar characteristic of labour that creates exchange value or manifests itself in exchange values – the *nature* of this labour'.[137]

Why does Ricardo never investigate the nature of value-creating labour? Why does he conflate 'labour' with value-creating labour? What prevented him from grasping the historical specificity of value-creating labour? The answer for Marx, I would argue, is that Ricardo's theoretical categories did

---

135. Marx 1989a, p. 241. See also Marx 1989b, p. 373: 'During the Ricardian period of political economy its antithesis, communism (Owen) and socialism (Fourier, St. Simon, the latter only in its first beginnings), [come] also [into being]. According to our plan, however, we are here concerned only with that opposition which takes as its starting-point the premises of the economists'.

136. Marx 1989a, p. 389.

137. Ibid. See also Marx 1989b, p. 325: 'All commodities can be reduced to labour as their common element. What Ricardo does not investigate is the *specific* form in which labour manifests itself as the common element of commodities'.

not proceed from the standpoint of the subjectivity of the labourer. Ricardo is more interested in the *products* of labour than in the labourer. He wants to understand how products come into being (such as commodities, capital and money) and how their value is determined. The product (capital) is the subject of his analysis, not the human-being who creates and shapes it. He never conceptually looks into the factory to see what occurs in the 'storm and stress' of the actual production-process. As a result, he fails to distinguish between living labour as a generic activity and the peculiar alienated kind of labour that actually creates value.

The manuscript of 1861–3, when read as a whole, shows that Marx took a very different approach. The section on Ricardo and other economists is preceded by a part on 'The Production Process of Capital'.[138] Marx here focuses on the central contradiction that is internal to the capitalist process of production – the contradiction between objectified labour and living labour. He writes, 'an increase in value means nothing more than an increase in objectified labour; but it is only through living labour that objectified labour can be preserved or increased'.[139] He refers to living labour as the 'subject' of this process – since no value can be created without it – while showing that living labour becomes subsumed by objectified labour: 'A further antithesis is this: in contrast to money (or value in general) as *objectified labour*, labour capacity appears as a capacity of the living subject; the former is past labour, labour already performed, the latter is future labour, whose existence can only be the living activity, the currently present activity of the living subject itself'.[140] Marx has entered into the heart of the process of production by showing what occurs *within* the factory. Not only are products being produced by workers, the workers themselves become transformed from living, creative, subjective agents into mere appendages of the machine. A split occurs between the subjectivity of the labourer and the labour that they perform. Marx describes this split in terms that recall, but also further extend, his earlier formulations of 1844:

> The labour goes over from the form of activity to the form of being, the form of the object. As alteration of the object it alters its own shape. The form-giving activity consumes the object and itself; it forms the object and materializes itself; it consumes itself in its subjective form as activity and

---

138. This is actually how the 1861–3 manuscript begins. The subject-matter of this section does not appear in *A Contribution to the Critique of Political Economy,* nor is it explicitly spelled out in the *Grundrisse.* It largely corresponds to what later becomes Part Two of Volume I of *Capital,* 'The Transformation of Money into Capital'.
139. Marx 1988, p. 36.
140. Marx 1988, p. 41.

consumes the objective character of the object, i.e., it abolishes the object's indifference towards the purpose of the labour.[141]

By directly exploring the contradictions internal to the capitalist labour-process, what becomes visible is the specific *kind* of labour that creates value. This becomes of critical importance in his criticism of Ricardo. Whereas, prior to 1861, Marx often credited Ricardo for pinpointing the determination of value by labour-time, he now emphasises his radical departure from him. Marx indicates that positing labour as the source of value fails to get to the critical issue – the kind of labour that creates value. When the latter is passed over, it becomes hard to see *why* living labour serves the *substance* of value. Marx is suggesting that it is not enough to ameliorate the *quantitative* inequities associated with the determination of value by labour-time; instead, what is most needed is to *qualitatively* eliminate the kind of labour that creates and constitutes value in the first place.

This has important ramifications for a Marxian understanding of a post-capitalist society. This can best be discerned when Marx's critique of Ricardo and post-Ricardians is considered in light of his preceding discussion in 'The Production Process of Capital'.[142] Marx argues that Ricardo's failure to grasp the nature of the labour that creates value leads to an erroneous theory of *money*. Ricardo argues that money, like other market-phenomena, only *appears* to contradict the determination of value by labour-time insofar as its value is determined by supply and demand, instead of by the amount of labour-time that it takes to produce it. Ricardo seeks to dispel what he considers this false appearance by arguing that money, like the market-price of a commodity, is ultimately reducible to the determination of value by labour-time. He '*directly* seeks to prove the congruity of the economic categories with one another'.[143] By reducing market-phenomena to the determination of value in an unmediated fashion, Ricardo posits an *identity* of essence and appearance. Marx argues that this is even truer of John Stuart Mill, who 'transforms the unity of opposites into the direct identity of opposites'.[144]

---

141. Marx 1988, p. 59.

142. The fact that Marx's critique of Ricardo and the post-Ricardians was separated out from the rest of the manuscript of 1861–3 and published as *Theories of Surplus Value* has made it difficult to appreciate the central point he was driving at in his critique of these and other theorists – namely, that a failure to specify the form of value results from keeping one's conceptual distance from the standpoint of the worker or what happens to the worker inside the factory.

143. Marx 1989a, p. 390.

144. Marx 1989b, p. 278. See also Marx 1989b, p. 290: 'The logic is always the same. If a relationship includes opposites, it comprises not only opposites but also the *unity* of opposites. It is therefore a *unity without opposites*. This is Mill's logic, by which he

Marx does not deny that the determination of value by labour-time is an essential economic category of capitalism, which is hidden and distorted by transactions on the phenomenal level of the market. What he denies is that there is a direct, *unmediated* connection between the law of value and market-phenomena. Prices *must* diverge from value, Marx contends, because of the specific kind of labour that creates value – abstract or *indirectly* social labour. Since 'the definite, particular labour of the private individual must manifest itself as its opposite, as equal, necessary, general labour',[145] the exchange-value of the commodity obtains an *independent* existence in money. Exchange-values calculated in money, or price, can therefore never be *directly* reduced to the commodity's 'real' value. While the sum of all prices is equal to the sum of all values, the price of any given commodity generally diverges from its value, because abstract labour is measured by a social average that is constantly fluctuating and changing, especially because of technological innovation. Value becomes price through *a transformation into opposite*; the two are not identical, even though they exist in a state of dialectical unity.

The reason why Ricardo and the neo-Ricardians *force* the opposites of price and value[146] into an unmediated unity is that they fail to comprehend the historical specificity of value-creating labour. They do not grasp that the concrete labour of individuals in capitalist society *must* be represented in terms of its 'immediate opposite, abstract, general labour'. Essence and appearance cannot be made to coincide so long as abstract or alienated labour persists, since 'Only by its alienation does individual labour manifest itself as its opposite'.[147]

By failing to grasp this, Ricardo and his school present 'the whole bourgeois system of economy as subject to one fundamental law, and extract the quintessence out of the divergency and diversity of the various phenomena'.[148] While this has the advantage of concentrating attention on the determination of value by labour-time, it is outweighed by its disadvantages: 'As the work proceeds, there is no further development. Where it does not consist of a monotonous formal application of the same principles to various extraneous matters, or of polemical vindication of these principles, there is only repetition or amplification'.[149]

---

eliminates the "contradictions".' Later, in Volume I of *Capital*, Marx ties this criticism to categories from Hegel's *Logic*.

145. Marx 1989b, p. 317.

146. Marx will also contend that this is true of their understanding of the relation of surplus-value and profit as well.

147. Marx 1989b, p. 323.

148. Marx 1989a, p. 394.

149. Marx 1989a, pp. 394–5. Marx's comments bring to mind Hegel's criticism of formal abstraction in the *Phenomenology of Spirit*: 'The Idea, which is of course true

Although Marx states that he intends to focus on the classical-political economists like Smith, Ricardo and Mill and not on the radical or socialist thinkers who were influenced by them, he does venture into a critical discussion of the latter. He does not dispute the contention of an important American advocate of free trade and critic of Ricardo, Henry Charles Carey, that Ricardo's economic theories made him 'a father of communism' in many respects.[150] The manuscript of 1861–3 also contains an extended section on 'Proletarian Opposition on the Basis of Ricardo', in which he discusses such thinkers as Thomas Hodgskin, George Ramsey, and Richard Jones.[151] Marx's analysis indicates that it should come as no surprise that the socialist followers of Ricardo adopted the notion that money could be replaced by another means of measuring the quantity of labour-time, such as time-chits or labour-tokens. They found no fault with Ricardo's purely quantitative analysis of value-production since they also did not ask the question of what specific kind of labour creates value. Like Ricardo, the post-Ricardian socialists simply assumed that it was a natural property of labour to serve as the substance of value. For this reason, they thought it is possible to replace money by a direct determination of value by labour-time, instead of relying on the indirect medium of price-formation on the market. Marx contends that they shared with Ricardo a failure to understand that money – or any alternative medium that is adopted as a universal equivalent – is not just the expression of a *quantity* of labour-time, but of a specific *quality* of labour, namely, abstract labour denuded of its particularity. This is why they held that the ills of capitalism could be remedied by eliminating the 'anarchy' of the market, such as by replacing money with labour-tokens.

Marx does not share their conception of the alternative to capitalism because he does not hold that price-formation on the market is 'arbitrary' and contingent whereas value-production is predictable and transparent. The arbitrary and contingent nature of market-phenomena is itself a reflection of the irrational and indirect nature of value-production. Instead of contrasting the transparency of value-production to the opaqueness of market-transactions, Marx sees both of these as irrational and contradictory forms. As long as the production-relations of capitalism are presupposed as natural and eternal, it is impossible to overcome the irrational and crisis-ridden nature of capital:

---

enough on its own account, remains in effect always in its primitive condition, if its development involves nothing more than this sort of repetition of the same formula...Rather it is a monochromatic formalism which only arrives at the differentiation of its material since this has been already provided and is by now familiar'. See Hegel 1977, p. 9.

150. Marx 1989a, p. 392.
151. See Marx 1991, pp. 253–371.

'[I]t is quite clear, that between the starting-point, the prerequisite capital, and the time of its return at the end of one of these periods, great catastrophes must occur and elements of crisis must have gathered and developed, and these cannot in any way be dismissed by the pitiful proposition that products exchange for product'.[152] As Marx also puts it, '*Crisis* is nothing but the forcible assertion of the unity of phases of the production process which have become independent of each other'.[153]

Ricardo himself, Marx notes, denies the possibility of crises that are endemic to value-production[154] because he posits an identity between production and consumption, as well as between purchase and sale. This implies that society,

> as if according to a plan, distributes its means of production and productive forces in the degree and measure which is required for the fulfilment of the various social needs, so that each sphere of production receives the quota of social capital required to satisfy the corresponding need. This fiction arises entirely from the inability to grasp the specific form of bourgeois production and this inability in turn arises from the obsession that bourgeois production is production as such, just like a man who believes in a particular religion and sees it as the religion, and everything outside of it only as *false* religions.[155]

Marx's statement that Ricardo assumes that the disproportionalities of value-production can be smoothed out 'as if according to a plan' is striking in light of the experience of the state-controlled 'planned' economies in the USSR and elsewhere in the twentieth century. By 1943, Soviet economists admitted that the law of value continued to operate in their putatively 'socialist' society. They contended, however, that because of state-planning the disproportionalities inherent in value-production had been overcome.[156] That they failed to succeed in actually overcoming such disproportionalities is rather clear, given the history of the Soviet economy. Similar to the socialist neo-Ricardians of the nineteenth century subject to Marx's critiques, they thought it was pos-

---

152. Marx 1989b, p. 126.
153. Marx 1989b, p. 140.
154. Ricardo held that economic crises are merely an exogenous hangover of feudal appendages, such as legislation preventing free trade and competition.
155. Marx 1989b, p. 158.
156. See the anonymous article 'Teaching of Economics in the Soviet Union', which was translated and published in the *American Economic Review*, vol. 34, no. 3 (September 1944), pp. 501–30. The article originally appeared in the Russian journal *Pod Znamenem Marxizma*, nos. 7–8 (1943). Whereas previously Soviet textbooks had argued that the law of value did not operate under socialism, the article now proclaimed that it was an operative principle of the Soviet economy. For the debate touched off by this declaration, see Dunayevskaya 1944; Baran 1944; Lange 1945; and Rogin 1945.

sible to eliminate indirect and 'anarchic' market-relations while maintaining a system of value-production based on indirectly social labour.[157]

Marx's discussion lends credence to Postone's contention that Marx's critique of capital applies to what he calls 'traditional' or 'Ricardian Marxism'.[158] The manuscript of 1861–3 indicates that Marx's criticism of Ricardo and the neo-Ricardians sheds illumination on the shortcomings of various 'alternatives' to capitalism proposed or implemented during the twentieth century. In fact, Marx goes so far as to view various socialist tendencies as expressing the logic of capital. This is particularly evident when he takes issue with those who confuse the abolition of interest-bearing or monetary capital with the elimination of the capitalist mode of production. He writes,

> It is thus clear why superficial criticism – in exactly the same way as it wants [to maintain] commodities and combats money – now turns its wisdom and reforming zeal against interest-bearing capital without touching upon real capitalist production, but merely attacking one of its consequences. This polemic against interest-bearing capital, undertaken from the standpoint of capitalist production, a polemic which today parades as 'socialism', occurs, incidentally, as a phase in the development of capital itself...[159]

The 1861–3 draft of *Capital* also introduces a new concept that is not explicitly developed in the *Grundrisse* – commodity-fetishism, although he does not actually employ the term 'fetish' or 'fetishism' at this stage.[160] Marx argues that in capitalism 'the social character of labour "manifests itself" in a perverted form – as the "property" of things: that a social relation appears as a relation between things (between products, value in use, commodities)'.[161]

---

157. The Soviet theoreticians *claimed* that their society had eliminated indirectly social labour, since the economy was governed by a central plan; however, that claim was controverted by their own admission that value-production continued to operate in it. That they neglected to acknowledge the inherently self-contradictory nature of such a position had less to do with their lack of skills in formal logic than their effort to produce an apologia and justification for existing conditions in the USSR.

158. I am referring only to Postone's contention that many twentieth-century Marxists were 'Ricardian' insofar as they focused on the magnitude of value rather than on the dual character of labour. As indicated above, I do not share his view that those who consider workers as revolutionary subjects are 'Ricardian Marxists' – especially since thinkers in the tradition of 'Marxist-Humanism' long ago emphasised the centrality of the dual character of labour while *affirming* the importance of subjective forces of resistance. For more on this, see Hudis 1995 and Hudis 2004c.

159. Marx 1989b, pp. 452–3.

160. Although the concept is not spelled out in the *Grundrisse*, Marx does refer to the phenomena of social relations appearing in 'perverted' form several times in it as well as in *A Contribution to the Critique of Political Economy*. See Marx 1987a, pp. 275–6 and pp. 289–90.

161. Marx 1989b, p. 317.

This is not simply an illusory appearance. Social labour *necessarily* appears as a property of things because the labour that creates value, abstract or alienated labour, is homogeneous and thing-like.

Marx notes, 'As a commodity, a commodity can only express its value in other commodities, since general labour time does not exist for it as a commodity'.[162] Labour-time serves as the determination of value only when it exists in an *objectified* form, in the shape of a *thing* or a commodity. It therefore appears that what establishes the exchangeability of a given set of commodities is their thing-like nature – their natural properties. Value appears as a property of the object. Value, however, is not a property of objects but 'only a *representation* in objects, an objective expression, of a relation between men, a social relation, the relationship of men to their reciprocal productive activity'.[163] It appears that value is an attribute of the things-in-themselves, instead of a *representation* of specific social relations. Value-production becomes *naturalised* in appearing to be a property of things-in-themselves. And it must appear this way so long as the peculiar social form of labour that characterises capitalism remains intact. Here we see why so many defenders and even critics of capitalism assume that value-production is 'natural'.[164]

Marx is engaging in a kind of phenomenological reduction in showing that what appears to exist independently of us is actually a representation of our *human* relations. As he puts it, 'Thus commodities, things in general, have value only because they *represent* human labour, not in so far as they are things in themselves, but in so far as they are incarnations of social labour'.[165] The fetishism of viewing the commodity as a thing-in-itself, which he considers 'perverse',[166] is *inevitable* so long as value-production persists.

Marx is not arguing that fetishism is simply a mental defect that can be stripped away by enlightened critique. Although fetishising the products of our own creation is surely alienated, it cannot be avoided so long as the dis-

---

162. Marx 1989b, p. 329.
163. Marx 1989b, p. 334. My emphasis.
164. Marx expresses this as follows: 'Thus the participants in capitalist production live in a bewitched world and their own relationships appear to them as properties of things, as properties of the material elements of production'. See Marx 1991, p. 514.
165. Marx 1989b, p. 336.
166. The German term used by Marx is *verkehrt*, which can also be translated as 'inverted' or 'turned upside down.' It can also be rendered as 'mad'. For Marx, a world in which the relation of subject and predicate is *inverted* through a process in which we become subordinated to the products of our own creation is indeed a *mad* world.

torted system of value-production is maintained. Marx takes issue with fellow socialists on this:

> The *capitalist*, as capitalist, is simply the personification of capital, that creation of labour endowed with its own will and personality which stands in opposition to labour. Hodgskin regards this as a pure subjective illusion which conceals the deceit and interests of the exploiting classes. He does not see that the way of looking at things arises from out of the actual relationship itself; the latter is not the expression of the former, but vice versa. In the same way, English socialists say: 'We need capital, but not the capitalist.'[167]

Marx does not oppose the capitalists on the grounds that they treat human-beings as objects – as if they had any choice in the matter. Capitalists treat human-beings as objects insofar as capital remains the defining principle of social organisation. In arguing that human relations appear as relations between things because that is what they truly are in capitalism, Marx is fully breaking from what he considers to be the illusions of both Ricardo and the neo-Ricardian socialists. Marx therefore does not propose replacing the capitalists with some other agency that can more rationally allocate resources according to the determination of labour-time. Instead, he writes: 'Where labour is communal, the relations of men in their social production do not manifest themselves as "values" of "things".'[168] Marx's critique of other theorists in the manuscript of 1861–3 thus speaks directly to his view of a postcapitalist society.

There are several other ways in which the 1861–3 draft speaks to the nature of a postcapitalist society. Marx returns to and further develops his argument from the *Grundrisse* that capitalism stimulates the development of new needs and capacities that provide a material foundation for a higher form of social existence. He writes,

> But it is a law of the development of human nature that once the satisfaction of a certain sphere of needs has been assured *new needs* are set free, created. Therefore when capital pushes labour time beyond the level set for the satisfaction of the worker's natural needs, it impels a greater division of social labour – the labour of society as a whole – a greater diversity of production, an extension of the sphere of social needs and the means for their satisfaction, and therefore also impels the development of human productive capacity

---

167. Marx 1989b, p. 429.
168. Marx 1989b, pp. 316–17.

and thereby the activation of human dispositions in fresh directions. But
just as surplus labour time is a condition for free time, this extension of the
sphere of needs and the means for their satisfaction is conditioned by the
worker's being chained to the necessary requirements of his life.[169]

Marx is emphasising the *contradictory* character of capitalism's development
of new needs and capacities – something that is not as explicitly spelled out
in the *Grundrisse*, which tended to emphasise capital's positive contributions.
While capital 'activates' new 'dispositions in fresh directions', the contrary
development also occurs: 'Once the *commodity* becomes the general form of
the product, or production takes place on the basis of exchange value and
therefore of the exchange of commodities, the production of each individual,
first of all, becomes one-sided, whereas his needs are many-sided'.[170] Marx is
acknowledging that, with the development of capitalism, workers (as well as
others) 'loses room for intellectual development, for that is time'.[171] People
are deprived of a host of 'pleasures of life', leading to 'the vacuity of their
lives.'[172] However, he contends, '[A]lthough at first the development of the
capacities of the *human* species takes place at the cost of the majority of
human individuals and whole human classes, in the end it breaks through
this contradiction and coincides with the development of the individual; the
higher development of individuality is thus only achieved by a historical
process during which individuals are sacrificed'.[173]

Hence, as Marx develops his discussion of the contradictions inherent to
capital's generation of new needs and capacities, he looks ahead to what
would characterise a postcapitalist society once such contradictions are
transcended:

> *Time of labour*, even if exchange value is eliminated, always remains the
> creative substance of wealth and the measure of the cost of its production.
> But *free time, disposable time*, is wealth itself, partly for the enjoyment of the
> product, partly for *free activity* which – unlike labour – is not determined by
> a compelling extraneous purpose which must be fulfilled, and the fulfilment
> of which is regarded as a natural necessity or a social duty, according to
> one's inclination.[174]

---

169. Marx 1988, p. 199.
170. Marx 1988, p. 298.
171. Marx 1988, p. 301.
172. Marx 1988, p. 302.
173. Marx 1989a, p. 348.
174. Marx 1989b, p. 391.

In a new, postcapitalist society, in which exchange-value is 'eliminated', the amount of time that individuals spend on the production and reproduction of basic necessities will remain an important factor. However, such labour-time – and indeed labour-time in general – will cease to be the *determining* principle governing such a society. Labour that is engaged in material production and reproduction, even when creating wealth, instead of value, is still determined by 'extraneous' purposes insofar as it is subject to some degree of natural necessity. Human activity can therefore not be its own end where labour remains the determining principle of social reproduction. A truly free society, according to Marx, is not governed by labour-time engaged in material production but by free time – the time taken to express the totality of one's sensuous and intellectual capacities. Marx spells out the nature of such a new society thusly:

> It is self-evident that if *time of labour* is reduced to a normal length and, furthermore, labour is no longer performed for someone else, but for myself, and, at the same time, the social contradictions between *master and men*, etc., being abolished, it acquires a quite different, a free character, it becomes real social labour, and finally the basis of *disposable time* – the *time of labour* of a man who also has *disposable time* must be of a much higher quality than that of the beast of burden.[175]

The length of labour-time dramatically declines in a new society at the same time as its character is qualitatively transformed with the abolition of class-divisions and social domination. What provides the material condition for this reduction of labour-time to a minimum is the development of capital itself, which relentlessly increases labour's productivity as it seeks to augment value. At the same time, however, capital's thirst for self-expansion is inseparable from a drive to appropriate ever-more unpaid hours of living labour. To put an end to this contradictory process, a new *kind* or form of labour and human activity is needed. Marx writes, 'The capitalist mode of production disappears with the form of alienation which the various aspects of social labour bear to one another and which is represented in *capital*'.[176] Therefore, he concludes, 'Just as one should not think of sudden changes and sharply delineated periods in considering the succession of the different geological formations, so also in the case of the creation of the different economic formations of society'.[177]

---

175. Ibid.
176. Marx 1989b, p. 446.
177. Marx 1991, p. 442.

Nevertheless, while the new society emerges from within the womb of the old one, the former represents a qualitative break and leap from the latter. Marx never ceases to stress the radically different way in which time would be treated in the new society: 'But *time* is *in fact* the active existence of the human being. It is not only the measure of human life. It is the space for its development'.[178]

---

178. Marx 1989b, p. 493.

Chapter Three

The Vision of the New Society in Marx's *Capital*

Volume I of *Capital*

Volume I of *Capital* is Marx's most important work and represents the culmination of over a quarter-century of intense research and philosophical development. It consists of an analysis of *capitalist* production and *only* capitalist production. Since its purpose is to discern the 'law of motion' of *existing* society, it might seem to have little to say about a future society. Some of Marx's own words tend to reinforce this perception. His 'Postface to the Second Edition' notes that a reviewer of the first edition 'reproaches me for, on the one hand, treating economics metaphysically, and, on the other hand – imagine this! – confining myself merely to the critical analysis of the actual facts, instead of writing recipes (Comtist ones?) for the cook-shops of the future'.[1] At the same time, Marx does not deny that his critique of capitalism is intended at least to indicate or intimate its future transcendence. In this regard, he cites positively the review by the Russian economist I.I. Kaufman, who wrote, 'For [Marx] it is quite enough, if he proves, at the same time, both the necessity of the present order of things and the necessity of

---

1. Marx 1976e, p. 99. The 'Postface to the Second [German] Edition' is dated January 1873. At the time Marx was also preparing the French edition of *Capital*, which appeared in serialised form between 1872–5. These editions, especially the French edition, introduced several important changes and additions to the first German edition of 1867.

another order into which they first must inevitably pass over, and it is a matter of indifference whether men believe or do not believe, whether they are conscious of it or not'.[2] Thus, I will be arguing that while the scope of *Capital* is restricted to an analysis of capitalism, an examination of its most important theoretical concepts shows that Marx's most important work contains some important material regarding his view of a postcapitalist society.

One of the most fundamental concepts in *Capital*, which is a novel theoretical development as compared with his earlier work, is that Marx explicitly distinguishes between exchange-value and value.[3] As we have seen, Marx's previous work treated exchange-value and value as more or less interchangeable.[4] This was even true as late as the first edition of Volume I of *Capital*, published in 1867. In contrast, the second German edition of 1872 states, 'Exchange value cannot be anything other than the mode of expression, the "form of appearance" [*Erscheinungsform*] of a content distinguishable from it'.[5] Marx adds, 'The progress of the investigation will lead us back to exchange-value as the necessary mode of expression, or form of appearance, of value. For the present, however, we must consider the nature of value independently of its form of appearance'.[6]

Why does Marx make this explicit distinction between exchange-value and value, and what is its significance? The answer lies in the peculiar or specific nature of value-production itself. Value, Marx writes, 'does not have its description branded on its forehead'.[7] Value does not exist on its own account, independently of the products in which it is embodied. It first appears as a *quantitative* relationship – one commodity can be exchanged for another because both contain equal *quantities* or *amounts* of (socially average) labour-time. Value is therefore never *immediately* visible: it *necessarily* first *appears* as exchange-value, as a quantitative relation between *things*. However, the exchange of things is not only a *quantitative* relation, since there must be a *quality* common to the things that can enable them to be exchanged for one another. Without a commensurate quality or substance, the exchange of

---

2. Marx 1976e, p. 101.
3. For an important discussion of this issue, see Kliman 2000.
4. As late as the first (1867) edition of the first volume, Marx writes, 'When we employ the word value with no additional determination, we refer always to exchange value [*Wenn wir künftig das Wort 'werth' ohne weitere Bestimmung brauchen, so handelt es sich immer vom Tauschwerth*]'. See Marx 1983b, p. 19. With the second German edition of 1872 Marx makes a clear distinction between exchange-value and value, even though it is implied in the 1867 edition.
5. Marx 1976e, p. 127.
6. Marx 1976e, p. 128.
7. Marx 1976e, p. 167.

discrete products is not possible.[8] Two commodities can enter into a *quantitative* relation only if they share a common *quality*. This quality, Marx shows, is abstract or homogenous labour: 'Equality in the full sense between different kinds of labour can be arrived at only if we abstract from their real inequality, if we reduce them to the characteristic they have in common, that of being the expenditure of human labour power, of human labour in the abstract'.[9] Abstract labour – labour expended without regard for the usefulness or use-value of the product – is the *substance* of value. But, since abstract labour is objectified in products, value first appears (and *must* appear) as a quantitative relationship between products – as exchange-value. So overpowering is this appearance that Marx himself does not explicitly delineate exchange-value, with its specific *forms* of value, as distinct from value itself, until relatively late in his development of *Capital*.

Marx contends that neither the greatest philosophers, such as Aristotle, nor the greatest classical-political economists, such as Ricardo, were able to go beyond the *appearance* of value-in-exchange to the examination of value itself.[10] This limitation has *objective* roots. It flows from the fact that value 'can only appear in the social relation between commodity and commodity'.[11] The essence, value, appears, and *must* appear, as exchange-value. Since 'reflection begins *post-festum*, and therefore with the results of the process of development ready at hand',[12] it is virtually inescapable, at least initially, to conflate value with exchange-value. So objective is this conceptual barrier that, as we have seen, even Marx does not explicitly single out the distinction between exchange-value and value in *The Poverty of Philosophy*, the *Grundrisse*, or the 1861–3 draft of *Capital*. It is only with Chapter One of *Capital* that Marx writes,

---

8. Marx quotes Aristotle on this: 'There can be no exchange without equality, and no equality without commensurability'. See Marx 1986e, p. 151. See also Aristotle 2002, p. 90 [1133b16–19]: 'So the currency, like a unit of measure, equalises things by making them commensurable, for there would be no community if there were not exchange, and no exchange if there was not equality, and no equality if there were not commensurability'.

9. Marx 1976e, p. 166. See also Marx 1976e, pp. 140–1: 'It is overlooked that the magnitudes of different things only become comparable in quantitative terms when they have been reduced to the same unit. Only as expressions of the same unit do they have a common denominator, and are therefore commensurable magnitudes'.

10. See Marx 1976e, p. 151: 'Aristotle therefore himself tells us what prevented any further analysis: the concept of value. What is the homogenous element, i.e. the common substance, which the house represents from the point of view of the bed, in the value expression for the bed? Such a thing, in truth, cannot exist, says Aristotle'.

11. Marx 1976e, p. 139.

12. Marx 1976e, p. 168.

When at the beginning of this chapter, we said in the customary manner that a commodity is both a use value and an exchange value, this was, strictly speaking, wrong. A commodity is a use value or object of utility, and a 'value'. It appears as the twofold thing it really is as soon as its value possesses its own particular form of manifestation, which is distinct from its natural form. The form of manifestation is exchange value, and the commodity never has this form when looked at in isolation, but only when it is in a value-relation or an exchange relation with a second commodity of a different kind.[13]

How does Marx finally get to specify explicitly the difference between exchange-value and value, and how does it impact his understanding of the alternative to capitalism? Marx proceeds phenomenologically, by beginning with the appearance of value in the relation between discrete commodities. After delineating the quantitative determination of value (two different commodities can be exchanged for each other insofar as they contain equal *amounts* of socially-necessary labour-time), he probes into the conditions that make this exchange possible. He discovers that the condition for the possibility of magnitudes of labour-time to be exchanged for one another is a common quality or element. That common element is abstract or undifferentiated labour. Marx's delineation of the dual character of labour – which he calls his unique contribution to the critique of political economy[14] – brings to light the substance of value, abstract labour. That in turn makes it possible to conceptualise value, independently of its form of appearance. He writes, 'In fact, we started from exchange value, or the exchange relation of commodities, in order to track down the value that lay hidden within it'.[15]

The movement from exchange-value (appearance) to value (essence) is not only the course by which Marx structures his argument, but it also corresponds to the historical development of economics. Economic theory develops from

---

13. Marx 1976e, p. 152. Aristotle explicitly distinguishes between the 'natural' form of wealth and its 'social' form, the latter which he derides as unnatural, in Book I of the *Politics*: 'Natural wealth acquisition is a part of household management, whereas commerce has to do with the production of goods, not in the full sense, but *through their exchange*...The wealth that derives from this kind of [unnatural] wealth acquisition is without limit'. See Aristotle 1998, p. 17 [1257b19–25] (emphasis in original). By failing to distinguish between exchange-value and value, however, Aristotle proved unable to grasp or delineate the *forms* of value.

14. Marx 1976e, p. 132: 'I was the first to point out and examine critically this twofold nature of the labour contained in commodities'. To my knowledge, this is the only time that Marx uses the first person in *Capital*, aside from the prefaces and postfaces.

15. Marx 1976e, p. 139.

classical-political economy's emphasis on the quantitative determination of value, in which commodities exchange against one another based on given magnitudes of labour-time they embody, to Marx's emphasis on the *kind* of labour that enables this exchange to occur – abstract, homogenous labour. The development from classical-political economy to Marx's own critique of political economy is a movement from quantity to quality, from the appearance of exchangeability to the identification of the conditions that make such exchangeability possible. Marx does not arrive at this result by jumping to the absolute like a shot out of a pistol, which Hegel famously warned us against. Instead, he traverses the pathway initially laid out by classical-political economy by beginning with the appearance of value as exchange-value and then proceeding to discover what makes this quantitative relation possible. By explicitly distinguishing value from exchange-value, he succeeds in overcoming the historical limits reached by classical-political economy.

It bears repeating that value cannot be conceptualised in an unmediated fashion, without going through a conceptual detour that proceeds *from* appearance, because value shows itself in the exchange-relation of commodity to commodity. We *must* begin with the form of appearance of exchange-value and 'track down' the value-relation that is immanent in it. It is not possible to proceed the other way around, by proceeding from value to exchange-value, because the essence (value) is not immediately accessible. However, the fact that the 'identical social substance' that enables one commodity to exchange for another can be grasped only by proceeding *from* the exchange-relation *to* that which makes exchange possible carries with it a grave risk: namely, that consciousness will get stuck in the detour by stopping at the phenomenal manifestation of value without inquiring into the conditions of its possibility. Since value can only show itself as a social relation between one commodity and another, it all too readily *appears* that relations of exchange are responsible for value-production. So powerful is that appearance that even Marx does not explicitly pose the difference between exchange-value and value itself until quite late in the development of *Capital*.

That Marx ultimately makes this distinction is of critical importance, since it suggests that attempting to ameliorate the deleterious aspect of value-production by altering the exchange-relation is fundamentally flawed. Since exchange-value is a manifestation of value, whose substance is abstract labour, the essential problem of capitalist production can be addressed only by altering the nature of the labour-process itself.

Marx points to this when he writes, 'Our analysis has shown that the form of value, that is, the expression of the value of a commodity, arises from the nature of commodity-value, as opposed to value and its magnitude arising

from their mode of expression as exchange-value'.[16] This helps to illuminate *why* many fail to correctly identify the central problem of capitalism –
including some of its most vociferous critics. Since value *must* show itself as
exchange-value, it *appears* that uprooting value-production depends upon
altering relations of exchange. However, altering relations of exchange in lieu
of changing conditions of labour cannot eliminate value-production, even
though value-production is inseparable from relations of exchange. While
altering the exchange-relation can influence the quantitative determination of value, it cannot change its qualitative determination, the *substance* of
value itself. Yet the peculiar nature of capitalism's social relations, in which
the substance of value appears in quantitative proportions in the exchange
of products, makes it *appear* as if altering the exchange-relation is of cardinal
importance. In sum, it lies in the very nature of capitalist value-production
that its true nature will be misunderstood. *Mystification is inseparable from the
very existence of the value-form.*

As Marx will indicate throughout *Capital*, the fundamental problem of capitalism is not its exchange-relations as much as the specific form assumed by
labour – abstract or alienated labour. For this reason, he is not satisfied with the
classical-political economists' discovery that labour is the source of all value.
Far more important, Marx argues, is the *kind* of labour that creates value and
serves as its substance. Only when this is recognised is it possible to focus on
the social relation that defines capitalism and that needs to be uprooted. He
insists, 'It is not sufficient to reduce the commodity to "labour"; labour must
be broken down into its twofold form – on the one hand, into *concrete labour
in the use-values of the commodity*, and on the other hand, into *socially necessary
labour* as calculated in *exchange value*'.[17] It is all too easy to hold stubbornly
to a vantage-point that never gets to the critical issue, precisely because of
the specific nature of value-production itself. As Marx puts it, 'But it does
not occur to the economists that a purely quantitative distinction between the
kinds of labour presupposes their qualitative unity or equality, and therefore
their reduction to abstract human labour'.[18]

Another major conceptual innovation in *Capital* is its discussion of commodity-fetishism. While Marx refers implicitly to the fetishism of commodities a number of times in his earlier work, it is only in *Capital* that he devotes
a full section (in the first chapter) to delineating it.[19] Georg Lukács was one of
the first post-Marx Marxists to call attention to its central importance:

---

16. Marx 1976e, p. 152.
17. Marx 1976e, p. 992.
18. Marx 1976e, p. 173.
19. Although the first German edition of 1867 discussed commodity-fetishism, it
did not contain the section entitled 'The Fetishism of the Commodity and its Secret.'

It has often been claimed – and not without a certain justification – that the famous chapter in Hegel's *Logic* treating of Being, Non-Being, and Becoming contains the whole of his philosophy. It might be claimed with perhaps equal justification that the chapter dealing with the fetish character of the commodity, contains within itself the whole of historical materialism and the whole self-knowledge of the proletariat seen as the knowledge of capitalist society.[20]

The basis of commodity-fetishism is that value *appears* to be an attribute of the physical or thing-like character of products of labour. Marx writes, 'The fetishism peculiar to the capitalist mode of production…consists in regarding *economic* categories, such as being a *commodity* or *productive* labour, as qualities inherent in the material incarnations of these formal determinations of categories'.[21] Marx asks *why* this 'folly of identifying a specific *social relationship of production* with the thing-like qualities of certain articles'[22] arises. 'Whence, then, arises the enigmatic character of the product of labour, as soon as it assumes the form of a commodity?'[23] Marx provides the following answer:

> Clearly, it arises from this form itself. The equality of the kinds of human labour takes on a physical form in the equal objectivity of the products of labour as values; the measure of the expenditure of human labour-power by its duration takes on the form of the magnitude of the value of the products of labour; and finally the relationships between the producers, within which the social characteristics of their labours are manifested, take on the form of a social relation between the products of labour.[24]

Marx is here returning to and deepening a concept that was integral to his work from as early as 1843–4 – the inversion of subject and predicate. Value is a *product* of a definite form of human labour; it is the predicate of human activity. So why does value take on a life of its own, insofar as it appears to be the property of the thing-like character of objects? Why does the predicate come to dominate the subject, the active agents who create value in the first place? Why is it that 'Their own movement within society has for them the

---

For an English translation of the original 1867 version of Chapter One of *Capital*, see Marx 1976f, pp. 1–78.

20. Lukács 1968, p. 170.

21. Marx 1976e, p. 1046. This is from the famous planned 'Chapter Six' of *Capital*, entitled 'Results of the Immediate Process of Production'.

22. Marx 1976e, p. 998.

23. Marx 1976e, p. 164.

24. Ibid.

form of a movement made by things, and these things far from being under their control, in fact control them'?[25]

Marx's answer is that the mysterious character of the product of labour, wherein the product is the subject instead of the predicate, arises from the *form* of the commodity itself – from the fact that value appears in the form of a relation between products of labour that are exchanged for one another. The product appears as the active agent because its value can only show itself as an exchange-relation between the products. Hence, the real subject, the labour that assumes a peculiar social form and is responsible for the ability of the products to exchange against one another, is rendered invisible by the *necessity* for value to appear as a relation between things, as exchange-value – even though value itself has nothing to do with the physical properties of these things.

In sum, the subject appears to be the predicate and the predicate appears to be the subject because that is how things really are in capitalist society. Marx writes, 'To the producers, therefore, the social relations between their private labours appear as what they are, i.e. they do not appear as direct social relations between persons in their work, but rather as material relations between persons and social relations between things'.[26]

The fetishism of commodities is no mere illusion that can be stripped away by an Enlightenment-style critique. It is a valid and *adequate* form of consciousness corresponding to the actual conditions of capitalist production. Abstract labour, the equality of all labours, takes on a physical form in being materialised or objectified in a commodity. The value of the commodity is measured by the magnitude of time that it takes to create it. Its value cannot be discerned independently of this quantitative measurement. Hence, the relation of producers that create value appears as a property of the thing-like character of the commodities and not of their own labour. Fetishism arises from the *necessity* for value to assume a form of appearance that is contrary to its essence. This mystified form of appearance is *adequate to its concept*, for it corresponds to the nature of the actual labour-process in capitalism in which living labour, an activity, is transformed into a *thing* in the process of production: 'It is nothing but the definite social relation between men themselves which assumes here, for them, the fantastic form of a relation between things'.[27] Marx sums it up as follows: 'This fetishism of the world of commodities arises from the peculiar social character of the labour that produces them'.[28]

---

25. Marx 1976e, pp. 167–8.
26. Marx 1976e, pp. 165–6.
27. Marx 1976e, p. 165.
28. Ibid.

This fetishism of commodities is so overpowering that even Smith and Ricardo fell victim to it. Despite their important discovery that labour is the source of value, they viewed this source, living labour, as a *thing* or a commodity that could be bought and sold. In doing so they fell prey to the fetishism that treats value as a property of *thing*s, instead of as the expression of social relations that take on the form of things. Marx avoids this problem by distinguishing between labour and labour-power. Living labour is not a thing; nor is it a commodity. It is an *activity*. The commodity is labour-power, the *capacity* to labour. By distinguishing between labour and labour-power, Marx also avoids falling victim to the fetishism that ascribes value to the physical character of things. As Dunayevskaya argues,

> [Marx] rejected the concept of labour as a commodity. Labour is an *activity*, not a *commodity*. It was no accident that Ricardo used one and the same word for the activity and for the commodity. He was a prisoner of his concept of the human labourer as a thing. Marx, on the other hand, showed that what the labourer sold was not his labour, but only his capacity to labour, his *labour power*.[29]

The question that still needs to be answered, however, is what enabled Marx to make this conceptual distinction that went beyond the framework of classical-political economy? If commodity-fetishism is an *adequate* expression of existing social relations, how does Marx manage to penetrate through the mystified veil of commodity-fetishism in such a way as to show the inadequacy and transitory nature of existing social relations? After all, as Marx writes in Chapter One of *Capital*, 'The categories of bourgeois economics…. are forms of thought which are socially valid, and therefore objective, for the relations of production belonging to this historically determined mode of social production, i.e. commodity production'.[30] If this is so, how does it become possible to avoid falling prey to the fetishism of commodities?

Marx himself provides the answer: 'The whole mystery of commodities, all the magic and necromancy that surrounds the products of labour on the basis of commodity production, vanishes therefore as soon as we come to other forms of production'.[31] *The only way to overcome the fetishism that attaches itself to products of labour, he argues, is to step outside of capitalism's confines and examine it from the standpoint of non-capitalist social relations.* Marx therefore proceeds to examine value-production from the vantage-point of both pre-capitalist *and* postcapitalist social relations. In doing so he returns to, and

---

29. Dunayevskaya 2000, p. 108.
30. Marx 1976e, p. 169.
31. Ibid.

further concretises, his conception in the *Grundrisse* that 'the correct grasp of the present' hinges on 'the understanding of the past' which 'leads to points which indicate the transcendence of the present form of production relations, the movement coming into being, thus *foreshadowing* the future...for a new state of society'.[32]

After discussing the precapitalist relations of feudal Europe in which 'the social relations between individuals in the performance of their labour appear at all events as their own personal relations, and are not disguised as social relations between things',[33] he writes: 'Let us finally imagine, for a change, an association of free men, working with the means of production held in common, and expending their many different forms of labour-power in full self-awareness as one single social labour'.[34] In one of the most explicit and direct discussions of the transcendence of capitalist value-production found in any of his writings, Marx outlines the following about such a future state of affairs:

First, he nowhere refers to value or exchange-value in discussing this future non-capitalist society. All products are 'directly objects of utility'[35] and do not assume a value-form. Second, what characterises this postcapitalist society is 'an association of *free* men' – not a mere association as such. He notes that pre-capitalist feudal societies were characterised by 'directly associated labour'.[36] Yet such societies were not free since they were based on 'patriarchal' and oppressive social relations. The new society, in contrast, is one in which social relations are *freely* constituted. Third, the individuals in this freely-associated society directly take part in producing, distributing, and consuming the total social product. There is no objectified expression of social labour that exists as a person apart from the individuals themselves.

Marx spells this out as follows: 'The total product of our imagined associa-tion is a social product'.[37] One part of the aggregate social product serves to renew or reproduce the means of production. It 'remains social' since it is not individually consumed. The other part of the aggregate social product

---

32. Marx 1986a, p. 389.
33. Marx 1976e, p. 170.
34. Marx 1976e, p. 171.
35. Ibid.
36. Ibid. This point is overlooked by Ernest Mandel in his Introduction to the Ben Fowkes translation of Volume I of *Capital*, in which he says that Marx aimed to show 'why and how capitalism created, through its own development, the economic, material and social preconditions for society of associated producers'. This overlooks the radical difference between precapitalist forms of association, based on force and compulsion, and those delineated by Marx as constituting the operative principle of a *non-capitalist* society. See Mandel 1976, p. 17.
37. Marx 1976e, p. 171.

'is consumed by members of the association as means of subsistence'.[38] How is this division of the aggregate product to occur? No mechanism independent of the free association of the producers decides this for them. It is decided by the conscious deliberation of the free association itself. Marx does not go into any details of how this would be arranged, since it 'will vary with the particular kind of social organization of production and the corresponding level of social development attained by the producers'.[39]

Marx seems reticent about going into too many details about this new society. This is because of his emphasis on the freely-associated character of such a society. The specific manner in which the total social product is divided between individual consumption and means of production depends on a number of variables that cannot be anticipated in advance. Marx is wary of suggesting any mechanism or formula that operates irrespective of what the freely-associated individuals decide to do based upon their specific level of social development.

Marx then writes, 'We shall assume, but only for the sake of a parallel with the production of commodities, that the share of each individual producer in the means of subsistence is determined by his labour time'.[40] He suggests that labour-time plays a double role in this new society. First, it functions as part of 'a definite social plan [that] maintains the correct proportion between the different functions of labour and the various needs of the associations'.[41] Labour-time is divided up or proportioned in accordance with the need to replenish the means of production as well as meet the consumption needs of individuals. He continues, 'On the other hand, labour time also serves as the measure of the part taken by each individual in the common labour, and of his share in the part of the total product destined for social consumption'.[42] The specific share of each individual in social consumption is determined by the actual amount of labour-time that they perform in the community.

Since this passage has been subject to a wide variety of interpretations, it is important to pay close attention to Marx's specific wording. Although he speaks of a 'parallel' with commodity-production insofar as 'the share of each individual producer in the means of subsistence is determined by his labour time', Marx is not suggesting that the new society is governed by *socially-necessary* labour-time. As noted earlier, there is a vast difference between *actual* labour-time and *socially-necessary* labour-time. Under capitalism, actual

---

38. Marx 1976e, p. 172.
39. Ibid.
40. Ibid.
41. Ibid.
42. Ibid.

labour-time does not create value; instead, the social *average* of *necessary* labour-time creates value. That he does not envisage the latter operating in a postcapitalist society is indicated by the sentence that concludes his discussion: 'The social relations of the individual producers, both towards their labour and the products of their labour, are here transparent in their simplicity, in production as well as in distribution'.[43] Social relations based on necessary labour-time are anything but transparent since they are established behind the backs of the producers by a social average that operates outside of their control. This is part of what he meant by commodity-fetishism. If social relations in the new society are 'transparent in their simplicity', this can only mean that the social product is distributed not on the basis of socially-necessary labour-time but rather on the actual amount of time that the individual engages in material production. Such a principle is completely alien to capitalist value-production.

The distinction between actual labour-time and socially-necessary labour-time is of cardinal importance, since conflating the two leads to the erroneous conclusion that Marx posits value-production as continuing to operate in a postcapitalist society. Georg Lukács fell into this problem in his *Ontology of Social Being* and *The Process of Democratization*. In the latter work, for example, he writes,

> For Marx, labour exploitation can exist under socialism if labour time is expropriated from the labourer, since 'the share of every producer to the means of production is determined by his labour time'...For Marx, the law of value is not dependent upon commodity production...according to Marx these classical categories are applicable to any mode of production.[44]

Lukács misreads Marx's phrase 'for the sake of a parallel with the production of commodities' as suggesting not just a parallel but an *identity* between commodity-production and forms that prevail in a postcapitalist society.

Marx mentions this parallel only to emphasise the role that labour-time would play in the future. But what does he mean by labour-time? The actual labour-time that operates *after* capitalism is far from identical with the socially-average necessary labour-time that operates *in* capitalism. In Lukács's reading the two become conflated, even though the latter implies value-production whereas the former implies its transcendence. Marx never mentions value or exchange-value in discussing the new society in Chapter One, and for good reason: he holds that the new society's social relations are 'transparent in their

---

43. Ibid.
44. Lukács 1991, pp. 120–1.

simplicity'. Lukács does not mention Marx's discussion of the 'transparent' nature of social relations in the future, even though Marx repeats it on several occasions.[45] If Lukács had paid greater attention to this issue, he would have recognised that Marx is not referring to socially-necessary labour-time in discussing the operative principles of a postcapitalist society.

Why, however, does Marx suggest in Chapter One of *Capital* that in a new society 'the means of subsistence is determined by labour time' when he has spent many years attacking Proudhon and the socialist neo-Ricardians for their proposals to 'organise' exchange along the lines of labour-vouchers and time-chits? Why does he do so when he continues to criticise these utopian experiments in *Capital* itself?[46] Again, the answer lies in the distinction between actual labour-time and socially-necessary labour-time. The socialist neo-Ricardians presumed that *actual* labour-time is the source of value. Like Ricardo himself, they focused on the quantitative determination of value by labour-time without ever inquiring into what *kind* of labour creates value in the first place. They conflated actual labour-time and socially-necessary labour-time and therefore imagined that a 'fair exchange' of labour-time for means of subsistence is possible on the basis of value-production. Marx castigated their position as completely utopian because it is impossible, he shows, to establish social equality on the basis of inequitable social relations in which the very activity of the labourer is treated as a thing. As Marx reiterates in Chapter Three of *Capital*, 'private labour cannot be treated as its opposite, directly social labour'[47] because social relations based on value-production are inherently indirect.

The situation becomes very different, however, with the abolition of value-production. But how exactly is value-production to be eliminated? The question centres on the issue of *time*. With the creation of a free association of individuals who consciously plan out the production and distribution of the social product, labour ceases to be subject to the dictatorship of time as an external, abstract, and impermeable force governing them irrespective of their will and needs. Once time becomes the space for the individuals'

---

45. See Marx 1976e, p. 173: 'The religious reflections of the real world can, in any case, vanish only when the practical relations of everyday life between man and man, and man and nature, generally present themselves to him in a transparent and rational form'.

46. See especially Chapter Two, where Marx takes issue with 'the craftiness of petty-bourgeois socialism, which wants to perpetrate the production of commodities while simultaneously abolishing the "antagonism between money and commodities", i.e. abolishing money itself, since money only exists in and through this antagonism. One might as well abolish the Pope while leaving Catholicism in existence'. See Marx 1976e, p. 181.

47. Marx 1976e, p. 188.

deliberation and development, social relations become 'transparent', since they are no longer governed by an abstract average that operates behind their backs. 'Society' no longer appears as a person apart, but rather as the sum total of the free and conscious activity of individuals. Labour again becomes directly social, but on the basis of freedom. Once the dictatorship of abstract time over the social agents is abolished in the actual process of production, it becomes possible to distribute the social product on the basis of the actual amount of time that they contribute to society, since production-relations have been transformed in such a way as to make such a distribution possible.

Marx addresses this by contrasting the utopian schemes of Proudhon and the socialist neo-Ricardians to what he considers the more practical approach of Robert Owen:

> Owen presupposes directly socialized labour, a form of production diametrically opposed to the production of commodities. The certificate of labour is merely evidence of a part taken by the individual in the common labour, and of his claim to a certain portion of the common product [that] has been set aside for consumption. But Owen never made the mistake of presupposing the production of commodities, while, at the same time, by juggling with money, trying to circumvent the necessary conditions of that form of production.[48]

Marx's comments on the new society in Chapter One of *Capital* are brief and somewhat cryptic. However, they represent an important development in exhibiting a willingness on his part to directly discuss the nature of a postcapitalist society.[49] What is most striking about Marx's discussion is the suggestion that it is impossible to penetrate through the mystified veil of commodity-fetishism unless the critique of capitalist value-production is made from the standpoint of its transcendence. The fact that the section on commodity-fetishism was finalised only *after* the experience of the 1871 Paris Commune – the first time in history that a mass revolt attempted an exit from capitalism – suggests the importance of analysing the present from the vantage-point of the future.[50] This may be what Rosa Luxemburg had

---

48. Marx 1976e, pp. 188–9.

49. This will take on even more importance following his completion of *Capital*, as is indicated by his *Civil War in France* (1871) and *Critique of the Gotha Programme* (1875). This will be discussed in Chapter Four, below.

50. See Dunayevskaya 2000, pp. 101–2: 'The totality of the reorganization of society by the Communards shed new insight into the perversity of relations under capitalism...The richness of human traits, revealed in the Commune, showed in sharp relief that the fetishism of commodities arises from the commodity form itself. This deepened the meaning of the form of value as both a logical development and as a social phenomenon'.

in mind when she wrote, 'The secret of Marx's theory of value, his analysis of money, his theory of capital, his theory of the rate of profit, and consequently of the whole existing economic system is – the transitory nature of the capitalist economy, its collapse: thus – and this is only another aspect of the same phenomena – the final goal, socialism. And precisely because, *a priori*, Marx looked at capitalism from the socialist's viewpoint, that is, from the historical viewpoint, he was enabled to decipher the hieroglyphics of capitalist economy'.[51]

As Marx himself puts it at the end of Chapter One, 'The veil is not removed from the countenance of the social life-process, i.e. the process of material production, until it becomes production by freely associated men, and stands under their conscious and planned control'.[52]

Although no section of Volume I of *Capital* takes up the new society as directly as the concluding pages of Chapter One, Marx's discussion of a number of critical theoretical categories in the rest of the volume illuminates his understanding of the alternative to capitalism. I will focus on four such categories: (1) the transformation of money into capital; (2) the nature of wage-labour; (3) the 'despotic form' of capital at the point of production; and (4) the distinction between two kinds of private property in the means of production, with which *Capital* ends.

Much of the first volume of *Capital* is concerned with how money becomes transformed into capital. The transformation is by no means self-evident. Marx holds that since 'the value of a commodity is expressed in its price before it enters into circulation' it is 'therefore a pre-condition of circulation, not its result'.[53] At the same time, money cannot become transformed into capital without the process of circulation. Although the *creation* of value precedes circulation, the transformation of money into capital cannot occur without a process of circulation. He concludes, 'Capital cannot therefore arise from circulation, and it is equally impossible for it to arise apart from circulation. It must have its origin both in circulation and not in circulation'.[54]

Marx wrestles with this contradiction – which may appear to be rather puzzling – throughout the rest of the book. In order to transform money into capital, the capitalist must find on the market a commodity that produces a value greater than itself. There is only one commodity that meets this requirement – labour-power. The transformation of money into capital requires the purchase and sale of labour-power. To put it differently, money

51. Luxemburg 2004, p. 151.
52. Marx 1976e, p. 173.
53. Marx 1976e, p. 260.
54. Marx 1976e, p. 268.

cannot be transformed into capital in the absence of a labour-market. By purchasing labour-power the capitalist can compel the labourers to create a value greater than the value of their labour-power or means of subsistence. The increased value is what Marx calls 'surplus-value'. Money is transformed into capital through the production of surplus-value.

However, what allows for the existence of a market in labour-power? The mere act of buying and selling labour-power is not enough. The labourers have to be *compelled* to sell their labour-power by being separated from the objective conditions of production – from the land and control over their labour. A market in labour-power can arise only if the workers become dispossessed of the ownership of possession of anything except their labour-power, which they sell for a wage in order to survive. Marx contends, 'In themselves, money and commodities are no more capital than are the means of production and subsistence. They need to be transformed into capital. But this transformation can itself only take place under particular circumstances'.[55] The most important of these circumstances is the creation of a class of 'free' wage-labourers – 'Free workers, in the double sense that they neither form part of the means of production themselves, as would be the case with slaves, serfs, etc. nor do they own the means of production, as would be the case with free peasant proprietors'.[56]

Hence, although a market for labour-time is an essential condition for the transformation of money into capital, the separation of the worker from the objective conditions of production is an essential condition for the existence of a labour-market. In the absence of a generalised labour-market, surplus-value and capital cannot become the determinative factors of social production and reproduction. The mere existence of a *commodity*-market does not therefore imply capitalist relations of production. Capitalist relations of production arise on the basis of a generalised *labour*-market that enables money to be converted into capital. But the emergence of that labour-market depends in turn upon a transformation of specific *production*-relations – most of all the separation of the labourer from the objective conditions of production.[57] Marx

---

55. Marx 1976e, p. 874.
56. Ibid.
57. There are many forms that this separation can take. It need not take the form of eliminating the commons by privatising social relations through the formation of a market-economy, as occurred in Europe during the transition from feudalism to capitalism. It can also take the form of eliminating the commons by statifying social relations through the elimination of a competitive market involving small peasant-proprietors, as occurred in the Soviet Union in the 1920s and 1930s and in China in the 1950s and 1960s, as well as elsewhere. Just as there are many paths to heaven, so there are many to purgatory.

therefore argues, 'The production of commodities leads inexorably to capitalist production, once the worker has ceased to be a part of the conditions of production (as in slavery, serfdom), or once primitive common ownership has ceased to be the basis of society (India)'.[58]

The transformation of money into capital therefore occurs in two 'wholly distinct, autonomous spheres, two entirely separate processes'.[59] One is the realm of circulation – the buying and selling of labour-power in the market-place. The other is *the consumption of the labour-power that has been acquired*, i.e. the process of production itself'.[60] Both are necessary, but the latter makes the former possible. What makes it possible for a market in labour-power to arise, and for money to be converted into capital, is the existence of alienated or abstract labour. It is crucial that,

> [T]hese means of production and these means of subsistence confront *labour-power*, stripped of all material wealth, as autonomous powers, personified in their owners. The objective conditions essential to the realization of labour are *alienated* from the worker and become manifest as *fetishes* endowed with a will and a soul of their own. *Commodities*, in short, appear as the purchasers of *persons*.[61]

Marx thus indicates that the market is not the primary object of his critique of capital. Even when discussing the market in labour-power, without which the transformation of money into capital cannot occur, he emphasises the formation of specific (alienated) relations of production that make such a market possible. The implication is that ending the separation of the labourers from the objective conditions of production would render superfluous the necessity of a labour-market.

This carries over into Marx's detailed analyses of wage-labour. The existence of wage-labour is the key to capital-formation. He writes, 'The capitalist form presupposes from the outset the free wage labourer who sells his labour power to capital'.[62] He adds, 'The whole system of capitalist production is based on the worker's sale of his labour power as a commodity'.[63] And he notes that the means of production and subsistence 'become *capital* only because of the phenomenon of *wage labour*'.[64] However, it takes a lot more than the existence of money or a commodity-market to generate wage-labour.

---

58. Marx 1976e, p. 951.
59. Marx 1976e, p. 1002.
60. Ibid.
61. Marx 1976e, p. 1003.
62. Marx 1976e, p. 452.
63. Marx 1976e, p. 557.
64. Marx 1976e, p. 1005.

Wage-labour can only arise if workers have become separated from the objective and subjective conditions of production. They must be torn from the land, from their instruments of production, and most of all, from control over their own labouring-activity. *Only then* do the labourers become compelled to sell themselves for a wage. Marx writes that this means, 'In reality, the worker belongs to capital *before* he has sold himself to the capitalist'.[65]

It *appears* from the purchase and sale of labour-power that the market-transaction between buyer and seller is the defining feature of capitalist social relations. But Marx insists that the worker 'belongs to capital' even *before* the worker is offered up for sale on the market. The sale of labour-power is merely the consequence of a much more oppressive experience that occurs within the work-process itself. Marx writes: 'The starting point of the development that gave rise to the wage labourer and to the capitalist was the enslavement of the worker'.[66] The critical determinant of both wage-labour and capital, each of which cannot exist without the other, is this:

> The capital-relation presupposes a complete separation between the workers and the ownership of the conditions for the realization of their labour. As soon as capitalist production stands on its own feet, it not only maintains this separation, but reproduces it on a constantly extending scale. The process, therefore, which creates the capital-relation can be nothing other than the process which divorces the worker from the ownership of the conditions of his own labour.[67]

This has a number of implications in terms of conceptualising an alternative to capitalism. Marx is suggesting that a postcapitalist society must eliminate wage-labour. *Marx consistently makes this point throughout his published and unpublished work.* As he states in his lectures on 'Value, Price and Profit' – delivered as he was completing Volume I of *Capital* – 'the final emancipation of the working class…[is] the ultimate abolition of the wages system'.[68] The end of wage-labour in turn suggests that a labour-market would not exist in a new society. However, the abolition of the labour-market does not hinge upon the abolition of money and the commodity-market, as much as upon the transformation of the process of production. *More specifically, the split between the worker and the objective conditions of production would have to be healed.* It is surely possible to conceive of a society without money and commodity-markets, but which still leaves this separation unhealed. And such a society

---

65. Marx 1976e, p. 723. My emphasis.
66. Marx 1976e, p. 875.
67. Marx 1976e, p. 874.
68. Marx 1985b, p. 149.

would be one in which wage-labour continues to prevail, but such a society is far removed from Marx's concept of socialism.

What has often stood in the way of this realisation is the assumption that Marx counterposed the 'anarchy of the market' to the social 'organisation' found in the capitalist process of production. A long line of thinkers in the radical tradition have argued in favour of correcting the inefficiencies and 'anarchy' of markets by extending the presumably more 'rational' and ordered mechanisms of the production-process into the sphere of distribution. Marx's discussion of *the despotic form of capitalist production* tends to undermine claims that he favoured this approach. He writes, 'If capitalist direction is thus two-fold in content, owing to the twofold nature of the process of production which has to be directed – on the one hand a social labour process for the creation of a product, and on the other hand capital's process of valorization – in form it is purely despotic'.[69]

This despotism is contained in the fact that 'it is not the worker who employs the conditions of his work, but rather the reverse, the conditions of work employ the worker'.[70] It is true that Marx refers to 'the anarchic system of competition' that he calls 'the most outrageous squandering of social means of production'.[71] However, he notes, 'the immanent laws of capitalist production *manifest themselves* in the external movement'[72] of individual units of competing capitals. He contends that the 'scientific analysis of competition is possible only if we can grasp the inner nature of capital'. 'Anarchic' competition is not the cause but the consequence of despotic relations of production.

According to Marx, what makes such relations of production despotic is the subordination of living labour by 'dead labour'. He argues in 'The Results of the Immediate Process of Production', 'In fact, the rule of the capitalist over the worker is nothing but the rule of the independent *conditions of labour* over the *worker*, conditions that have made themselves independent of him'.[73]

Viewed from this perspective, neither the 'anarchy of the market' nor even the actions of the capitalists *vis-à-vis* the workers serve as the essential objects of the Marxian critique of capital. The capitalist, also, is merely the expression of the separation of the worker from the objective conditions of production. For once these conditions become independent from the worker, the *necessity* arises for a discrete class of capitalists to chain the workers to an alienated

---

69. Marx 1976e, p. 450.
70. Marx 1976e, p. 548.
71. Marx 1976e, p. 667.
72. Marx 1976e, p. 433. My emphasis.
73. Marx 1976e, p. 989.

labour-process.[74] This suggests that even the elimination of the personifications of capital does not suffice to free the worker, so long as the breach between the worker and the objective conditions of production remains unhealed. On these grounds, Marx often criticises his fellow socialists for advocating capital without the capitalists. He argues,

> The *functions* fulfilled by the capitalist are no more than the functions of capital – viz. the valorization of value by absorbing living labour – executed *consciously* and *willingly*. The capitalist functions only as *personified* capital, capital as a person, just as the worker is no more than *labour* personified…Hence the rule of the capitalist over the worker is the rule of things over man, of dead labour over the living, of the product over the producer.[75]

The fullest indication that Marx neither posits the market as the major object of his critique, nor conceives of its abolition as the key to creating an alternative to capitalism, is contained in a paragraph added to 'The General Law of Capitalist Accumulation' in the French edition of *Capital*, in 1872–5. In discussing the concentration and centralisation of capital to its ultimate limit, he writes: 'In any branch of industry centralization would reach its extreme limit if all the individual capitals invested there were fused into a single capital. In a given society this limit would be reached only when the entire social capital was united in the hands of either a single capitalist or a single capitalist corporation'.[76] This indicates that, for Marx, capitalism's law of motion would not be radically altered even if 'the *entire* social capital' became united 'in the hands of either a single capitalist or a single capitalist corporation'. Such a situation would, of course, imply the effective abolition of a competitive free market. But it need not imply the end of capitalism itself. Capitalism could survive, Marx is suggesting, with a variety of forms of circulation and distribution. It is at least *theoretically* possible that capitalist social relations could persist even in the absence of an anarchic or competitive 'free' market.[77]

---

74. The process becomes reciprocal, of course, in turn.

75. Marx 1976e, pp. 989–90.

76. Marx 1976e, p. 779. For a discussion of how this passage proved of critical importance in developing the theory that 'Soviet-type' societies were state-capitalist, see Dunayevskaya 1992 and 2002.

77. This is not to suggest that such an extreme form of concentration and centralisation of capital would necessarily be more productive or efficient. Volume III of *Capital* suggests that a radical suppression of competition between individual units of capital would be likely to deprive capitalism of its vivacity. Marx writes, 'And if capital formation were to fall exclusively into the hands of a few existing big capitals, for whom the mass of profit outweighs the rate, the animating fire of production would be totally extinguished. It would die out. It is the rate of profit that is the driving force

This does not mean, however, that capitalism could exist if all of *global* capital were concentrated in the hands of a single state or single capitalist corporation. The passage at the end of Volume I of *Capital* on concentration and centralisation reaching its 'extreme limit' refers to a given *national* unit of capital. It is impossible, however, given the nature of value-production, for all of global capital to be concentrated into a single hand. Marx earlier directly spoke to this in the *Grundrisse*:

> Since value constitutes the basis of capital, and capital thus necessarily exists only through exchange for a *counter-value*, it necessarily repels itself from itself. A *universal capital*, not confronted by alien capitals with which it exchanges – which from our present standpoint nothing confronts it but wage labour or itself – is consequently an impossibility. The mutual repulsion of capitals is already inherent in capital as realised exchange value.[78]

Taken together with the statement at the end of Volume I of *Capital* on the concentration and centralisation of capital, the implication is clear enough: the control of capital by a single state or entity is incompatible with Marx's conception of 'socialism' or 'communism', while any effort to achieve this on a global level is completely quixotic. Socialism or communism, as Marx earlier stated in *The German Ideology*, can only arise as part of a *world*-system, a *global* transformation. But such a transformation does not consist of concentrating and centralising capital in a single entity.

Marx carries out a further discussion of the possibility of a unit of national capital existing without 'free market' competition, in his discussion of two kinds of 'private property' at the end of the first volume of *Capital*. In discussing the 'So-Called Primitive Accumulation of Capital', he points to the destruction of *two kinds* of private property in the means of production. One is 'the dissolution of the private property based on the labour of its owner'. This refers to 'The private property of the worker in his means of production'.[79] This property is based on small-scale land-holding and industry. This kind of private property is ruthlessly and violently destroyed by the process that brings modern *capitalist* private property into being. Modern capitalism arises most of all from the eviction of the peasant-proprietors from the land, from the *destruction* of their private property.

---

in capitalist production, and hence nothing is produced save what can be produced at a profit'. See Marx 1981a, p. 368.

78. *Grundrisse*, Marx 1986a, p. 350. This passage tends to undercut theories of 'ultra-imperialism' which were later formulated by such thinkers as Karl Kautsky, and which have become *au courant* in some of the contemporary literature on globalisation.

79. Marx 1976e, p. 927.

Although Marx sharply criticises the way in which capitalist private property supplants the private property of the direct producer, he does not advocate returning to the landowning-patterns that characterised precapitalist societies in the West.[80] Such small, isolated, and relatively fragmented landowning patterns do not befit the higher form of social organisation that will follow capitalism. But they do indicate that forms of private ownership and possession have existed that are qualitatively different from capitalist private property, which is based on the complete separation of the labouring populace from the objective conditions of production.

Marx refers explicitly to the Hegelian concept of 'the negation of the negation' to characterise this process. The first negation is large-scale capitalist private property that supplants the small-scale property of artisans and peasants. But as capitalism undergoes a further concentration and centralisation in fewer and fewer hands, the point is reached where this negation is itself negated: 'But capitalist production begets, with the inexorability of it a natural process, its own negation'.[81] This *second negation* does not reestablish the fragmented and isolated parcels of precapitalist property, but it does end the breach between the labourers and the objective conditions of production. What emerges is 'cooperation and the possession in common of the land and the means of production produced by labour itself'.[82] The new society, for Marx, represents a reversal of the basic principle of capitalism, which was 'the annihilation of that private property which rests on the labour of the individual himself'.[83] Instead, a free association of producers overcomes the separation between individuals and the conditions of material wealth. This entails something far more emancipatory than the transformation of private property into state-property; indeed, Marx never mentions the state once in this chapter that concludes Volume I of *Capital*. His analysis of the two kinds of private property at the end of the first volume of *Capital* shows once again that he is not limiting his horizon to the contrast of private versus collective property. Instead, he is focusing on the contrast between property-relations that fragment individuals from their natural and subjective capacities and ones that overcome this separation. The latter, for Marx, constitutes the substance of a new society.

---

80. The situation is quite different in the non-Western world, where communal property predominated. Especially in his later writings, Marx tends to see these communal property forms as a possible material condition for enabling developing societies to shorten or even bypass the stage of capitalist industrialisation, if they could link up with socialist transformation in the industrialised West.

81. Marx 1976e, p. 929.

82. Ibid.

83. Marx 1976e, p. 940.

Volumes II and III of *Capital*

Volumes II and III of *Capital* are integral to Marx's overall theoretical project. In one outline he gave of his critical of political economy, Marx planned for Volume I to deal with the process of production, Volume II with the process of circulation, and Volume III with the process of capitalist production as a whole.[84] He only lived to complete the first volume, even though most of the manuscripts of what became Volumes II and III were written prior to the publication of the first volume in 1867. Volumes II and III have to be read with a degree of caution, since they were edited and published after Marx's death by Engels (Volume II appeared in 1885; Volume III appeared nearly a decade later). It is therefore unlikely that either volume would have appeared in its present form and content had Marx succeeded in completing it.[85] Volume II clearly lacks the polish as well as literary quality of the first volume, and its more rarefied subject-matter makes it perhaps one of the least amenable to immediate application on behalf of political or social causes amongst all of his writings. Volume III has given rise to far more discussion and debate in the critical literature on Marx, largely because it deals with topics that touch directly on matters of concern to traditional economists, such as credit, interest, rent, the rate of profit, speculative capital and the causes of crises. Given the great span of topics covered in these two volumes (most of which are not touched upon in Volume I at all), I must limit myself to those passages that directly speak to the subject-matter of the present work.

Although Volume II of *Capital* deals with circulation, it would be a mistake to assume that it deals with the circulation of *commodities*, since that is analysed in the first part of Volume I. Rather, the second volume deals with the circulation of *capital*. The circulation of capital comprises three component parts – money-capital, productive capital, and commodity-capital. These are not three independent classes of capital, but rather three forms of *industrial capital*, separate moments of the same aspect of the economy. Capital of necessity takes on these three modes of existence: they are 'different forms with which capital clothes itself in its different stages'.[86] Their inter-relation is Marx's primary object of investigation in the second volume.

---

84. As noted earlier, he also intended that what became published after his death as *Theories of Surplus Value* should serve as *Capital's* concluding volume.

85. *MEGA²* has published Marx's original manuscripts for Volumes II and III, which for the first time has allowed scholars to critically evaluate Engels's role in editing the manuscripts for publication. This debate falls outside the scope of this study and is not discussed here.

86. Marx 1978, p. 109.

Marx's aim is to describe how these circuits operate in a chemically-pure *capitalist* economy. He writes, 'In order to grasp these forms in their pure state, we must first of all abstract from all aspects that have nothing to do with the change and constitution of the forms as such'.[87] He abstracts from contingent or secondary factors that get in the way of grasping the object of his analysis by assuming: (1) commodities are sold at their value; (2) no revolutions in value occur in the circulation-process;[88] (3) there is no foreign trade: 'We therefore completely abstract from it here, and treat gold as a direct element of the annual [domestic] production';[89] and (4) there are no crises of realisation. Marx is not leaving aside these factors in order to create a purely abstract model of capitalist accumulation that has little or no bearing on reality: instead, he is stripping away secondary or tertiary phenomena that get in the way of delineating capitalism's actual law of motion. According to Marx, capital can 'only be grasped as a movement, not as a static thing'.[90] He employs this method of abstraction in order to present the circuits of capital in the clearest possible terms.

Given its relatively rarified subject matter, it is surprising that Volume II contains any discussion of a postcapitalist society at all. However, a close analysis shows that several passages address the issue. What grounds much of Marx's discussion of the issue is a concept that is discussed in the opening pages of Volume II – the 'distribution of the elements of production'. This does not refer to the distribution of relations of circulation as opposed to those of production. Instead, it refers to how one class – the workers – are torn from the objective conditions of production and become 'distributed' as 'free' wage-labourers, while another class – the capitalists – effectively own them. As Marx puts it:

> Thus the situation that underlines the act of M-C (L/MP) is one of distribution; not distribution in the customary sense of distribution of the means of consumption, but rather the distribution of the elements of production themselves, with the objective factors concentrated on one side, and labour-power isolated from them on the other. The means of production, the objective productive capital, must thus already face the worker as such, as capital, *before* the act M-L can become general throughout society.[91]

---

87. Ibid.
88. Marx does so because such revolutions do not alter the proportions of the elements of value in terms of its various components so long as they are universally distributed.
89. Marx 1978, p. 546.
90. Marx 1978, p. 185.
91. Marx 1978, p. 116.

The importance of this concept becomes clearer later in the third part of Volume II, 'The Reproduction and Circulation of the Total Social Capital'. This part has a largely *polemical* thrust, in that Marx aims to show what he considers the erroneous nature of two prevailing tendencies in political economy. One is that of Adam Smith, who 'spirited away' constant capital by arguing that it is ultimately consumed as revenue. The other is under-consumptionism, as represented by such figures as Sismondi, Malthus, and Rodbertus (and more recently, one could argue, by Paul Sweezy, Ernest Mandel and David Harvey), which argues that the critical determinant in capital-accumulation is a level of effective demand sufficient to buy up the surplus-product.

Marx counters Smith's view by arguing that the value of constant capital does not dissolve into wages and profits, since a considerable portion of it is consumed productively. There are *two* reasons for Marx's criticism of Adam Smith on this issue. The first, and most obvious, is that if Smith were right that the value of constant capital ultimately dissolves into revenue, there would be no reason for workers to fight against the appropriation of their unpaid hours of labour by the capitalists. Although that is doubtless an important consideration, there is also a deeper issue involved in Marx's critique of Smith than the alienation of the product from the producer. For Marx, I would argue, the most egregious aspect of Smith's error is that it conceals how constant capital is the instrument through which the capitalist gains mastery over the worker. If the value of constant capital dissolves into revenue, the domination of dead over living labour dissolves as well. Thus, Smith completely obscures what Marx considers to be the crux and the distinctiveness of the class-relation of capitalist society.

Some of the same considerations explain Marx's objection to under-consumptionism – the notion that the central contradiction of capitalism is the inability of workers to buy back the surplus-product. Of course, Marx knows full well that the purchasing power of the workers does not enable them to buy back the surplus-product. But the *reason* for this, he contends, is not the lack of effective demand: instead, the lack of effective demand is a result of a deeper problem. Although crises often *manifest* themselves in an inability to sell the surplus-product, they 'first become evident not in the direct reduction of consumer demand, the demand for individual consumption, but rather a decline in the number of exchanges of capital for capital, in the reproduction process of capital'.[92] Marx counters the under-consumptionist argument as follows:

---

92. Marx 1978, pp. 156–7.

It is a pure tautology to say that crises are caused by the scarcity of solvent consumers, or of a paying consumption. The capitalist system does not know any other modes of consumption than a paying one...But if one were to attempt to clothe this tautology with a semblance of profounder justification by saying that the working class receives too small a portion of their own product, and the evil would be remedied by giving them a larger share of it, or raising their wages, we should reply that crises are always preceded by a period in which wages rise generally and the working class actually gets a larger share of the annual product intended for consumption.[93]

Marx objected to under-consumptionism because it tends to locate the central contradiction of capitalism in the *market* instead of in *production*. To Marx, this not only gets the *facts* of capitalism wrong; it also misconstrues how to correct them. If capitalism's main problem is the lack of effective demand, it follows that resolving it centres on paying workers better wages and benefits. The need to uproot the domination of dead over living labour becomes just as readily obscured as by Smith's error.

Marx's view, which is spelled out in the formulas of expanded reproduction, did not at all satisfy critics such as Rosa Luxemburg. As she saw it, Marx's assuming-away of realisation crises projects a tendency of unimpeded equilibrium or balanced growth. As she wrote in *Accumulation of Capital*, 'The complicated problem of accumulation is thus converted into a diagrammatic progression of surprising simplicity. We may continue the above chain of equations *ad infinitum* so long as...a certain increase in the constant capital in Department I[94] always necessitates a certain increase in the variable capital'.[95] She found the implications of this profoundly disturbing, for some of the same reasons that a number of economists have found it appealing – that it *seems* to suggest the possibility of infinite capitalist expansion.[96]

---

93. Marx 1978, pp. 486–7.

94. Marx distinguishes between two departments of social production. Department I is means of production, consisting of: a) the value of means of production consumed in creating means of production (which Marx calls 'productive consumption'); b) the value of means of production laid out in labour-power (or the sum of wages paid out in the sphere of production); and c) the profits of the industrial capitalist. Department II is means of consumption, consisting of: a) the value of means of production transferred to commodities that are individually consumed by workers and capitalists; b) the value of the labour-power that produces such consumption-goods; and c) the profits of the capitalists accrued from it. Surplus-value is embodied in both departments.

95. Luxemburg 1968, p. 118.

96. For more on this, see Desai 2002.

Luxemburg's sharp criticism of Marx's presentation of the formulae of expanded reproduction did not stop her, however, from suggesting that it offered a possible model of a postcapitalist society that overcomes the 'anarchic' character of capitalism. She wrote in *The Accumulation of Capital*: 'Marx's diagrams of enlarged reproduction has objective validity – *mutatis mutandis* – for a planned society'.[97] While she held that Marx's formulas failed to present the actual dynamic of *capitalism* by ignoring effective demand and realisation-crises, they are valid, she wrote, for a 'planned' economy in which 'market-anarchy' is overcome.

Three years earlier, and writing from the very different perspective of dis-proportionality-theory, Rudolf Hilferding had argued that Marx's formulae suggest the kind of normative balance between production and consumption that could be achieved through state-intervention in the economy. Whereas Luxemburg criticised Marx's formulae on the grounds that they suggest balanced growth, Hilferding embraced them for – so he presumed – offering a model of balanced growth. As one recent study puts it, 'By assuming balance in the reproduction schema, co-ordination is established between capital and consumer-good producing sectors. For some Marxists, writing at the start of the twentieth century, this provided a seductive insight into how governments might impose order on the economic system'.[98]

A more recent articulation of Hilferding's view was expressed by Ernest Mandel, author of the introduction to the most recent English translation of *Capital*. He writes, 'It follows logically from this idea that if the capitalists were capable of investing "rationally," i.e., so as to maintain proportions of equilibrium between the two main sectors of production, crises could be avoided'.[99] Mandel denies that *capitalists* can or will rationally plan; he instead calls for rational planning based on the elimination of private property and private capitalists by bringing capital-accumulation under the management of a state-plan. His position owes much to the efforts of such thinkers as Wassiley Leontief, who earlier sought to apply Marx's theory of expanded reproduction to the state-centralised economies of the USSR.

The problem with these approaches – whether of Luxemburg, Hilferding, and Mandel/Leontief – is that *the formulae of expanded reproduction*, as is true of Marx's analysis of capitalist production as a whole, are not applicable to

---

97. Luxemburg 1968, p. 131.
98. Trigg (ed.) 2006, p. 64. In *Finance Capital*, Hilferding argued that 'order' could only be established by 'subordinating the whole of production to conscious control'. It is instructive that this *fetishism of the plan*, which later became so pronounced in Stalinist Russia and China, had its origins in the Second International.
99. Mandel 1962, p. 366.

any society other than capitalism. This is because, as I have been arguing, the value-production upon which they are based is applicable only to capitalism. Moreover, there is little or no textual evidence to suggest that Marx's aim in presenting the schemata of expanded reproduction was to imply anything about a postcapitalist society, one way or the other. Although he emphasises the material form of constant capital, he deals with constant capital – as all of the factors of production and circulation – in *value*-terms. And for Marx value-production is the *differentia specifica* of *capitalism*.[100]

Nonetheless, while Marx does not address the nature of a postcapitalist society in his formulae of expanded reproduction, he touches on it in a number of other places in Volume II of *Capital*. For example, in the middle of an analysis of the exchange between the two departments of social capital in the chapter on 'Simple Reproduction', Marx suddenly breaks into a discussion of a new society: 'If production were social instead of capitalist, it is evident that these products of department I would be no less constantly redistributed among the branches of production in this department as means of production, according to the needs of reproduction; one part directly remaining in the sphere of production from which it entered as a product, another part being shifted to other points of production'.[101] Here, Marx is suggesting that the *form* of the distribution of the elements of production is of decisive significance for any social order. In capitalism, this distribution occurs behind the backs of the producers, according to the dictates of value-production. In socialism, the distribution would be based on the needs of the human agents of reproduction itself. This distribution is of a radically different kind under socialism, since the producers allocate a given amount of material wealth to replenish means of production and another amount to supply their consumption-needs. *At this point, value-production does not enter the picture at all.*[102]

To take another example, in Chapter Sixteen on 'The Turnover of Variable Capital', Marx goes into much greater detail by discussing what prevails 'If we were to consider a communist society in place of a capitalist one': 'Money capital would immediately be done away with, and so too the disguises that

---

100. Although Marx's formulae are specifically directed to the analysis of *capitalism*, this does not mean that some kind of simple or expanded reproduction would not exist in a postcapitalist society. Such a process would not, however, represent a process of accumulation of *capital*. Marx's formulae of expanded reproduction, which illustrate the dynamic of capital-accumulation, cannot therefore be directly grafted onto efforts to envisage a postcapitalist society.

101. Marx 1978, pp. 500–1.

102. It is important to note that Marx is here discussing the distribution of the elements *of production*, not distribution in the sense of the sphere of circulation, which is of secondary and derivative importance.

transactions acquire through it. The matter would be simply reduced to the fact that the society must reckon in advance how much labour, means of production and means of subsistence it can spend, without dislocation'.[103] Since value-production ceases in a postcapitalist society, there is no reason for its transactions to occur through the medium of monetary capital; society itself, through the free association of producers, would 'reckon in advance' how the elements of social wealth are to be produced and distributed.

Marx elaborates upon this in even more detail in Chapter Eighteen:

> With collective production, money capital is completely dispensed with. The society distributes labour power and means of production between the various branches of industry. There is no reason why the producers should not receive paper tokens permitting them to withdraw an amount corresponding to their labour time from the social consumption fund. But these tokens are not money; they do not circulate.[104]

This passage builds upon and extends his discussion of the new society at the end of the first chapter of Volume I of *Capital*, since Marx explicitly refers to receiving tokens or vouchers based on the *amount* of labour-time contributed by the individual to the community. It is just as necessary for a socialist society to distribute the elements of production as any other. In contrast to capitalist society, however, this distribution does not occur through an autonomous force that is independent of the producers. The distribution of the elements of production is not computed on the basis of an abstract social average of labour-time, but on the actual amount of labour-time contributed by the individual. Labour-time under socialism, as Marx has earlier indicated in Volume I of *Capital*, simply refers to the *amount* of physical hours employed in a given enterprise. One receives, in the form of tokens, a share of the common goods of society that is materially equivalent to the actual amount of time engaged in producing them for the community.

Interestingly, none of Marx's discussions of a postcapitalist society in Volume II of *Capital* mention the state. He instead refers to the control of the elements of production and distribution by *society*. Nor, as we have seen, does he mention the state in his discussion of a postcapitalist society in the first chapter of Volume I of *Capital*.

While Marx's comments in Volume II on postcapitalism are hardly systematic or detailed, they are conceptually consistent with his comments on the subject in Volume I of *Capital*. From his earliest writings of the 1840s to his late

---

103. Marx 1978, p. 390.
104. Marx 1978, p. 434.

ones, Marx insisted that the aim of capitalist society is not to enrich human needs and capabilities, but rather to augment value. Capitalism is an abstract form of domination that has one over-riding goal: to accumulate value for its own sake. A new society would need to radically reverse this. On these grounds, Marx writes in Chapter Four of Volume II, 'For capitalism is already essentially abolished once we assume that it is enjoyment that is the driving principle and not enrichment itself'.[105]

Volume III of *Capital* may seem to be even less likely than the second volume to venture into a discussion of a new society, since it is largely devoted to a detailed analysis of such economic phenomena as profit-rates, credit, interest, rent, and speculative capital and crises. Yet, even in the course of discussing these issues, Marx makes some important comments about what is to follow a capitalist society.

This can be seen especially in Marx's analysis of credit. He shows that credit works to accelerate and amplify the concentration and centralisation of capital, as it enables larger units of capital to buy up and absorb their competitors. This leads to the formation of joint-stock companies (publicly-held corporations based on stock-ownership) and mega-firms. Publicly-held corporations allow for an enormous development of economies of scale and output that small, individual units of capital find impossible to match. Private capital is increasingly forced out by what Marx calls 'social capital', that is, a collectivity of capitalists, in short, the investor-class. He writes, 'Capital...now receives the form of social capital (capital of directly associated producers) in contrast to private capital, and its enterprises appear as social enterprises as opposed to private ones. This is the abolition of capital as private property within the confines of the capitalist mode of production itself'.[106] Here, among other things, Marx is indicating that the capitalist mode of production does not necessarily depend upon capital taking the form of private property. In the joint-stock company, the individual entrepreneur loses private ownership of the enterprise. As the firm becomes larger and more complex, capitalist private property becomes socialised. Of course, here it is not socialised either by, or in the interest of, the workers. But this process still represents 'the abolition of capital as private property'. He adds,

> In joint-stock companies, the function is separated from capital ownership, so labour is completely separated from ownership of the means of production and of surplus labour. This result of capitalist production in its highest development is a necessary point of transition towards the transformation

---

105. Marx 1976e, p. 199.
106. Marx 1981a, p. 567.

of capital back into the property of the producers, though no longer as the private property of individual producers but rather as their property as associated producers, as directly social property. It is furthermore a point of transition towards the transformation of all functions formerly bound up with capital ownership in the reproduction process into simple functions of the associated producers, into social functions.[107]

Joint-stock companies further extend the alienation and dispossession of the labourer. The workers – as well as the capitalists – cease to have even an indirect ownership-stake in the enterprise. The firm becomes completely autonomous from the social forces that comprise it. The joint-stock company can therefore in no way be considered an expression of 'socialism'. At the same time, the joint-stock company represents a possible *transitional* form *towards* a new social order, in that it undermines the principle of private ownership of the means of production. In doing so, it helps prepare the ground for a form of socialisation that can overcome the separation of the labourers from the conditions of production.

Marx is not suggesting that the formation of the credit-system and joint-stock companies *on their own* impel the formation of a socialist society. He directly criticises those 'socialists' who have 'illusions' about the ability of mega-firms to directly lead to a new society:

> Finally, there can be no doubt that the credit system will serve as a powerful lever in the course of transition from the capitalist mode of production to the mode of production of associated labour; however, only as one element in connection with other large-scale organic revolutions in the mode of production itself. On the other hand, illusions about the miraculous power of the credit and banking system, in the socialist sense, arise from complete ignorance about the capitalist mode of production and about the credit system, as one of its forms.[108]

Marx's above description of the joint-stock company as a possible *transitional* form (among others) to a new society, even though it is firmly within the confines of the capitalist mode of production, makes clear that he does not conceive of it as part of a distinct phase *between* capitalism and socialism.

---

107. Marx 1981a, p. 568.
108. Marx 1981a, p. 743. Marx's criticism of the illusions about the joint-stock company 'in the socialist sense' anticipates what became the standard orthodoxy in much of the Second International after his death. Its leading theoreticians (such as Kautsky and Hilferding) argued that such formations would naturally 'grow over' into socialism on their own. The consequences of such gradualism set the stage for the Second International's demise in 1914.

The joint-stock company is firmly embedded within the capitalist mode of production – indeed, it can be considered its 'highest' expression.

And yet this highest expression of *capitalism* represents a possible transitional form to a *future* society. This suggests that, for Marx, the transitional formation that leads to socialism is nothing other than *capitalism*. He contends,

> This is the abolition of the capitalist mode of production within the capitalist mode of production itself, and hence a self-abolishing contradiction, which presents itself *prima facie* as a mere point of transition to a new form of production. It presents itself as such a contradiction even in appearance. It gives rise to monopoly in certain spheres and hence provokes state intervention. It reproduces a new financial aristocracy, a new kind of parasite in the guise of company promoters, speculators, and merely nominal directors; an entire system of swindling and cheating with respect to the promotion of companies, issues of shares and share dealings. It is private production unchecked by private ownership.[109]

Marx's discussion of the 'swindling' and 'cheating' that characterise the mega-firm indicates that he is by no means embracing it as a liberatory form. Nor does he view in a positive light the tendency of these mega-firms to 'provoke state-intervention' in the economy, since he says that that produces a parasitic financial aristocracy.

Still less does he contend that the joint-stock company represents a form of socialised *production*. He explicitly refers to it as '*private* production unchecked by private ownership'. Precisely because no single individual or unit of capital has complete ownership of the mega-firm, the latter *extends* rather than mitigates the central problem of capitalism – the separation of the producers from the conditions of production.

As Marx shows at the end of Volume I of *Capital*, the distinguishing mark of *capitalist* private property is not that private individuals own property. Non-capitalist producers also own property, but it is often *destroyed* by capitalist private property. The distinguishing mark of capitalist private property is that it rests upon the dispossession of the labourer. This is why Marx holds that private ownership can be eliminated without eliminating private production. He makes this explicit by writing that the joint-stock system 'is an abolition of capitalist private industry on the basis of the capitalist system itself'.[110] Nevertheless, the separation of the enterprise from the control of private capitalists creates a material condition on the basis of which the workers could

---

109. Marx 1981a, p. 569.
110. Marx 1981a, p. 570.

eventually create genuinely socialised relations – once, that is, they manage to strip the cooperative content of labour from its despotic form by achieving an 'organic revolution in the mode of production'.

This leads Marx into a direct discussion of what *can* produce such a transition from the old society to the new one – worker-owned and managed cooperatives. On the one hand, Marx was very interested in workers' cooperatives and did not downplay their importance, including when undertaken by such utopian socialists as Fourier and Owen. On the other hand, he was very critical of socialists who disparaged such efforts, like Saint-Simon.[111] Marx writes of workers' cooperatives,

> The cooperative factories run by workers themselves are, within the old form, the first examples of the emergence of a new form, even though they naturally reproduce in all cases, in their present organization, all the defects of the existing system, and must reproduce them. But the opposition between capital and labour is abolished here, even if at first only in the form that the workers in association become their own capitalist, i.e., they use the means of production to valorize their own labour. These factories show how, at a certain stage of development of the material forces of production, and of the social forms of production corresponding to them, a new mode of production develops and is formed naturally out of the old. Without the factory system that arises from the capitalist mode of production, cooperative factories could not develop.[112]

There is much to be said of this passage. First, Marx avers explicitly that workers' cooperatives represent a new *form* of production. He does not say that of the joint-stock company, which he sees as the highest expression of *capitalist* production. The fact that the latter does away with private ownership does not change that one iota. This is an important consideration, since it was already misunderstood by many socialists of the time (as well as afterwards) who held that the credit-system would enable capitalism to naturally evolve directly into socialism.[113]

---

111. See Marx 1981a, p. 740: 'All his earlier writings are in fact simply a glorification of modern bourgeois society against feudal society, or of the industrialists and bankers against the marshals and law-mongers of the Napoleonic era. How different from the contemporary writings of Owen!'

112. Marx 1981a, p. 571.

113. This was one of the central issues in the dispute between Rosa Luxemburg and Eduard Bernstein, who held such an evolutionary position based upon stressing the growing importance of large-scale credit and centralisation of capital. This debate consumed the German Social-Democratic movement in 1898–9 and afterwards. See Luxemburg 2004.

Second, Marx holds that workers' cooperatives represent a new form of production insofar as they overcome the opposition between capital and labour, at least initially and provisionally. This is because 'In the case of the cooperative factory, the antithetical character of the supervisory work disappears, since the manager is paid by the workers instead of representing capital in opposition to them'.[114]

Third, despite the importance of these cooperatives in foreshadowing the future, they are limited by the fact that the 'workers in association become their own capitalist' insofar as the collectively-owned and managed enterprise remains subject to value-production. They still 'valorise their own labour'. Marx does not go on to explain exactly *how* they valorise their own labour, but he appears to be suggesting that since these cooperatives exist as islands in a capitalist ocean they cannot avoid operating in accordance with the law of value. In this sense, they still remain within capitalism, even as they contain social relations that point to its possible transcendence.[115]

It may seem that workers who take over a productive enterprise and run it as their own cooperative have freed themselves from the capital-relation, and, in one sense, they have. They have certainly eliminated the need for the capitalist. As Marx puts it, 'the capitalist vanishes from the production process as someone superfluous'.[116] At the same time, Marx repeatedly criticises the socialists of his time for 'wanting capital without the capitalist'.[117] While the workers who take over the productive enterprise may free themselves from the need to subject themselves to a capitalist, that does not necessarily mean that they have freed themselves from the social power of capital. Workers' cooperatives that exist in a context in which exchange-value continues to govern the production and circulation of commodities eventually discover that they have less freedom and control than may at first appear. For while there is no longer a particular capitalist within the enterprise to tell them what to do, the system of value-production informs or governs their decisions as to what to produce, how much to produce, how fast to produce, and in what form to produce. The more social cooperatives continue to operate as islands within a sea of value-production, the less *real* social power the workers actually have as they find themselves subject to an autonomous force of value-production.

---

114. Marx 1981a, p. 512.

115. Needless to say, this would characterise not only a *particular* cooperative that is surrounded by a sea of capitalism, but also even large-scale *networks* of cooperatives that failed to be supplemented by a systemic transformation of capitalist production on an international as well as national level. Whether such cooperatives can *inspire* such a transformation remains an important, and open, question.

116. Marx 1981a, p. 511.

117. Marx 1986a, p. 229.

This does not prevent, however, worker-owned cooperatives from constituting a transitional form to socialism – any more than the fact that the joint-stock company is firmly rooted in capitalism prevents it from constituting a possible transitional form to a new society. *That is because capitalism, for Marx, is itself the transitional form for a socialist reorganisation of social relations.* Marx writes, 'Capitalist joint-stock companies as much as cooperative factories should be viewed as transition forms from the capitalist mode of production to the associated one, simply that in the one case the opposition is abolished in a negative way, and in the other, in a positive way'.[118]

In Marx's last discussion of a new society in Volume III of *Capital*, he speaks of the kind of social relations that will directly characterise it. In one of the most explicit discussions of a socialist society anywhere in his writings, he states:

> The realm of freedom really begins only when labour determined by necessity and external expediency ends; it lies by its very nature beyond the sphere of material production proper. Just as the savage must wrestle with nature to satisfy his needs, to maintain and reproduce his life, so must civilized man, and he must do so in all forms of society and under all possible modes of production. This realm of natural necessity expands with his development, because his needs do too; but the productive forces to satisfy these expand at the same time. Freedom in this sphere, can consist only in this, that socialized man, the associated producers, govern the human metabolism with nature in a rational way, bringing it under their collective control instead of being dominated by it as a blind power; accomplishing it with the least expenditure of energy and in conditions most worthy and appropriate of their human nature. But this always remains a realm of necessity. The true realm of freedom, the development of human powers as an end in itself, begins beyond it, though it can only flourish with this realm of necessity as its basis.[119]

Thus, for Marx, the realm of freedom, begins when humanity no longer has to define itself by labouring-activity. To be sure, he is not suggesting that labour as such literally comes to an end. He explicitly states that labour exists in all forms of society and under all possible modes of production.[120] In a truly free society, however, human life-activity is no longer

---

118. Marx 1981a, p. 572.
119. Marx 1981a, pp. 958–9.
120. See Marx 1976e, p. 290.

defined by labour engaged in material production. It is not defined by external or natural necessity.[121]

According to Marx, the amount of time engaged in material production would be drastically reduced in the new society, thanks to technological innovation and the development of the forces of production. At the same time, labour, like all forms of human activity, would become *freely* associated and not subject to the autonomous power of capital that operates behind the backs of individuals.

Here is the most important determinant in Marx's concept of the new society: social relations must cease to operate independently of the self-activity of the associated individuals. Marx will oppose any power – be it the state, a social plan, or the market itself – that takes on a life of its own and utilises human powers as a mere means to its fruition and development. Marx's opposition to the inversion of subject and predicate constitutes the reason for his opposition to all forms of value-production. It is also what grounds his conception of socialism. Human power, he insists, *must* become a self-sufficient end – it must cease to serve as a means to some other end. He will project this concept even more explicitly in his last writings, which contain his most detailed discussion of the content of a postcapitalist society.

---

121. Marx's statement renders implausible the claim made by N.R. Berki, that 'In *Capital* Marx more or less completely acquiesces in the continuing – and indeed, *permanent* – superiority of nature over the human species. And correspondingly his earlier vision of "labour" as integrated species-activity, as full and free individual self-realization, is all but completely overshadowed by a decidedly pessimistic view of labour as *eternal* toil and drudgery'. See Berki 1983, p. 134.

Chapter Four

Marx's Late Writings on Postcapitalist Society

The impact of the Paris Commune on Marx

There is no question that the Paris Commune of 1871 had an enormous impact on Marx. Although it was restricted to the city of Paris and lasted only six weeks, the Commune marked the first time in Marx's life that the working class seized hold of a major urban area and attempted to reorganise social relations in a revolutionary direction. Although he was living in London at the time, Marx was in close contact with events on the ground, thanks to his network of correspondents and his role in the International Workingmen's Association, or First International.[1] In addition, he made an important study of the Commune in his pamphlet *The Civil War in France*.

Marx was deeply impressed with the liberatory content of the Commune. In the matter of a few weeks, the populace of Paris put an end to the Second Empire of Louis Napoleon by eliminating the standing army; stripped the police-force of its political powers; established the separation of church and state; organised the production and distribution of foodstuffs and other goods through deliberative bodies of workers; and arranged for municipal officials to be democratically elected and subject to

---

1. Marx composed *The Civil War in France* as an address of the General Council of the International Workingmen's Association (also known as the 'First International').

immediate recall. It placed 'the whole initiative hitherto exercised by the State...into the hands of the Commune'. It compelled the 'old centralised government' to 'give way to the self-government of the producers'.[2] All of this was achieved without a single party or political tendency monopolising power.[3] For these reasons, Marx considered the Commune to be 'a thoroughly expansive political form, while all previous forms of government had been thoroughly repressive'. He viewed it as 'the political form at last discovered under which to work out the economical emancipation of labour'.[4]

To get a sense of how far the Commune changed Marx's perspectives on revolution, recall that in the *Communist Manifesto* he had written, 'The proletariat will use its political supremacy to wrest, by degrees, all capital from the bourgeoisie, to centralize all instruments of production in the hands of the State, i.e., of the proletariat organised as the ruling class; and to increase the total productive forces as rapidly as possible'.[5] In contrast, in *The Civil War in France* he writes, 'But the working class cannot simply lay hold of the ready-made State machinery and wield it for its own purposes'.[6] His first draft of the address notes that earlier revolutions were 'forced to develop, what absolute monarchy had commenced, the centralization and organization of state power, and to expand the circumference and the attributes of the state power'.[7] He adds, 'All revolutions thus only perfected the state machinery instead of throwing off this deadening incubus.'[8] The Paris Commune, in contrast, sought to *dismantle* the machinery of the state through decentralised, democratic control of society by the freely-associated populace:

> This was, therefore, a Revolution not against this or that, legitimate, constitutional, republican, or Imperialist form of State Power. It was a Revolution against the *State* itself, this supernaturalist abortion of society, a resumption by the people for the people, of its own social life. It was not a revolution to transfer it from one fraction of the ruling classes to the other, but a Revolution to break down this horrid machinery of class domination itself.[9]

---

2. Marx 1986c, p. 332.
3. Numerous clubs, organisations, and political parties participated in the Commune. The most predominant political tendency was the Proudhonists. Marx's own followers represented a relatively small minority among the Communards.
4. Marx 1986a, p. 334.
5. Marx and Engels 1976b, p. 504.
6. Marx 1986c, p. 328.
7. Marx 1986b, p. 484.
8. Ibid.
9. Marx 1986b, p. 486.

All of this marks a distinct departure from the view of the state expressed in the *Manifesto*. The Paris Commune led Marx to conclude, more explicitly than ever before, that the state is not a neutral instrument that could be *used* to 'wrest' power from the oppressors. *Its very form is despotic*. In recognising this, the Communards did not aspire to *centralise* power into the hands of a state of their own.[10] Instead, they aimed for 'the destruction of the State power which claimed to be the embodiment of that unity independent of, and superior to, the nation itself, from which it was but a parasitic excrescence'.[11]

Far from being a neutral instrument, the state is a disfiguring outgrowth of society. Society gives birth to this monstrosity, which takes on a life of its own and operates behind its back. 'The centralized state machinery...entoils (inmeshes) the living civil society like a boa constrictor'.[12] A *social* revolution aims to reverse this reversal: 'The Communal Constitution would have restored to the social body all the forces hitherto absorbed by the State parasite feeding upon, and clogging the free movement of, society'.[13] The Paris Commune is therefore not a new form of the state. Instead, 'this new Commune...breaks the modern State power'.[14] It aspires to 'the reabsorption of the State power by society'.[15]

The Paris Commune was unlike anything that had emerged in previous revolutions. Marx generalises its experience by contending that it discloses the proper political form that can enable revolutions to break free from the despotism of capital: 'The Commune was therefore to serve as a lever for uprooting the economical foundations upon which rests the existence of classes, and therefore of class rule'.[16] Since the new society consists of freely-associated producers planning and allocating social wealth, it must be created by means of such a free association. The vision is fundamentally democratic. 'Such is the *Commune – the political form of the social emancipation*, of the liberation of labour from the usurpation of the (slaveholding) monopolies of the means of labour'.[17]

---

10. Marx praises the Commune for centralising legislative and executive functions in the hands of its self-governing popular assemblies, but this is quite different from centralising these branches of government into a single agency of the *state*. One of the most outstanding achievements of the Commune was its degree of the *decentralisation* of power.

11. Marx 1986c, p. 332.

12. Marx 1986b, p. 483.

13. Marx 1986c, p. 333.

14. Ibid.

15. Marx 1986b, p. 487.

16. Marx 1986c, p. 334.

17. Marx 1986b, p. 490.

This stands at quite a distance from the view of the state as the principal instrument of revolutionary transformation, which tended to dominate efforts at social transformation in the twentieth century. The Commune was a cooperative form of administration that was not weighed down by being dominated by one political party or tendency, centralised or otherwise. Yet it managed to institute a series of wide-ranging transformations in social relations that have attracted the imagination of people around the world ever since.[18] Marx now conceives of an association of freely-associated cooperatives as the most effective form for making a transition to a new society.[19]

The Commune was the political *lever* or *form* for the transformation of the despotic relations of capital, but it did not yet *constitute* the transcendence of capital – nor could it in the mere six weeks of its existence. Marx never claimed that Paris was a socialist society under the Commune. It rather marked the self-government of the producers on a *municipal* scale. It could only have constituted a transitional form to socialism had it been allowed to survive and spread. As Marx notes in his comments on cooperatives in Volume III of *Capital*, a liberatory form that exists within a capitalist context can still represent, taken together with other factors, the transition to a new society, so long as a number of historical conditions are present.

Marx himself notes, 'The working class did not expect miracles from the Commune. They have no ready-made utopias to introduce *par décret du peuple*'.[20]

> They know that in order to work out their own emancipation, and along with it that higher form to which present society is irresistibly tending by its economical agencies, they will have to pass through long struggles, through a series of historic processes, transforming circumstances and men. They have no ideas to realise, but to set free the elements of the new society with which the old collapsing bourgeois society itself is pregnant.[21]

Note that Marx does not say that the formation of specific social structures will by themselves produce the liberated individual; instead, he says that the transformation of individuals, through long and difficult struggles, is

---

18. Among these were the dramatic changes it began to introduce in gender-relations. For more on this, see Thomas 2007.

19. As one recent study puts it, 'Therefore, when Marx criticized Bakunin, he did it not as an authoritarian. Rather, he took the antimony that Proudhon pointed out much more seriously than Bakunin did. What is more, Marx praised the Paris Commune, carried out mainly by Proudhonists, in which he found the vision of "possible communism"...Marx also speculated that an "association of associations" would replace the capitalist nation-state'. See Karatani 2003, p. 178.

20. Marx 1986c, p. 334.

21. Marx 1986c, p. 335.

needed in order to effectively form social institutions that can realise their social potential. While the seeds of the new society are contained in the old one, people must transform themselves through a long and arduous series of revolutionary struggles in order to bring them to fruition.

At several points, Marx emphasises not only the achievements but also the limitations of the Commune – of which, he contends, the Communards were fully aware:

> They know that the superseding of the economical conditions of the slavery of labour by the conditions of free and associated labour can only be the progressive work of time, (that economical transformation) that they require not only for a change of distribution, but a new organization of production, or rather the delivery (setting free) of the social forms of production in present organised labour (engendered by present industry) of the trammels of slavery, of their present class character, and their harmonious national and international coordination.[22]

Marx does not hesitate to emphasise how laborious the process of creating a new society is, since it depends not only upon national, but international cooperation, as well as transforming not only the relations of distribution, but also those of production. Marx was outraged by the bloody suppression of the Commune by the forces of reaction. Yet, not long afterwards, he became even more disappointed at the realisation that even his own followers had failed to learn its lessons. Nowhere is the depth of Marx's dissatisfaction expressed more sharply than in his work composed four years after the Commune's defeat, the *Critique of the Gotha Programme*.

The *Critique of the Gotha Programme*

Marx's *Critique of the Gotha Programme* of 1875 contains his most sustained, detailed, and explicit discussion of a postcapitalist society. It was not written, however, as part of an effort to provide a blueprint as to the kind of society that would follow capitalism. Rather, its composition was driven by *organisational* considerations within the socialist movement. The German socialist movement comprised two tendencies in the 1860s and 1870s. One was the General Union of German Workers, whose founder was Ferdinand Lassalle. It was the first nationwide socialist organisation of the German proletariat, and its energetic and charismatic leader helped make it the largest and best-known socialist organisation in Europe, except for the International itself, of

---

22. Marx 1986b, p. 491.

which it was a part. After a period of collaboration, Lassalle and Marx had a bitter breakup in the 1860s, largely occasioned by what Marx considered Lassalle's unprincipled interest in forging alliances with sections of German officialdom in order to secure organisational legitimacy for his party and social reforms.

The other tendency of the German workers' movement were the much-smaller Eisenachers (named after the city in which they were founded), led by August Bebel and Wilhelm Liebknecht, who considered themselves Marx's followers. In 1875, the two groups entered into unity-negotiations in the city of Gotha, and formed a united organisation against Marx's wishes, based on a brief programme named after the site of the conference. This marked the birth of what later was known as the German Social-Democratic Party, which became the largest socialist organisation in European history after Marx's death.

Marx was furious when he read the Gotha Programme, which he considered to be a complete capitulation to Lassallean principles.[23] He threatened to break off relations with his German followers unless they disavowed the decisions made at the unity-congress. They refused to do so, but Marx decided not to go through with his threat and in the end chose not to make his denunciation public, in part because Bismarck had just jailed several leading Eisenachers.

There were a number of formulations in the Gotha Programme that infuriated Marx,[24] whether on the state or the class-struggle, but none more so than its brief discussion of the alternative to capitalism. Point three of the Programme stated, 'The emancipation of labour demands the raising of the means of labour to the common property of society and the collective regulation of the total labour with a fair distribution of the proceeds of labour'.[25]

---

23. Lassalle had died a decade earlier, in 1864. Although the extent of Marx's differences with Lassalle became public knowledge only decades after his death, when his correspondence began to be published, many of the Eisenachers were well aware of Marx's longstanding hostility to Lassallean conceptions and practices, among which was Lassalle's theory of 'the iron law of wages'. Many commentators on Marx have sought to minimise these differences. One exception to this can be found in Dunayevskaya 1981 and 2000.

24. Marx particularly castigates the programme's opening declaration, 'Labour is the source of all wealth'. He counters, 'Labour is *not the source* of all wealth. *Nature* is just as much the source of use values…as labour, which itself is only the manifestation of a force of nature, human labour power'. Labour is instead the source of *value*. Despite Marx's criticism, the false conflation of wealth and value has been ubiquitous in discussions of Marx's work for over a century. See Marx 1989d, p. 81.

25. Marx 1989d, p. 83.

Here, the Gotha Programme was not referring to distribution of the elements of production. Rather, it was referring to the distribution of the social product, which Marx saw as a wholly secondary and subsidiary matter. In fact, the Gotha Programme failed to refer at all to production-relations or their transformation. Instead, it focused on the 'fair' distribution of the products of labour in a new society.

Marx sharply attacks the claims, as he puts it, that in a future communist society every worker must receive his 'undiminished' Lassallean 'proceeds of labour'.[26] He denies that workers would receive an 'undiminished' share of the total social product, since a number of deductions would be needed to pay for depreciation of the means of production, the expansion of production, and for an insurance-fund against accidents. None of these factors can be calculated in advance, since they depend on an assortment of contingent conditions. Moreover, additional deductions from the now-'diminished' proceeds of labour would be needed to pay for the costs of social administration, schools and health-services, and compensation for those too old or too ill to work. These would increase 'considerably in comparison with present-day society and it grows in proportion as the new society develops'.[27] Marx thoroughly rejects the claim that workers in a new society would obtain the full equivalent of the 'value' of their labour.

Marx is clearly irritated at having to write this criticism of the Gotha Programme. As he puts it in a letter to one of the Eisenachers, Wilhelm Bracke, 'it was by no means a pleasure to write such a lengthy screed'.[28] He is not issuing his critique in order to delineate the nature of distribution in the new society; the matter is clearly of secondary interest to him. But he is deeply concerned at the implications of the Gotha Programme's focus on distribution to the exclusion of emphasising the need to transform relations of production.

For this reason, he directly addresses the form of collective ownership of the means of production in a society that *does* manage to radically transform production-relations – a matter that was not discussed in the Gotha Programme itself. He writes,

> Within the collective society based on common ownership of the means of production, the producers do not exchange their products; just as little does the labour employed on the product appear here *as the value* of these products, as a material quality possessed by them, since now, in contrast

---

26. Marx 1989d, p. 84.
27. Marx 1989d, p. 85.
28. Marx 1989d, p. 77.

to capitalist society, individual labour no longer exists in an *indirect* fashion
but *directly* as a component part of the total labour.[29]

Again, his categories of directly versus indirectly social labour are brought
to bear upon the issue of a postcapitalist society.

Marx leaves no doubt that his description of such a state of affairs represents a socialist or communist society, which to him were indistinguish-
able terms: 'What we are dealing with here is a communist society, not as it
has *developed* on its own foundations, but on the contrary, just as it *emerges*
from capitalist society, which is thus in every respect, economically, morally,
and intellectually, still stamped with the birth-marks of the old society from
whose womb it emerges'.[30]

This represents the first time in any of his writings that Marx explicitly
refers to two 'phases' of a new society. These are not two distinct *stages* that
are respectively termed 'socialism' and 'communism'. For Marx, the terms
'socialism' and 'communism' – along with 'free association', 'society of free
individuality', or simply 'the new society' – are completely interchangeable.[31]
The later notion that 'socialism' and 'communism' represent distinct stages of
social development – a staple of Stalinist dogma – was alien to Marx's thought
and only entered the lexicon of 'Marxism' after his death.

To see why Marx contends that neither value-production nor the exchange
of products characterises the initial phase of socialism or communism, it is
necessary to closely examine his statement that individual labour exists as a
direct component part of the sum of social labour in a new society. The total
sum of labour can be treated as an aggregate, just like the amount of labour
performed by an individual can be treated as a discrete unit. In the capitalist
mode of production, individual labour exists *indirectly* as a part of the sum
of total labour, since the only labour that counts is that which corresponds to
the average amount of time socially necessary to create a product. Individual
labour that fails to conform to that average is socially useless and expend-
able. It does not *directly* figure into the aggregate. This situation prevails so
long as actual labour-time is subsumed by socially-necessary labour-time.
Individual labour can exist or count only *indirectly* 'as a component part of
the total labour' so long as capitalist relations of production and distribution
are maintained.

With socialism or communism, on the other hand, the disregard of actual
labour-time in favour of socially-necessary labour-time is abolished. The

---

29. Marx 1989d, p. 85.
30. Ibid.
31. For more on this, see Chattopadhyay 2010.

exertion of concrete acts of labour in producing use-values, performed by freely-associated individuals, becomes the one and only expression of living labour. No longer does a force operate behind the backs of the producers – socially-necessary labour-time – that renders their individual activity useless or unproductive if it fails to meet an abstract standard. The dominance of time as an abstract standard is shattered through the formation of *freely*-associated production-relations, in which the producers organise the manner, form, and content of their activity on basis of their actual capabilities. The *replacement of the dictatorship of abstract time with time as the space for human development serves as the basis for a new kind of labour – directly social labour*. With this momentous transformation, the split between abstract and concrete labour is healed. With the elimination of the dual character of labour, the substance of value – abstract labour – drops out of existence. As a result, value-production itself ceases to exist. Therefore, the 'labour employed on the products' therefore no longer appears in the form of 'the value of these products'.

With the abolition of the conditions of value-production, value's form of appearance – exchange-value – likewise ceases to exist. Value *must* take on a form of appearance distinct from itself, as exchange-value; but *exchange-value can only be the appearance of something if there is something to appear*. Exchange-value is readily visible, but it is far more difficult, as *Capital* shows, to 'track down' the value immanent in it. So difficult is it to discern value independent of its manifestations that it appears to be a property of the physicality of things, instead of the peculiar social form of labour in capitalism. Yet, with the abolition of this peculiar social form, the conditions for the possibility of both value and exchange-value cease to exist. Labour now becomes directly social on a free basis, instead of indirectly social, as in capitalism.

However, if value and exchange-value cease to exist, how is the mutual and universal exchangeability of products of labour possible? As we have seen, products of labour, as well as labour-power, can be rendered mutually-exchangeable only if there is an abstract denominator or principle of *equality* that makes such exchangeability possible. The universal exchange of discrete products requires a commensurate quality or substance: 'There can be no exchange without equality, and no equality without commensurability', as noted over two thousand years ago by Aristotle.[32] This equal quality is value, and abstract labour is its substance. But the production-relations of a socialist or communist society eliminate abstract labour. The actions and predispositions of individuals are no longer subject to an abstract average that operates regardless of them. With this transformation, which involves the abolition of

---

32. Aristotle 2002, p. 90 [1133b16–19].

alienated labour, value-production comes to an end. How is it possible, then, for products of labour to be mutually-exchangeable in such a society? *The answer is that they can not be mutually exchangeable*. This is why Marx writes that, even in the initial phase of a socialist or communist society, 'the producers do not exchange their products'.

This indicates that a socialist or communist society, as Marx envisages it, eliminates the possibility of a market in which products of labour are mutually and universally exchanged. A commodity-market cannot exist if there is no substance that renders different magnitudes qualitatively equal. Once the breach between abstract and concrete labour is healed, the substance of value is annulled, and with it, the market itself.

Does this mean that markets in *any* possible sense of the word cannot exist in a new society? Marx does not directly address the question. However, given the logic of his argument, it does not necessarily follow that the answer is in the affirmative. First, as Marx often notes, markets existed long before capitalism. The mere existence of some form of market, at least in a limited and subsidiary sense, is not therefore *ipso facto* evidence of capitalist relations of production. Second, the object of Marx's critique of capitalism is not the market; it is the relations of production and the distribution of the conditions of production. Third, in the *Critique of the Gotha Programme*, Marx is responding to what he considers the erroneous theoretical statements in a programme of a political party. He does not intend for his critique to be read as a detailed blueprint that accounts for any and all possible conditions and institutions of a postcapitalist society.

This much is clear: a *generalised* commodity- or labour-market, in which products of labour are mutually interchangeable, cannot exist if the substance of value, abstract labour, ceases to exist. A society cannot be characterised or dominated by market-transactions or a market of any kind if the conditions for its possibility are not present. And the condition of possibility for a market is the existence of indirectly social labour – a condition that is annulled in the new society. It is one thing, however, for a *generalised* commodity-market to exist, and quite another for far-more restricted markets to persist (especially temporarily) in a completely *subordinate* and *subsidiary* role in comparison to a society's governing social relations.

A few years before the *Critique of the Gotha Programme*, Marx wrote in *The Civil War in France*:

> If cooperative production is not to remain a sham and a snare; if it is
> to supersede the capitalist system; if united cooperative societies are to
> regulate national production upon a common plan, thus taking it under
> their own control, and putting an end to the constant anarchy and periodical

convulsions which are the fatality of capitalist production – what else, gentlemen, would it be but Communism, 'possible' Communism?[33]

For cooperative production not to be 'a sham and a snare', it has to be under the control of the workers themselves. But what does he mean by *control*? Surely, Marx is referring to effective as well as formal control. And the workers would not have effective control of their cooperative production if an independent pricing mechanism acted in disregard of their collective deliberations by dictating the manner, form, and nature of their labouring activity. Marx's conception of socialism is fundamentally *democratic*, and to be meaningful, such a democracy must exist on the economic as well as the political level. Throughout his writings, Marx never wavers from his emphasis on the need for the producers to have power and control over the process of forming the social product. He is conceiving of a new society in which the products of human activity can no longer take on an autonomous power independent of the producers. He opposes the existence of a market insofar as its existence implies the existence of such an autonomous force.

As Marx repeatedly stresses, the process of creating a society is a long and labourious one. The effort extends far beyond the moment of revolution itself. It is impractical to presume that a new society can emerge *sui generis*, without bearing the birthmarks of the society from which it emerges. At the same time, Marx wishes to emphasise that a socialist or communist society represents a qualitative *break* from the conditions and social forms that define capitalism. This two-fold concern governs his discussion through the rest of the *Critique of the Gotha Programme*.

As noted earlier, Marx explicitly states that his discussion thus far is of 'a communist society, not as it has developed on its own foundations, but on the contrary, just as it emerges from capitalist society', and is 'still stamped with the birth-marks of the old society from whom womb it emerges'. So how would workers be remunerated in the lower phase of a new society? Since, for Marx, a radical break occurs between capitalism and even the most initial phase of socialism or communism, it is crucial that the defining characteristics of capitalism be eliminated from the outset. And one of the most defining characteristics of capitalism, for Marx, is wage-labour. He makes it clear that there is no place for it in the initial phase of a new society by spelling out an alternative form of remuneration. This form is as follows: each individual *gives to* society 'his individual quantum of labour', which is measured in 'the sum of hours of work'. The 'individual labour-time of the individual' represents the individual's share in society, and the individual receives back from

---

society a corresponding amount of means of subsistence. 'The individual producer receives back from society – after the deductions have been made – exactly what he gives to it. What he has given to it is his individual quantum of labour'.[34] Individuals receive from society a voucher or token that they have 'furnished such and such an amount of labour (after deducting his labour for the common funds)' and from it obtains from 'the social stock of means of consumption as much as the amount of labour costs'.[35] Remuneration is based on an 'equal standard' – the *actual amount* of labour-time performed by the freely-associated individuals.

Marx is *not* saying that the worker's labour is computed on the basis of a social *average* of labour-time. Here, labour-time simply refers to the amount of actual hours of work performed by the individual. Remuneration is based on 'the individual labour time of the individual producer'. This is completely different from capitalism, where remuneration is based on *socially-necessary* labour-time. As Marx puts it, 'The same *amount* of labour which he has given to society in one form he receives back in another'.[36] This also would include kinds of work that are not valued under capitalism, such as women's domestic labour, child-rearing, and pre-school education.

Marx states, 'Here obviously the same principle prevails as that which regulates the exchange of commodities, as far as this is the exchange of equal values'. He is referring to values in the *generic* sense of an exchange of equal *quantities*, of equal sums of actual (concrete) labour-time. Yet the 'content and form' of this exchange are radically distinct compared with what occurs in capitalism, since 'nothing can pass to the ownership of individuals except individual means of consumption'.[37]

Why does he compare remuneration by labour-time to the 'principle' of commodity-exchange? Simply because there is an exchange of two items of equal worth: one hour of actual labour is exchanged for goods or services produced in the same amount of time, just two commodities are exchanged on the basis of an equality between them. However, the exchange of labour-time for goods and services in the initial phase of a new society is radically different in form and content from capitalist commodity-relations, since the former is based on the equality of concrete magnitudes posited by the producers – not on an abstract average that operates independently of them.

It is important to emphasise that Marx is not suggesting that remuneration in this lower phase of socialism or communism is based on the level of

---

34. Marx 1989d, p. 86.
35. Ibid.
36. Ibid. My emphasis.
37. Ibid.

productive output by the labourer. Rather, it is based on 'the natural measure of labour'[38] – *time*, the actual number of hours performed by the individual. The difference between labour and labour-time is a critical analytical distinction, and conflating the two readily leads to misconstruing Marx's position. He is not suggesting that the operative principle of the lower phase of socialism or communism is 'from each according to their ability, to each according to their work'. No such formulation appears either in the *Critique* or in any of Marx's work. Yet it became the widespread interpretation of Marx in the statist-'communist' régimes of the twentieth century. As János Kornai writes,

> Under classical socialism the principle of socialist distribution stated in every textbook is, 'To each according to his work'. But the question remains of how performance can be measured and what the income proportionate with the performance should be. To an extent the principle 'distribution according to work' applies under capitalism as well, at least in the case of earned income. There performance is measured and rewards are set mainly (but not exclusively) by an anonymous, decentralized process: the labour market, on which the relative wages emerge. Whereas in a classical socialist economy the question of what income is due for what quantity and type of work is decided arbitrarily by persons appointed to do so.[39]

Kornai is correct that 'distribution according to work' became the justification by which the centralised command-economies in the USSR, Eastern Europe and China imposed draconian social control upon the workforce. Far from representing a form of the 'new' society, it became an administrative formula for getting the workers to produce under degrading conditions for the sake of 'catching up with the West'. He is also correct that 'distribution according to work' is not at odds with the principle by which *capitalism* operates.

Kornai fails to notice, however, that Marx was fully aware of this, *which is why no such formulation or conception enters his own discussion of a postcapitalist society*.[40] Marx is not concerned with the form by which the worker is compelled to provide greater and greater amounts of work for the controlling agents of society. He is not concerned with whether the mechanism that

---

38. Engels used this phrase in his *Anti-Dühring* in explaining why distribution according to actual time worked in a new society does not imply value-production. See Engels 1987, p. 288. The book was written shortly after Marx composed the *Critique of the Gotha Programme*, and Marx was very familiar with its content.

39. Kornai 1992, p. 324.

40. Although Kornai quotes from the *Critique of the Gotha Programme*, he neglects to mention Marx's all-important concept of remuneration based on labour-time. It is ironic that many critics of 'actually-existing socialism' fail to take issue with its central ideological premise – namely, the claim that it operated according to principles laid down by Marx.

compels the workers to produce more than they consume is accomplished through the arbitrary vehicle of the market or through the equally arbitrary whims of government-officials. Both forms 'reward' labourers based on their productive output; they are made to produce more and more within a unit of time in accordance with the average amount of time that it takes to produce the product on the world-market. In this sense, both forms rest upon the existence of wage-labour, which is inseparable from the despotic plan of capital.

In direct contrast, Marx's concept of socialism or communism is premised upon the abolition of wage-labour and of capital and value-production, as seen from his discussion of remuneration by labour-time in the *Critique of the Gotha Programme*. The worker receives an amount of means of subsistence based on the unit of *time* worked, not on the amount of productive output within that unit. Labour-time is a varying and contingent standard, based on a given hour of actual labour performed by the individual in specific circumstances. The workers are not 'paid' according to whether or not their *labour* conforms to some invariable standard over which they have no control. The latter, distribution according to labour, is entirely consistent with value-production, whereas the former, distribution according to actual labour-time, represents a break from value-production altogether.

Yet if this is the case, why does Marx write in the *Critique*, 'Labour, to serve as measure, must be defined by its duration or intensity'?[41] Does this imply 'distribution according to work'? At issue is what Marx means by 'intensity'. Many have assumed that Marx is referring to how much is produced in a given unit of time (for instance, one worker who makes three shoes an hour would receive less goods from the common storehouse than another who makes six shoes an hour. And one who makes twelve shoes an hour would 'earn' more than both). In this scenario, workers are not being remunerated for their labour-time but for their labour-output. This would mean that the governing principle of such a society would be 'from each according to their ability, to each according to their work'.

Yet if this were the case, it is hard to see how the lower phase of socialism or communism would be significantly different from what prevails under capitalism, *even if the workers had political control over the economic process*. As in capitalism, their performance would be measured by the intensity of labour, as reflected in the wage-relation. Hence, 'the workers in association [would] become their own capitalist, i.e. they use the means of production to valorize their own labour'.[42] So why does Marx state that 'labour, to serve as a measure,

---

41. Marx 1989d, p. 86.
42. Marx 1981a, p. 740.

must be defined by its intensity or duration'? I would suggest that the answer is that by *intensity* Marx is not referring to the quantity of output within a given unit of time. Rather, he is referring to the output of *energy* in a given unit of time. For instance, a teacher of autistic children may expend more energy in four hours of instruction than someone who spends the same amount of time teaching non-autistic children. Should not the former be compensated for the intensity of their labour? The added intensity can be taken into account without violating the principle of remuneration according to labour-time *so long as the output of energy, and not the output of the quantity of the product, is taken as the determining factor.*[43] In this scenario, the society of freely-associated producers would need to determine if a particular kind of labour requires more energy or intensity than another, and if so, how much it should be quantified in terms of actual labour-time. Such a determination could involve a good deal of discussion and debate. But there would be no value-production, since production would not occur in accordance with an abstract average that operates behind the backs of the producers. On these grounds, the claim that Marx's discussion of 'intensity or duration' implies 'distribution according to work' becomes eminently implausible.

Marx's discussion in the *Critique of the Gotha* Programme is his most detailed discussion of a postcapitalist society, but it is entirely consistent with his previous writings on the issue in the drafts of *Capital* as well as in its published versions.

His critique of Proudhonian proposals for utilising time-chits or labour-vouchers in *The Poverty of Philosophy* and the *Grundrisse* is based on the conflation of actual labour-time with socially-necessary labour-time. He rejects such proposals because they are premised upon the *existing* system of commodity-production. Exchange-relations cannot be rendered transparent or rational by being grafted onto a system of commodity-production that is itself irrational and mystified. Marx's sharp critique of his followers in 1875 for accepting the Lassallean notion that workers can obtain the full value of their product carries forth the critique he had earlier made of the Proudhonists for presuming that an 'equitable' distribution of the products of labour is consistent with value-production.

---

43. It may seem perverse to refer to 'quantity of output' when it comes to something like teaching, but this is precisely the direction in which the US educational system is going, as seen in the heightened emphasis on standardised testing. Students are increasingly treated as commodities, and the greater the quantitative output of students with high grades, the better the chance a teacher has of earning greater remuneration through promotion. Needless to say, all this is completely adequate to the concept of capital.

Marx's *Critique of the Gotha Programme* is also remarkably consistent with his comments about the new society in the first chapter of Volume I of *Capital*. This is especially seen from his statement in the *Critique*, 'Here obviously the same principle prevails as that which regulates the exchange of commodities....' Marx is restating his formulation at the end of Chapter One of Volume I of *Capital*, which stated, 'We shall assume, but only for the sake of a parallel with the production of commodities, that the share of each individual producer in the means of subsistence is determined by his labour time'.[44] In neither case is Marx suggesting that value-production prevails under 'socialism'. A fundamentally different content and form are operative in the new society, but they can be *compared* to the exchange of commodities insofar as an exchange of equal determinants occurs in both cases. What makes the two radically distinct is that in the new society the exchange of labour-time for social products is transparent, whereas in the old society it is not. And it is not transparent in the old society because labour is indirectly social. This is of cardinal importance, for it signifies that production-relations in the new society have become radically transformed.[45]

Marx's discussion in the *Critique of the Gotha Programme* is also consistent with his earlier discussions throughout the three volumes of *Capital*. These works emphasise the difference between actual labour-time and socially-necessary labour-time. These works state that remuneration in the society will at least initially be based on the labour-time of the individual, not on labour-output that is governed by an abstraction. Neither indicates that exchange-value or value exists in the new society. Moreover, Volume II of *Capital* explicitly endorses remuneration based on labour-tickets or vouchers along basically the same lines as the 1875 *Critique*. Volume II also states that money ceases to be the medium of social interaction in the new society and that the vouchers do not circulate, that is, they do not augment value.

There is, however, an important difference between the *Critique of the Gotha Programme* and these earlier writings, in that the *Critique* suggests for the first time that the postcapitalist relations under discussion thus far in Marx's work

---

44. Marx 1976e, p. 172.
45. Although a considerable amount of critical commentary has appeared on Marx's *Critique of the Gotha Programme*, almost none of it discusses his concept of the replacement of indirect social labour by direct social labour. This is true of Berki 1983, pp. 150–61, Hollander 2008, pp. 386–7, and Campbell 1996, pp. 206–8. The neglect of Marx's concept of direct versus indirect social labour also characterises many of those who have attempted to appropriate Marx's 1875 *Critique* for conceptualising a postcapitalist society. See especially Neurath 2005.

had pertained to the *initial* phase of the new society, which still is *defective* from the vantage-point of what eventually follows it.[46]

The initial phase of socialism or communism is defective for a number of reasons. Some degree of social inequality would exist, since some individuals would work more hours than others and would therefore obtain a larger amount of the means of consumption. Likewise, an individual who produces more in a given hour than another would not receive greater remuneration than one who labours for the same amount of time. Since 'one man is superior to another physically or mentally and so supplies more labour in the same time, or can work for a longer period of time',[47] the levels of remuneration would be unequal. Most important of all, remuneration takes into consideration 'a certain side only' of individuals – their contribution in terms of labour-time – 'everything else being ignored'.[48] Since labour-time – albeit in the radically-altered form of actual and not average labour-time – governs the distribution of the elements of production, social existence is still based on natural necessity. Marx therefore writes, 'Hence, *equal right* here is still in principle – bourgeois right, although principle and practice are no longer at loggerheads, while the exchange of equivalents in commodity exchange only exists *on the average* and not in the individual case'.[49] He introduces an important note of caution here, however: 'But these defects are inevitable in the first phase of communist society as it is when it has just emerged from capitalist society. Right can never be higher than the economic structure and its cultural development which this determines'.[50]

As Marx states in Volume III of *Capital*, 'The realm of freedom really begins only when labour determined by necessity and external expediency ends; it lies by its very nature beyond the sphere of material production proper'.[51] *True*

---

46. One exception to this is Marx's discussion of the 'realm of freedom' at the end of Volume III of *Capital*. 'The true realm of freedom, the development of human powers as an end in itself', resonates with Marx's 1875 discussion of a higher phase of communism.

47. Marx 1989d, p. 86.

48. Marx 1989d, p. 87. Marx is *not* suggesting by this that the only 'side' of individuals that matters in the lower phase of socialism or communism is their contribution in terms of labour-time. He is suggesting that this is all that matters when it comes to deciding upon how they are *remunerated*. Remuneration, as a factor of distribution, is a secondary and subsidiary issue for Marx. He is therefore not suggesting that what governs remuneration defines all social relations. In Marx's view, a socialist or communist society considers individuals from *many* sides. Their role as labourers is not the only, or even the most important aspect. It is capitalism, not socialism, that views individuals only in terms of their level of productive output.

49. Marx 1989d, p. 86.

50. Marx 1989d, p. 87.

51. Marx 1981a, pp. 958–9.

freedom represents a *higher* phase in which society is no longer *measured* by labour-time or *defined* by material production. This higher phase is 'the development of human power as an end in itself'.[52] At that point, 'a certain side' of the individual will no longer determine the *distribution* of the elements of production. Production and distribution, like social relations as a whole, would instead be based on the *totality* of the individual's needs and capacities.

Marx discusses the radically different distributive principle that governs a higher phase of communism[53] as follows: 'From each according to their abilities, to each according to their needs!' This represents a significant development as compared with the lower phase, since distribution no longer operates on the basis of an exchange of equivalents. The lower phase represents a radical departure from commodity-production, since there is an exchange of concrete, sensuous equivalents – so many hours of labour in exchange for so many goods and services produced in that amount of actual time. *But no such exchange occurs in a higher phase of socialism or communism.* 'From each according to their abilities, to each according to their needs' is not a *quid pro quo*. It is not as if one's needs are met only to the extent that they correspond to the expression of a given set of abilities. If such a principle prevailed, human relations would still be governed by natural necessity and external expediency. Society would remain governed by material production. But the *true* realm of freedom lies beyond all of this.

Moreover, a higher phase of communism is distinguished from the lower phase in that labour-time no longer serves as a measure. Even in the lower phase, of course, labour-time does not exist as a measure in the same way as socially-necessary labour-time does in capitalism. As Plato once famously noted, 'nothing that is imperfect is the measure of anything'.[54] Socially-necessary labour-time is a 'perfect' standard or measure, since even though its magnitude is constantly shifting and changing, it confronts the producers as a fixed form in the market that is not beholden to their particular needs and desires. Actual labour-time, on the other hand, is a very different kind of measure. It is *imperfect* since is it calculated on the basis of the varied and changing actions of discrete individuals. It does not confront the producers as a fixed form that is not beholden to their particular needs and desires.

---

52. Marx 1981a, p. 959.

53. As Chattopadhyay 2010 points out, Marx refers to *a* higher phase, not *the* higher phase. He also never refers to this higher phrase as an *ultimate* or *conclusive* stage. As I see it, this is consistent with Marx's earlier formulation from 1844 that 'communism as such is not the goal of human development, the form of human society'. Marx does not appear to have ever endorsed the notion that there is an endpoint or culmination of human history.

54. Plato 1961, p. 739 [504c2–3].

Nevertheless, by the time we reach a higher phase of socialism or communism, actual labour-time too ceases to be a measure. There is no longer a need for labour *in any form* to serve as a standard or measure.

This does not mean that labour as such vanishes in a higher phase of socialism or communism. Marx explicitly states that in such a higher phase, labour would no longer be 'only a means of life but life's prime want'.[55] Labour is now radically-transformed as compared with capitalism, since it serves not as a means to an end but as an end in itself. In a higher phase of socialism or communism, labour is fully inseparable from the individual's self-activity and self-development. It becomes a self-sufficient end.

It is not hard to see that Marx's vision of a higher phase of socialism or communism requires a momentous material and intellectual transformation. It certainly does not emerge overnight! Marx explicitly states that it cannot come into existence without a whole series of preconditions. These include the end of the separation between mental and manual labour; the transformation of labour from a means to an end to an end in itself; a dramatic increase of the productive forces such as to alleviate the possibility of poverty and want; and 'the all-round development of the individual'. *The 'subjective' development of the individual is as important a precondition of a truly new society as such 'objective' factors as the development of the forces of production.* Marx does not specify any time-frame for these transformations. He is always cautious about getting ahead of what individuals could or could not achieve in the course of their practical history, precisely because he is wary of imposing any conceptions upon individuals that are independent of their own self-activity.

This also explains the nature of his discussion of the distributive principles of lower and higher phases of a new society in the *Critique of the Gotha Programme*. He is not trying to formulate a normative model of how distribution *ought* to function in a new society. Instead, he is addressing what would occur of necessity if, and only if, a radical transformation occurred in production and human relations. Marx does not feel the need to *advocate* specific forms of distribution in a postcapitalist society, because they will arise, he contends, from the nature of the new forms of production. He insists, 'If the elements of production are so distributed, then the present-day distribution of the means of consumption results automatically. If the material conditions of production are the collective property of the workers themselves, then there

---

55. Marx 1989d, p. 87. Some translations give this passage as 'labour has become not merely a means to live but is in itself the first necessity of living'. See Marx 1933, p. 31.

likewise results a distribution of the means of consumption different from the present one'.[56]

This does not mean that Marx's discussion of the lower phase of socialism or communism is of incidental or passing importance. For Marx's discussion of the lower phase points to the specific conditions that are needed to make the principle 'From each according to their abilities, to each according to their needs' a reality. These conditions centre on the transformation of *human* relations through the abolition of indirectly social labour, wage-labour, the division between mental and manual labour and alienated man/woman relations. It is only through the transformation of these relations that it becomes possible to actualise the distributive principle of 'from each according to their abilities, to each according to their needs'. Each one of these relations arises only as a result of conscious, purposeful activity by *freely*-associated individuals. 'From each according to their ability, to each according their needs' cannot come into being through the imposition of some administrative formula. It is a product of a *free* society.

The nuances of Marx's discussion in the *Critique of the Gotha Programme* can be brought into focus by noting an important comment made by Herbert Marcuse on Marx's view of the new society. According to Marcuse, the problem of capitalism

> is to be solved by a revolution which brings the productive process under the collective control of the 'immediate producers'. But this is not freedom. Freedom is living without toil, without anxiety: the play of human faculties. The realization of freedom is a problem of *time*: reduction of the working day to the minimum which turns quantity into quality. A socialist society is a society in which free time, not labour time is the social measure of wealth and the dimension of the individual existence.[57]

Marcuse is certainly correct that for Marx the realisation of freedom centres on the problem of time. Marx repeatedly emphasises throughout his work that in a new society, time will become the space for human development. However, Marcuse also makes the questionable claim that, for Marx, the problem of time revolves solely around the reduction of the working day to an absolute minimum. Labour-time is not only a quantitative but also a qualitative determination. As can be seen from a careful reading of the *Critique of the Gotha Programme*, Marx's view is that labour-time does not

---

56. Marx 1989d, p. 88.
57. Marcuse 2000, p. xxiii.

cease to be a measure of social wealth in the lower or initial phase of socialism. This does not mean that Marx conceives of this initial phase as one in which freedom remains unrealised, since the creation of freely-associated, non-alienated labour shatters the dictatorship of time as an abstract, external, immutable entity that directs the will of the producers and consumers. Freedom defines every phase of the new society for Marx, even when that phase still operates in accordance with natural necessity, since it consists of 'free men' 'expending their many different forms of labour power in full self-awareness as one single social labour force'.[58] A society is unfree not because labour-time is a measure, but because socially-necessary labour-time is the measure. And socially-necessary time ceases to be the measure once individuals *as a social entity* freely organise social production and reproduction temporally and spatially in accordance with their natural and acquired talents and capabilities.

By failing to conceptually distinguish between actual labour-time and socially-necessary labour-time, Marcuse is led to conclude that a new society, for Marx, entails the abolition of labour *per se*.[59] As noted in Chapter One, Marx does speak of the abolition of labour in his early writings, but by that he means the abolition of *alienated* labour. Moreover, the *Critique in the Gotha Programme* explicitly states that labour exists not only in the initial phase of socialism but also in a higher phase insofar as labour becomes 'life's prime want'.[60] In a higher phase of socialism, but only in a higher phrase, labour engaged in material production ceases to be a measure of social relations. Freedom in the initial phase of socialism or communism remains defective insofar as it remains tied to the necessity of remunerating individuals based on actual labour-time. But that is a far cry from suggesting that that has anything to do with value-production.

---

58. Marx 1976e, p. 171.

59. Marcuse's position also seems to be premised upon the view that 'toil' necessarily involves 'anxiety'. This is clearly not Marx's view. As he writes in the *Grundrisse*, 'Adam Smith conceives labour to be a curse. To him, "rest" appears as the adequate state, as identical with "liberty" and "happiness"...for work to become *travail attractif*, to be the realization of the individual, in no way implies that work is pure fun, pure amusement, as in Fourier's childishly naïve conception. Really free work, e.g., the composition of music, is also the most damnably difficult, demanding the most intensive effort'. See *Grundrisse*, Marx 1986a, p. 530.

60. Marx's formulation causes considerable problems for Postone's interpretation of Marx as well, given his position that the elimination of labour as a socially-constitutive category is a pre-condition of a new society. He appears to sidestep the issue by not mentioning the *Critique of the Gotha Programme* in *Time, Labour, and Social Domination*.

'Socialism', for Marx, was never meant to serve as a transitional stage to some distant 'communist' formation. He is not pushing off the realm of freedom to some far horizon. *The realm of freedom emerges simultaneously with the elimination of capitalism.* Marx is realistic enough to understand, however, that a free society itself undergoes self-development. There would be no necessity for it to undergo further self-development if it did not contain some kind of internal defect that impels the forward movement.[61]

This is not to suggest that Marx did not conceive of a possible transitional stage *between* capitalism and the initial phase of socialism. He addresses this in the *Critique of the Gotha Programme* thusly: 'Between capitalist and communist society lies the period of the revolutionary transformation of the one into the other. Corresponding to this is also a political transition period in which the state can be nothing but *the revolutionary dictatorship of the proletariat.*'[62]

Based on the above discussion of the impact of the Paris Commune, it appears that Marx conceived of this transitional period along the lines of the non-statist and *freely-associated* form of self-governance that emerged in the Commune. Marx saw in the Commune an exemplar of the political form best-suited for exiting capitalism. It is a mediatory or transitional *political* stage in which capitalist social relations have not yet been fully overcome but which are in the process of being broken down.

For this reason, it is important to note that in the *Critique* Marx does not speak of the 'dictatorship of the proletariat' but of the *'revolutionary* dictatorship of the proletariat'.[63] He may have done so in order to distinguish his position from that of Lassalle, whom he attacked as 'a future workingmen's dictator'.[64] Marx does not advocate a 'revolutionary dictatorship' that rules *over* the proletariat through a political party; instead, he advocates *the rule of*

---

61. This would also apply, one can speculate, to that higher phase in which the totality of human sensuousness is allowed its full and free manifestation. Since intellectual and 'spiritual' growth is potentially infinite, there can be no 'end' to a society that allows for a 'totality of manifestations of life'. Perhaps this is why Marx held that 'communism as such is not the goal of human development' and why in the *Grundrisse* he speaks of an 'absolute movement of becoming'. Marx never explicitly addresses this issue in terms of a higher phase outlined in the *Critique of the Gotha Programme.*

62. Marx 1989d, p. 95. In his discussion of the *Critique of the Gotha Programme*, Campbell 1996, p. 207 refers to 'Marx's reference to socialism as the period of the dictatorship of the working class'. However, Marx does not refer the dictatorship of the proletariat as socialism. He clearly refers to it as lying '*between* capitalist and communist [or socialist] society'. This failure to distinguish the *political* form of transition *between* capitalism and socialism from socialism itself is extremely widespread in the secondary literature of Marx, but it has no basis in Marx's actual writings.

63. I wish to thank Karel Ludenhoff for bringing this to my attention, in private correspondence.

64. Marx 1985b, p. 467.

the proletariat itself as it works to progressively eliminate capital's all-consuming social dominance through democratic forms of deliberation and participation. Important though this stage is, however, it is not equivalent to the lower phase of socialism or communism. For, with Marx's lower phase, a decisive and qualitative break is made with capitalism.

Marx makes this explicit in his 'Notes on Bakunin's Statehood and Anarchy', written around the same time as the *Critique of the Gotha Programme*. It further reveals how Marx understood 'revolutionary dictatorship' – and how different his understanding of it was from most 'Marxists' who followed him. In response to Bakunin's question as to whether a working-class 'dictatorship' would consist, in the case of Germany, of all of the workers of the country, Marx replies, 'Certainly! For the system starts with the self-government of the communities'.[65] Marx identifies proletarian rule not with a party speaking in its name, but rather with its own 'communities' of association. He acknowledges that this can be termed 'a workers' state, if he wants to call it that'.[66] But what Marx means by this is that 'The class rule of the workers over the strata of the old world who are struggling against them can only last as long as the economic basis of class society has not yet been destroyed'.[67] This is not rule *for* the masses but *by* them. The masses make use of a tool or instrument of the old society, governmental power, insofar as the social transformations that can lead to the abolition of the state itself are not yet fully achieved; and yet this government-form, *unlike in capitalism*, is thoroughly *democratic* and *inclusive*. As the self-determining and participatory communities manage to abolish indirectly social labour and alienated human relationships, this governmental form would be superseded. As he puts it, 'This just means that when class rule has disappeared there will be no state in the present political sense'.[68] Moreover, when the workers' 'victory is complete, its rule too is therefore at an end, since its class character will have disappeared'.[69]

The notion that the lower phase of socialism or communism represents a 'proletarian dictatorship' in which value-production still prevails, which largely defined the discourse of established 'Marxist' thought in the twentieth century, is alien to Marx's thought. Such misreadings of his work had already begun to emerge in his own lifetime, and he lived long enough to directly

---

65. Marx 1989e, p. 519.
66. Marx 1989e, p. 520. Marx's use of this phrase calls into question Cyril Smith's claim that Marx never used the term 'workers' state'. See Smith 2005, pp. 143–56.
67. Marx 1989e, p. 521.
68. Marx 1989e, p. 519.
69. Ibid. Marx's comments of 1875 on the 'self-abolition' of proletarian rule is completely consistent with his earlier comments in *The Holy Family* and *The German Ideology*. See Chapter One, above.

answer them. One of his most poignant critiques is found in his 'Notes on Wagner's *Lehrbuch des politischen Ökonomie*', which was one of the first works by an academic economist to directly engage Marx's theoretical contribution:

> *Value.* According to Mr. Wagner, Marx's theory of value is the *'cornerstone of his socialist system'*. As I have never established a 'socialist system', this is a fantasy of Wagner, Schäffle *e tutti quanti*.... [I]n my *investigation* of value I have dealt with bourgeois relations, not with the application of this theory of *value* to a 'social state' not even constructed by me but by Mr. Schäffle for me.[70]

Marx's entire body of work shows that a new society is conditional upon a radical transformation of labour and social relations. The measure of whether such a transformation is adequate to the concept of a new society is the abolition of the law of value and value-production by freely-associated individuals.

This goal is not achieved, however, merely by some act of revolutionary will. It is achieved by discerning and building upon the elements of the new society that are concealed in the shell of the old one. This includes elucidating the forces of liberation that arise against capitalist alienation – which includes not only workers but all those suffering the ills of capitalist society, be they national minorities, women, or youth – which Marx referred to as the 'new forces and passions' for the 'reconstruction of society'.[71] It is the development of capitalism 'as such' and the myriad forms of resistance that arise against it – none of which can be anticipated in advance – that create the possibility for a new society. It is on these grounds that Marx argues, 'The capitalist mode of production is in fact a transitional form which by its own organism must lead to a higher, to a cooperative mode of production, to socialism'.[72]

---

70. Marx 1989h, pp. 533, 537.

71. Marx 1976e, p. 928.

72. See Marx 1989f, pp. 783–4: 'Daß die kapitalistische Producktionsweise eigentlich nur eine Übergangsform ist, die durch ihren eigenen Organismus zu einer höheren, zur *genossenschaftlichen* Productionsweise, zum Sozialismus führen *muß*'. I am indebted to Chattopadhyay 2010 for bringing this passage to my attention.

Conclusion

Evaluating Marx's Concept of a Postcapitalist Society

This study has shown that a coherent and vital concept of a new society is contained in the works of Marx, present from his early work of the 1840s to his last writings. From the inception of his philosophical project, Marx expressed strong opposition to any formation or situation in which individuals become dominated by social relations and products of their own making. His criticism of the inversion of subject and predicate, which is evident from his early writings on the state and civil society, carries over into his critique of the economic formations of capitalism, in which the self-development of individuals becomes thwarted by the products of their productive activity. This perspective is hardly restricted to his early writings. His two-decades-long process of developing *Capital*, as well as the content of *Capital* itself, shows that the primary object of Marx's criticism was the domination of things over individuals, of dead labour over living labour, of the object over the subject. It is on these grounds that he not only opposed capitalist commodity-production but also the system of value-production upon which it is based. Marx's critique of capital is part of a complex argument directed against all social phenomena that take on a life of their own and dictate the behaviour and actions of the social agents that are responsible for creating them.

Marx's philosophical approach, both to the critique of capitalism and to the delineation of its alternative, is rooted in a particular conception of *freedom*. Free development, for Marx, is not possible if human activity and its products take on the form of an autonomous power and proscribe the parameters in which individuals can express their natural and acquired talents and abilities. As I have sought to show, Marx's commitment to this concept of freedom owes much to his effort to re-think the status of human relations in the aftermath of the philosophical discoveries of German idealism, on the one hand, and the emergence of industrial capitalism and the formation of a radicalised working class opposing it, on the other. His conclusion that the modern world is a fundamentally inverted (and indeed a *mad*) phenomenon does not derive from an exaggerated commitment to 'rationalism' or speculative metaphysics; instead, it derives from his understanding of freedom as the subject's ability to feel at one with and at home in its objective manifestations, instead of being controlled and dominated by them.

This conception of freedom serves as the basis of Marx's objections to the myriad forms of social phenomena associated with modern capitalism – value, exchange-value, money, commodity-production and circulation, and not least, capital itself. It also grounds his criticism of the state and civil society. For this very reason, Marx does not object to capitalism because of the mere existence of the market and private property. He objects to the market and private property insofar as they are expressions of capital – a formation that crystallises the transformation of human relations into relations between things.

Marx's conception of a postcapitalist society is therefore radically different from what has characterised most approaches to 'socialism' and 'communism' in the century or more since his death. His critique of existing society goes much deeper than the contrast between the 'anarchic' market and the 'organised' factory, just as it extends beyond the boundaries of defining socialism as the mere abolition of private property and the market. Marx also goes further than merely condemning the *class*-relations of capitalist society, since, as I have shown, his foremost object of critique is alienated *human* relations – including those between men and women. In doing so Marx focuses on the need to eliminate the basis of both modern capitalism and its statist-'socialist' alternatives – value-production. Since he objects to value-production in so far as it crystallises the subjection of individuals to social relations of their own making, he can hardly conceive of its alternative as another structure in which human relations take on the form of things. Marx's conception that only *freely*-associated labour can strip the mystical veil from commodity-production is not a mere humanitarian adjunct to an otherwise objectivistic economic theory. His concept of the alternative to capitalism flows from the same normative concerns that govern his critique of capital itself. Just as he opposes any social formation that acts behind the backs of individuals, so he opposes any social solution that imposes itself irrespective of the self-activity of the subject.

Marx's conception of a postcapitalist society is therefore both expansive and visionary, in that it excludes any social formation that takes on an autonomous power at the expense of its creators. This is why even when he endorsed workers' cooperatives as a possible transitional form to socialism, he warned that they too can become a 'sham and a snare'[1] if they are not under the workers' actual, and not just formal, control. This is why even when he noted that the concentration and centralisation of capital points towards the socialised relations of the future, he argued that they could serve as the basis for a future society only if they there were accompanied by 'other large-scale organic revolutions in the mode of production'.[2] Marx never endorses a given social form as the solution, unless it avoids the tendency of human subjective activity to become constrained by forces of its own making.

At the same time, there is an underlying realism and sobriety in Marx's work that runs counter to the claim that his concept of a free society requires the existence of perfect and error-free individuals. Most of his discussions of postcapitalism actually deal with a socialist or communist society that is 'still stamped with the birthmarks of the old society from whom womb it emerges'.[3] This is especially the case with his discussions of the new society in Volumes I and II of *Capital*, and in much of the *Critique of the Gotha Programme*.

Marx understands that it is not possible to achieve complete social equality in the immediate aftermath of the demise of capitalism. Nor is it possible to leave behind such cardinal principles of the old society as basing remuneration on an exchange of labour-time for means of consumption – even though labour-time functions in a radically different form and content in his envisaged new society, as compared with the old one. It is indeed *fundamentally* different, since social relations become 'transparent in their simplicity' once the labourers put an end to alienated labour and the dictatorship of abstract time. Marx is *not* suggesting that *all facets of life* become transparent in the lower phase of socialism or communism; indeed, he never suggests this about conditions in a higher phase either.[4] He is addressing something much more

---

1. Marx 1986c, p. 335.
2. Marx 1981a, p. 743.
3. Marx 1989d, p. 85.
4. Despite the claims of some critics of Hegel, it is highly questionable that Hegel endorsed the idea that a complete transparency is possible between the self and the

specific: namely, the transparent nature of the exchange between labour-time and products of labour. This relation can never be transparent so long as there is value-production: it becomes transparent only once indirectly social labour is replaced by directly social labour.

The fact remains, however, that conditions in the lower phase of socialism or communism are defective and limited as compared to those that follow in a higher phase. Indeed, Marx contends that they are 'still stamped with the birthmarks of the old society' in '*every* respect, economically, morally, and intellectually'.[5] This is a far cry from someone who thinks that a socialist society entails the perfected human-being.

Marx does not, of course, limit his horizon to the initial phase of socialism or communism. He discusses it as part of understanding what is needed in order to bring to realisation the more expansive social relations of a higher phase of communism. Marx conceives of this phase as the passing-beyond of natural necessity – not in the sense that labour as such would come to an end, but rather that society would no longer be *governed* by the need for material production and reproduction. This higher phase, however, can only come into being as a result of a whole series of complex and involved historical developments, which include the abolition of 'the enslaving subordination of the individual to the division of labour, and thereby also the antithesis between mental and physical labour'.[6] It is impossible to achieve this, he reminds us, in the absence of highly-developed productive forces. Marx never conceived it as possible for a society to pass to 'socialism' or 'communism' while remaining imprisoned in conditions of social and technological backwardness.[7] And yet it is not the productive forces that create the new society: it is, instead, live men and women. '*For it is not the means of production that create the new type of man, but the new man that will create the means production*, and the new mode of activity will create the new type of human being, socialist man'.[8]

Other, let alone Marx – who often criticises Hegel for appearing to veer towards such a conception. For more on this, see Kain 2005.

5. Marx 1989d, p. 84.

6. Marx 1989d, p. 87.

7. Even when Marx, at the end of his life, entertained the possibility that a country like Russia could experience a socialist *revolution* ahead of the West, he held that it would not succeed unless the revolution was joined and supported by a proletarian revolution in the industrially-developed countries. He never held that Russia (or any other country for that matter) could create a *socialist* society in the absence of such an international transformation of social and production relations. See Marx 1983c, pp. 97–126. For more on this, see Hudis 2010 and Anderson 2010.

8. Dunayevskaya 1992, p. 20. This statement is contained in an essay first written in 1942, entitled 'Labor and Society'.

Marx's realistic *humanism* is most of all expressed in his insistence that the new society is contained in the womb of the old one. For Marx, there was never a question of calling socialism or communism into being through the projection of a subjective wish. The new society will immanently emerge from the existing conditions prepared by capitalist production and reproduction *and* the social struggles against them. If those conditions and struggles are not present, he held, it would not emerge at all, regardless of how much such a state of being may be desired by particular individuals. This is the reason that Marx devoted so much of his life to a detailed study and analysis of *existing* capitalist relations as well as revolutionary struggles and movements and why he spends so little time devising any kind of blueprint for the future.

That he said relatively *little* about the future, however, has been wrongly interpreted to mean that he said *nothing* about the future. Moreover, it has been wrongly interpreted to mean that one *ought* not to say anything about the future – presumably because normative considerations and 'oughts' are out of place for 'socialists' and 'historical materialists'. The self-refuting nature of the proposition is self-evident but is all-too-rarely reflected upon by its expositors. Normative considerations are as inescapable as language itself, precisely because what *ought* to be is inscribed within what *is*.[9] It is impossible to avoid reflection about the future, nor is it desirable to avoid it – at least so long as such reflection has some grounding in *reality*. The inescapable nature of normative statements about the future is evident from the content of Marx's own work. Much as he may have wanted to avoid speaking about the future, he often found it necessary to do so *precisely because the elements of the future are contained within the very structure of the present* that he subjected to such careful and painstaking critical examination.

Marx definitely understood his role as delineating the 'law of motion' of capitalism towards its collapse, but the very fact that he analysed it with this aim in mind suggests that he approached his subject matter with a conception of the necessity for its transcendence. If he did not have a specific kind of *future* in mind, why would he have adopted the specific argumentative approach found in his greatest theoretical work, *Capital*, which centres upon tracing out the processes towards *dissolution* of a given social phenomenon?

---

9. 'Many attempts have been made to deduce "ought" from "is" or to base it on some kind of "ought-free" being of facticity. These attempts are not based on the presupposition that "is" and "ought" are opposed, but instead on the hypothesis that the meaning of "is" or "being" is more universal or more fundamental than that of "ought", and that the latter can somehow emerge out of the former...In this hypothesis, "ought" and "is" are simultaneously given – they belong together – but our awareness of this belonging would require an awakening' (Peperzak 2004, p. 46).

Marx's entire vantage-point hinges on not just *having*, but also being *commit-ted* to, a specific vision of the future. Without it the very nature of his political, economic, and intellectual project could not have developed as it did.

Does this mean that Marx finds himself in something of a bind – want-ing to avoid 'utopian' speculation about the future, on the one hand, while not being able to avoid analysing the present on the basis of some (however general) conception of the future, on the other? Can he successfully carry out the 'scientific' and 'materialist' nature of his project while remaining wedded to a conception of how the future should or ought to evolve? It may appear that there is a tension between these two dimensions of Marx's project, and it would take an additional work to demonstrate the many ways in which Marx sought to navigate his way through this problem. However, it is possible that a famous analogy from an earlier philosopher may help illuminate how Marx managed to reconcile and overcome this apparent tension between the imma-nent and the transcendent. I am referring to Plato's conception of *maieutics* – of the philosopher as the *midwife* of knowledge.[10]

References and illusions to the new emerging from within the 'womb' of the old constantly appear in Marx's work. If there is one persisting and recurrent theme in Marx's analysis of capital, it is this: 'The development of the produc-tive forces of social labour is capital's historic mission and justification. For that very reason, it unwittingly creates the material conditions for a higher form of production'.[11] The new society, for Marx, always emerges from within the womb of the old one. But what does this say about Marx's own standpoint *vis-à-vis* the object of his investigation? He does not want to project a vision or concept of the new society from out of his head, irrespective of the social conditions and relations of reality itself. To do so, after all, would violate the very concept of freedom, since it would entail imposing a conception *upon* the subject from outside. Neither can he avoid speaking about the future in some way, however, since his conception of the future (in however general a form) has helped inform his very approach to the object of his investigation. He therefore adopts the approach of elucidating the elements of the future that he finds contained within the present, based on the series of values and premises that he brings to his analysis.

Marx's writings therefore serve as a kind of midwife of the new society. He does not give birth to the idea of socialism or communism: he elicits it from the movement of capitalism itself. In other words, it is not only that Marx

---

10. The concept is central to Plato's *Theaetetus*. The image of midwifery (*maieutics*) is mentioned 26 times in Plato's dialogues, 24 of them in the *Theaetetus* and once in the *Cratylus* and *Statesman*. See Brandwood 1976, p. 544.

11. Marx 1981a, p. 368.

holds that the new society will emerge from within the womb of the old one. It is that for this very reason he sees his role as being no more than the midwife who assists its delivery. By elucidating capitalism's *tendency* towards dissolution and collapse to the rising labour-movement, he is able to explain the main elements of that new society without falling prey to utopianism.

Given the tragic outcome of what has passed for 'Marxism' in the past century, how valid is such a methodological approach and perspective? In many respects, it remains extremely valuable, precisely because Marx's *maieutic* approach avoids the voluntarism and élitism that have marred far too many experiments at social transformation. The tragedy of 'Marxism' is that a philosophy that originated (at least in Marx's hands) with the aim of abolishing any social powers that operate behind the backs of the producers ended up creating dictatorial régimes that imposed their will on individuals without even a minimal degree of democratic control or public accountability. Nor was this only a political problem: the economic plans of the state-controlled economies operated no less outside the control of the producers, who were reduced to wage-slavery (where they were not subjected to forced labour of a more nefarious kind).[12] The notion that a 'new' society can be imposed behind the backs of the populace and irrespective of specific social conditions faced by that society has done enormous damage – not least in leading large numbers of people around the world to question whether a viable alternative to capitalism is even possible. Indeed, it can be argued that the greatest barrier in the way of a revolutionary challenge to capitalism today is not the *material* or *ideological* power of capital but rather the memory of the innumerable flawed and failed efforts to overcome it in the not-so-distant past. The past does hang like a dead weight upon the living – especially when alternative visions of a postcapitalist society that can animate the imagination of humanity are hard to come by.

It is not idle speculation to presume that Marx would be the first to criticise the flawed attempts at 'emancipation' made in his name, since, as I have shown, he *did* criticise many of them in his disputes with a number of socialist and communist tendencies of his era. At the same time, precisely because we live in the shadow of the crimes committed in Marx's name, it does not seem possible to fully renew the Marxian project of issuing a full-throttled challenge to capital if the conception of a new society found in his writings

---

12. It has been widely estimated that between 12 and 15 million citizens of the Soviet Union laboured in the forced labour-camps at any given time during and after the forced-industrialisation campaign under Stalin. This is not to count the millions of others, especially Ukrainians, Uzbeks, Crimean Tartars and others, who perished at his hands.

remains only implicit. This is not only because of the way in which the limitations and ultimate collapse of the state-capitalist régimes that called themselves 'socialist' or 'communist' helped give global capitalism a new lease on life. It is also because of a slew of social and ecological dangers facing us in the twenty-first century. Given the fact that time may well be running out on the effort to save the planet from capital's rapacious self-expansionary nature, as seen in the ecological crisis, it has become necessary to project a much more explicit notion of what constitutes a viable notion of the alternative to capitalism than Marx himself envisaged. After all, Marx did not live to witness the enormous destructive potential contained in the productive power of capital that is so evident today. Of necessity, he emphasised the need to *develop* the productive forces – whereas we are witnessing the need to *limit* the destructive power of much of these forces as much as and as soon as possible, even as the need to overcome the crushing poverty and economic under-development that afflicts much of the developing world remains one of the foremost problems facing us today.

Yet these very realities make Marx's critique of capital, and his conception of the alternative to it, more relevant than ever before. Precisely because every facet of life is today threatened by the all-dominating power of capital that Marx warned so eloquently against a century and a half ago, his conception of how to surmount the capital relation, which is itself inseparable from value-production, must be developed and projected today in a far more explicit and comprehensive manner than appeared necessary in the nineteenth century.

While the future may well be contained in the womb of the old, the events of the past hundred years make it painfully evident that there is nothing automatic or ensured about the emergence of the new. Although our age may still be defined as one of a 'birth-time of history',[13] we have also experienced all too many still-births – in large part because so many have misconstrued the nature of what constitutes a genuinely free, non-capitalist society. 'Marxism' has especially suffered from the tendency of many of its adherents to separate the 'factual' from the 'normative', the real from the ideal, the economic from the philosophical. We must put all this behind us. The history of the past hundred years makes it painfully evident that while the material conditions for the existence of socialism are a *necessary* condition for freedom, they are by no means *sufficient*. They can even lead to a new form of tyranny based on the despotic plan of capital, if the effort to elicit the emancipatory forms contained within the womb of the old is based on political shortsightedness

---

13. See Hegel 1978, p. 6: 'Besides, it is not difficult to see that ours is a birth-time and a period of transition to a new era'.

and philosophical miscomprehension. Precisely because we cannot do without the labour of thinking out *and working out* in everyday life an alternative to capitalism, we cannot do without rediscovering the invaluable insights that Marx left us as to how to surmount the capital-relation.

This is most of all needed because the lack of a viable alternative to both 'free-market' capitalism and what has called itself 'socialism' has acted as a serious impediment to social transformation over the past three decades. The barriers to generating mass opposition to capitalism surely cannot be explained by it having become a 'kindler and gentler' system over the past several decades: on the contrary, its drive for profit at the expense of human needs has only become more accentuated. So why have so many movements stopped short of challenging capital itself, in favour of instead emphasising relatively restricted social reforms and self-limiting revolutions? I would argue that given the absence of a viable alternative to capitalism, discontent with the many ills of existing society risks falling short of a serious challenge to the system as a whole. In this sense, a philosophically grounded alternative to capitalism is not only needed to further develop mass-opposition; it is needed to actually inspire it.[14]

This work has tried to show that a much deeper, richer, and more emancipatory conception of a postcapitalist society is found in Marx's work than has hitherto been appreciated. This is not to say that Marx provides anything in the way of a detailed answer as to what is a viable alternative to capitalism. His work does, however, contain crucial conceptual markers and suggestions that can help a new generation chart its way towards the future. Rather than wait upon 'a sunburst, which, in one flash, illuminates the features of the new world',[15] the realities of our time, in terms of its triumphs as well as its tragedies, calls on us to develop a much more explicit and articulated alternative to capitalism than appeared necessary in Marx's time, and even to Marx himself. We do the most justice to a thinker like Marx, not by repeating what he said and did, but by *rethinking* the meaning of his legacy for the realities of our times. It is to this end that this study is devoted.

---

14. For more on this, see Hudis 2005a.
15. Hegel 1978, p. 7.

Translation of Marx's Excerpt-Notes on the Chapter 'Absolute Knowledge' in Hegel's *Phenomenology of Spirit*

Note: Marx's notes on the chapter 'Absolute Knowledge' from Hegel's *Phenomenology of Spirit* have never before appeared in English translation. They were composed at the time Marx wrote the *Economic and Philosophical Manuscripts* of 1844, most likely as part of his work on the concluding part of the Third Manuscript, now known as 'Critique of the Hegelian Dialectic and Philosophy as a Whole'. The original can be found in *Karl Marx-Friedrich Engels Gesamtausgabe* [*MEGA²*] IV/2 (Berlin: Dietz Verlag), 483–500. Page numbers in the text (in brackets) are to the edition of the *Phenomenology* used by Marx (G.W.F. Hegel, *Phänomenologie des Geistes*, ed. Johann Schulze [Berlin, 1841]), as supplied by the editors of *MEGA²*.

Marx's notes consist mostly of copying out passages and paraphrasing parts of this final chapter of Hegel's *Phenomenology*. Places where Marx inserts his own comments are indicated by boldface. All emphases and ellipses are by Marx. The manuscript breaks off about two-thirds of the way into the chapter on 'Absolute Knowledge'. In translating these notes, I have consulted the translations of Hegel's *Phenomenology* by A.V. Miller and J.B. Baillie without, however, necessarily committing myself to their respective renderings of Hegel's text.

In the *Phenomenology*, *Absolute Knowledge* thus becomes described as:

1) In revealed religion the *actual* self-consciousness of Spirit is not yet the *object of its consciousness*; it and its moments fall within picture-thinking and in the form of objectivity. The content of this picture-thinking is absolute spirit; it is still a matter of transcending this *mere* form. [p. 574.]

2) This *surmounting of the object* of consciousness... is not to be taken in a one-sided manner, that the object showed itself returning into the self; rather, it is to be taken *specifically*... to not only mean that the object showed itself as returning into the self, but above all that the object presents itself not only as a vanishing factor but as the externalisation of self-consciousness that posits thinghood. This *externalisation* has not merely a negative but a *positive* meaning, not merely *for us* or in itself but for *self-consciousness itself*. The negative of the object, or its self-transcendence, has a positive meaning, *for* on the one side it *knows* this nothingness of the object that it itself externalises; – for in this externalisation it posits itself as the object or the object as the inseparable unity of *being-for-self*. On the other hand, there is also this other moment, that self-consciousness has equally transcended this externalisation and objectification as it has returned to itself, so that it is *with itself* in its otherness as such.

3) This is the movement of consciousness and herein is found the totality of its moments. – It must have taken up a relation to the object in the totality of its determinations and from the point of view of each of them. This totality of its determinations means the object is *in itself* a *spiritual* being and it is so because in truth consciousness apprehends each individual one of them as its *own self*, through the *spiritual relationship* just mentioned. [pp. 574–5.]

4) The *object* is thus the partly *immediate* being or the *thing* in general – corresponding to its immediate consciousness. It is partly a becoming other of itself, its *relationship* or *essential being is for another and for itself*; its determinateness – corresponds to *perception*, partly to essential being in the form of a universal corresponding to the understanding. **(Being, Essence, Concept; Universality. Particularity. Individuality. Position. Negation. Negation of the Negation; simple, differentiated, transcended opposition. Immediacy. Mediation. Self-transcending mediation. Being in itself. Externalisation. Return to itself from externalisation. In-itself. For-itself. In-and-for-itself. Unity. Differentiation. Self-differentiation. Identity. Negation. Negativity. Logic. Nature. Spirit. Pure Consciousness. Consciousness. Self-Consciousness. Concept. Judgement. Syllogism.)** It

is then a whole, a syllogism, or the movement of universality through particularisation to individuality, as also the reverse movement, from the individual through its transcendence or determination to the universal. – These are the three determinations by which consciousness must know the object *as itself*. This *knowing* of which we here speak is not that of the *pure comprehension* of the object; instead, this knowing is to be taken only as aspects or moments of its coming to be in the manner appropriate to consciousness as such, as moments of pure knowledge, the concept itself, in the form of shapes of consciousness. For this reason the object does not yet appear in consciousness as the spiritual essence that we have spoken of; the relationship of consciousness to it is not the view of this totality as such nor in its *pure* form as the concept. Instead, it is from one side a *shape* of consciousness in general, and from the other side a number of moments that we bring together, in which the totality of the moments of the object and the relations of consciousness to the object can be indicated only as resolving itself into its moments. [pp. 575–6.]

5) In regard to the *object* in so far as it is an immediacy, a being of *indifference*, we saw Observing Reason *seeking and finding* itself in this indifferent thing – that is, as equally conscious of its action being *external* to it, and as the object that is only known immediately...its specific determination is expressed in the infinite judgment that *the being of the I is a thing*. And moreover, the I is a being of sensuous immediacy; when the I is called a *soul* it is in fact represented as a thing, but as something invisible, intangible; in fact not as an immediate being, what one means by a *thing*. That *non-spiritual* judgment [2] is the concept of its spirituality. **Now to see how this *inner* sense becomes pronounced.** The *thing is I*, that is, the thing transcended; in itself it is nothing. It has meaning only in the *relation*, through the *I* and its *connections* with it. – This moment comes forth for consciousness in pure insight and enlightenment. Things are simply considered to be *useful* and are considered only in terms of their *utility*....The *cultivated* self-consciousness, which has traversed the world of self-alienated spirit, has through its externalisation produced the thing as its own self; it therefore retains it in itself, and knows that the thing has no independence, that the thing is *essentially* only *being for an other*; or, to provide complete expression to the *relationship*, to what here constitutes the nature of the object, the thing *exists as being-for-self*; it declares sense-certainty to be absolute truth; however, this *being for self* is itself declared a vanishing moment which passes into its opposite, into a being that is at the mercy of *another*. – But the knowledge of the thing is still not complete; it must become known not only in terms of the immediacy

of its being and determinateness, but rather also as *essence* or *inner being*, as *self*. This is present in *moral self-consciousness*. It knows its knowing to be what is *absolutely essential* or that *being* is pure will and pure knowledge; *it is nothing else* except this willing or knowing. Any other has only unessential being, that is, not *being in and for itself*, only its empty husk. In so far as the moral consciousness lets *determinate being* go forth freely from the self, so too it takes its conception of the world back into itself once again. Finally, as *conscience* it is no longer this ceaseless alteration of determinate being placed and displaced in the self; instead, it knows that its *determinate being* as such is this pure certainty of its own self; the objective element in which it puts itself is thus nothing other than pure *knowledge of itself by itself.* [pp. 576–7.]

6) These are the moments of which the reconciliation of spirit with its own particular consciousness is composed. By themselves they are single and solitary, and their spiritual unity alone provides the power of this reconciliation. The last of these moments is this unity itself and binds them all together into itself. *Spirit*, which in its determinate being is certain of itself, has for the element of its *existence* nothing else but this very knowledge of itself. The declaration that what it does is in accordance with the conviction of duty, it is the *valuing* (**Money**) of its action. – Action is the first *inherent* division of the simple unity of the notion and the return from out of this division. This first movement turns over into the second, in that this element of recognition posits itself as *simple* knowledge of duty as against the *distinction* and *diremption* that lie in action as such; in this way it constitutes a stubborn actuality confronting action. In *forgiveness* we saw how this hardness surrenders and divests itself. Actuality, therefore, as *immediate determinate being*, has no other significance for self-consciousness than that of being a pure knowing; – likewise, as *determinate* being or as relation, what is self-opposed is a knowing partly of this purely individual self and partly of knowledge as a universal. Herein it is equally posited that the third moment, the *universality* or *essence*, is valued only as *knowledge* for each of the two sides that stand in opposition to one another. Finally, they put an end to the empty opposition that still remains and are the knowledge of I = I – this *individual* self that is immediately a pure knowing or a universal. [pp. 577–8.]

[3] **How** reconciliation of consciousness with self-consciousness **comes about is stated in two ways:** 1) In religious spirit, 2) in the consciousness of itself as such. 1) Reconciliation in the form of being-in-itself; 2) in the form of being-for-itself. In our consideration of them they fall apart. The unity of the two sides is not exhibited: 1) Spirit *in itself*, absolute content;

2) for itself, contentless form or as the aspect of self-consciousness; 3) Spirit in and for itself. [pp. 578–9.]

7) This unification in religion, as present in the return of picture thinking into self-consciousness, but not however according to the intrinsic form, since the religious aspect is the aspect of the *in-itself*, which the movement of self-consciousness stands against. The unification belongs to this other aspect, which in contrast is the aspect of reflection into self; it contains itself and its opposite, not only implicitly but explicitly or in a developed and differentiated way. The content, as well as the other aspect of spirit, *as other*, have been brought forth and is here in its completeness; the unity, which is still lacking, is the simple unity of the concept. – It is as the particular shape of consciousness, the *beautiful soul*, the shape of self-certain spirit, in which the concept stands forth. Its realisation firmly opposed, it is the one-sided shape that vanishes into thin air but also positively externalises itself and moves forward. Through this realisation, the *determinateness* of the concept is raised up against its *fulfilment*; its self-consciousness attains the form of universality. The genuine concept is the *knowing* of *pure* knowledge as its being, as essential being that *this* pure self-consciousness, is equally a *genuine object*, for it is self-existent being itself. [pp. 579–80.]

The fulfilment of the concept is partly in the *acts* performed by Spirit, partly in *religion*.... In the prior shape the form is that of the self itself, in that it contains the self-certain spirit that *acts*; the *self realises the life of absolute spirit*. This shape is just that of the simple concept, which relinquishes its *eternal essence, it is there* or it acts. The *diremption* or coming forth out of its inwardness, lies in the purity of the concept, for this is the *absolute abstraction* of *negativity*. Similarly, it has the element of its being or reality in itself, for this is simple *immediacy*, which is *being* and *existence* as well as essence; the former the negative, the latter positive thought itself. **Hegel keeps developing the tedious process of the beautiful soul, whose result is** the *pure universality of knowledge,* which is self-consciousness. – The concept connects the *content* to itself; and the concept is the knowledge of the *self's act within itself* as all that is essential and all existence, the knowledge of this *subject* as *substance* and of substance as this knowledge of its own act. [pp. 580–82.]

8) *Spirit* knows itself in the *shape of spirit, comprehended knowing.* Truth not only *is itself* identical with *certainty*, but it also has the *shape* of *certainty* of its own self or its determinate being, that is, in the *form* of comprehended spirit that knows itself. Truth is the *content*, which in religion is still not identical with its certainty. This equality however is obtained, since the

concept has secured the shape of the self. In this way that which is the very essence has become the element of existence, or has become the *form of objectivity* for consciousness – that is, the concept. Spirit, *appearing* in this element in consciousness, or produced by consciousness, is *science*. It is the pure *being-for-self* of consciousness; it is I, that is this and no other I and is no less so an immediately *mediated* or transcended *universal* I. It has a *content* that it *differentiates* from itself; for it is pure negativity or diremption; it is consciousness. This content in its differentiation is the I itself, for it is the movement of transcending itself or the pure negativity that the I is. In it the I as differentiated, is reflected into itself; the content is grasped only when the I in its *otherness* is at one with itself. [pp. 582–3.]

[4] *This content*, stated more *specifically*, is nothing other than *the movement just spoken of*; for the content is the spirit that traverses its own self and does so *for itself* as spirit, by the fact that it possesses the shape of the concept in its objectivity. As regards the existence of this concept, *science* does not appear in time or reality until spirit has attained this consciousness of itself. As spirit that knows what it is, it exists not before and nowhere at all until after spirit has completed its work of overcoming its incomplete shape so as to secure for consciousness the shape of its essence – and in this way to equate its *self-consciousness* with its *consciousness*. **See the continuation, p. 583 ff. Being that is hidden to itself is *apparently only the certainty of itself*. The relationship of time to history.** Comprehended spirit the *annulling* of time. *Experience, Knowledge,* **transformation of substance into subject, the object of consciousness into the object of self-consciousness, that is, in** *as much as the transcended object or concept.* It is only as this reflection of itself into itself that it is the truth of spirit. In so far as spirit is of necessity this self-differentiation, its intuited whole appears over against this simple self-consciousness; and since the whole is differentiated, it is differentiated into its intuited pure concept – into time and the content of the *in-itself.* Substance as subject involves the *at-first inner necessity* to represent in itself what it inherently is as spirit. *The completed objective presentation* is equally the *reflection* of substance or its *development into* the self. Consequently, unless spirit *completes itself* in itself, has not done so as world spirit, it cannot reach its completion as *self-conscious* spirit. Therefore, the content of religion expresses earlier in time than science what *spirit is*; but science alone is the true knowledge of itself. *The movement, the form of its knowing as such* [pp. 583–5.]

References

Albritton, Robert 1999, *Dialectics and Deconstruction in Political Economy*, London: Macmillan.
—— 2004, 'Theorising Capital's Deep Structure and the Transformation of Capitalism', *Historical Materialism*, 12, 3: 73–92.
—— 2005, 'How Dialectics Runs Aground: The Antimonies of Arthur's Dialectic of Capital', *Historical Materialism*, 13, 2: 167–88.
—— 2008, *Economics Transformed: Discovering the Brilliance of Marx*, London: Pluto Press.
Anderson, Kevin 2010, *Marx at the Margins: On Nationalism, Ethnicity, and Non-Western Societies*, Chicago: University of Chicago Press.
Aristotle 1984, *Posterior Analytics* in *The Complete Works of Aristotle*, Volume 1, edited by Jonathan Barnes, Princeton: Bollington.
—— 1998, *Politics*, translation C.D.C. Reeve, Indianapolis: Hackett Pubishing Company.
—— 2002, *Nicomachean Ethics*, translation Joe Sachs, Newburyport: Focus Publishing.
Arthur, Christopher J. 1983, 'Hegel's Master-Slave Dialectic and a Myth of Marxology', *New Left Review*, I, 142: 67–75.
—— 1986, *Dialectics of Labour: Marx and His Relation to Hegel*, London: Blackwell.
—— 2002, *The New Dialectic and Marx's 'Capital'*, Historical Materialism Book Series, Leiden: Brill.
Avineri, Shlomo 1969, *The Social and Political Thought of Karl Marx*, Cambridge: Cambridge University Press.
Backhaus, Hans-Georg 1992, 'Between Philosophy and Science: Marxian Social Economy as Critical Theory', in *Open Marxism*, Volume 1: *Dialectics and History*, edited by Werner Bonefeld, Richard Gunn, and Kosmas Psychopedis, London: Pluto Press.
—— 1997, *Dialektik der Wertform. Untersuchungen zur Marxschen Ökonomiekritik*, Freiburg: Ça Ira.
Bailey, Anne M. and Josep R. Llobera (eds.) 1981, *The Asiatic Mode of Production: Science and Politics*, London: Routledge.
Baran, Paul 1944, 'New Trends in Russian Economic Thinking?', *American Economic Review*, 34, 4: 862–71.
Bellofiore, Riccardo and Roberto Fineschi (eds.) 2009, *Re-reading Marx: New Perspectives After the Critical Edition*, London: Palgrave Macmillan.
Berki, Robert N. 1983, *Insight and Vision: The Problem of Communism in Marx's Thought*, London: J.M. Dent & Sons.
Bidet, Jacques 2009, *Exploring Marx's 'Capital': Philosophical, Economic, and Political Dimensions*, Historical Materialism Book Series, Chicago: Haymarket Books.
Brandwood, Leonard 1976, *A Word Index of Plato*, Leeds: W.S. Maney and Son.
Campbell, David 1996, *The Failure of Marxism: The Concept of Inversion in Marx's Critique of Capitalism*, Aldershot: Dartmouth.
Chattopadhyay, Paresh 2010, 'Marx Made to Serve Party-State', available at: <http://www.usmarxisthumanists.org/?s=paresh>.
Cohen, G.A. 1989, *History, Labour and Freedom: Themes from Marx*, Oxford: Oxford University Press.
Desai, Meghnad 2002, *Marx's Revenge: The Resurgence of Capitalism and the Death of Statist Socialism*, London: Verso.

Draper, Hal 1977, *Karl Marx's Theory of Revolution*, Volume 1, *State and Bureaucracy*, New York: Monthly Review Press.

Dunayevskaya, Raya 1944, 'A New Revision of Marxian Economics', *American Economic Review*, 34, 3: 531–7.

—— 1981, *Rosa Luxemburg, Women's Liberation, and Marx's Philosophy of Revolution*, Champaign-Urbana: University of Illinois Press.

—— 1992, *The Marxist-Humanist Theory of State-Capitalism*, edited by Peter Hudis, Chicago: News and Letters.

—— 2000 [1958], *Marxism and Freedom, from 1776 Until Today*, Amherst: Humanity Books.

—— 2002, *The Power of Negativity: Selected Writings on the Dialectic in Hegel and Marx*, edited by Peter Hudis and Kevin B. Anderson, Lanham: Lexington Books.

—— 2003 [1973], *Philosophy and Revolution: from Hegel to Sartre and from Marx to Mao*, Lanham: Lexington Books.

Dupré, Louis 1966, *The Philosophical Foundations of Marxism*, New York: Harcourt, Brace and World.

Dussel, Enrique 1988, *Hacio un Marx desconocido, un comentario de los Manuscriptos del 1861–63*, Mexico City: Siglo XXI.

—— 2001a, 'The Four Drafts of *Capital*: Toward a New Interpretation of the Dialectical Thought of Karl Marx', *Rethinking Marxism*, 13, 1: 10–26.

—— 2001b, *Towards an Unknown Marx: A Commentary on the Manuscripts of 1861–63*, translation Yolanda Angulo, edited by Fred Moseley, London: Routledge.

Engels, Friedrich 1987 [1878], *Herr Eugen Dühring's Revolution in Science*, in *Marx and Engels Collected Works*, Volume 25, New York: International Publishers.

Engels, Friedrich and Karl Marx 1975 [1845], *The Holy Family*, in *Marx and Engels Collected Works*, Volume 4, New York: International Publishers.

Fineschi, Roberto 2009, '"Capital in General" and "Competition" in the Making of *Capital*: The German Debate', *Science and Society*, 73, 1: 54–76.

Foucault, Michel 2003 [1969], 'What Is an Author?', in *The Essential Foucault*, edited by Paul Rabinow and Nikolas Rose, New York: The New Press.

Hardt, Michael and Antonio Negri 2000, *Empire*, Cambridge, MA.: Harvard University Press.

—— 2004, *Multitude*, New York: Penguin Press.

Harris, Henry S. 1995, *Hegel: Phenomenology and System*, Indianapolis: Hackett Publishers.

Harstick, Hans-Peter (ed.) 1977, *Karl Marx über Formen vorkapitalistischer Produktion: Vergleichende Studien zur Geschichte des Grundeigentums 1879–80*, Frankfurt: Campus Verlag.

Hegel, Georg W.F. 1977 [1807], *Phenomenology of Spirit*, translation A.V. Miller, Oxford: Oxford University Press.

—— 1978 [1830], *Philosophy of Mind*, translation William Wallace, Oxford: Clarendon Press.

—— 1979a [1812], *Science of Logic*, translation A.V. Miller, Atlantic Highlands: Humanities Press.

—— 1979b [1801/2 and 1803/4], *System of Ethical Life* and *First Philosophy of Spirit*, edited by Henry S. Harris and T.M. Knox, Albany: SUNY Press.

—— 2008 [1807], *Phänomenologie des Geistes*, Hamburg: Felix Meiner Verlag.

Heinrich, Michael 1989, 'Capital in General and the Structure of Marx's *Capital*', *Capital & Class*, 13: 63–79.

Henry, Michel 1983, *Marx: A Philosophy of Human Reality*, translation Kathleen McLaughlin, Bloomington: Indiana University Press.

Hollander, Samuel 2008, *The Economics of Karl Marx, Analysis and Application*, Cambridge: Cambridge University Press.

Holloway, John 2002, *How to Change the World Without Taking Power*, London: Pluto Press.

Hook, Sidney 1968 [1936], *From Hegel to Marx: Studies in the Intellectual Development of Marl Marx*, Anne Arbor: University of Michigan Press.

Hudis, Peter 1989, 'Toward Philosophic New Beginnings in Marxist-Humanism', *Quarterly Journal of Ideology*, 13, 4: 87–96.

—— 1995, 'Labor, High-Tech Capitalism, and the Crisis of the Subject: A

Critique of Recent Developments in Critical Theory', *Humanity & Society*, 19, 4: 4–20.

—— 1998, 'Dialectics, "the Party" and the Problem of the New Society', *Historical Materialism*, 3: 95–117.

—— 2004a, 'Marx Among the Muslims', *Capitalism, Nature, Socialism*, 15, 4: 51–68.

—— 2004b, 'Review: "Change the World Without Taking Power"', *Herramienta*, available at: <http://www.herramienta.com.ar/debate-sobre-cambiar-elmundo/review-essay-rethinking-idearevolution>.

—— 2004c, 'The Death of the Death of the Subject', *Historical Materialism*, 12, 3: 147–69.

—— 2005a, 'Developing a Philosophically Grounded Alternative to Capitalism', *Socialism and Democracy*, 19, 2: 91–8.

—— 2005b, 'The Philosophic Ambiguities of C.L.R. James', *Socialism and Democracy*, 19, 2: 207–14.

—— 2007, 'Neue Einschätzungen zu Rosa Luxemburgs Shriften über die nicht-westliche Welt', in *China Entdeckt Rosa Luxemburg*, edited by Narihiko Ito, Teodor Bergmann, Stefan Hochstadt, and Ottokar Luban, Berlin: Dietz Verlag.

—— 2010, 'Accumulation, Imperialism, and Pre-Capitalist Formations: Luxemburg and Marx on the non-Western World', *Socialist Studies/Études socialistes*, 6, 2: 75–91.

Kain, Philip J. 2005, *Hegel and the Other: A Study of the Phenomenology of Spirit*, Albany: State University of New York Press.

Kant, Immanuel 1996a [1785], *Groundwork of the Metaphysics of Morals* in *The Cambridge Edition of the Works of Immanuel Kant: Practical Philosophy*, translated and edited by Mary J. Gregor, Cambridge: Cambridge University Press.

—— 1996b [1797] *Metaphysics of Morals* in *The Cambridge Edition of the Works of Immanuel Kant: Practical Philosophy*, translated and edited by Mary J. Gregor, Cambridge: Cambridge University Press.

Karatani, Kojin 2003, *Transcritique: On Kant and Marx*, translation Sabu Kohso, Cambridge, MA: The MIT Press.

Kierkegaard, Søren. 1992 [1846], *Concluding Unscientific Postscript to Philosophical Fragments*, Volume 2, translated and edited by Howard V. Hong and Edna H. Hong, Princeton: Princeton University Press.

Kliman, Andrew 2000, 'Marx's Concept of Intrinsic Value', *Historical Materialism*, 6: 89–113.

Kolakowski, Leszek 1978, *Main Currents of Marxism: Its Rise, Growth, and Dissolution*, Volume 3: *The Breakdown*, Oxford: Oxford University Press.

Kornai, János 1992, *The Socialist System: The Political Economy of Communism*. Princeton: Princeton University Press.

Kosik, Karel, 1976 [1964], *Dialectics of the Concrete: A Study on the Problems of Man and World*, Dordrecht: D. Reidel.

Kouvelakis, Stathis 2003, *Philosophy and Revolution: From Kant to Hegel*. London: Verso Books.

Lange, Oscar 1945, 'Marxian Economics in the Soviet Union', *American Economic Review*, 35, 1: 127–33.

Leopold, David 2007, *The Young Karl Marx: German Philosophy, Modern Politics, and Human Flourishing*, Cambridge: Cambridge University Press.

Levinas, Emmanuel 1969 [1961], *Totality and Infinity: An Essay on Exteriority*, translation Alphonso Lingis, Pittsburgh: Duquesne University Press.

Lifshitz, Mikhail 1973 [1933], *The Philosophy of Art of Karl Marx*, translation Ralph B. Winn, London: Pluto Press.

Lobkowicz, Nicholas 1967, *Theory and Practice: History of a Concept from Aristotle to Marx*, Notre Dame: University of Notre Dame Press.

Löwy, Michael 2005, *The Theory of Revolution in the Young Marx*, Chicago: Haymarket Books.

Lukács, Georg 1968 [1923], *History and Class Consciousness: Studies in Marxist Dialectics*, translation Rodney Livingstone, London: Merlin Press.

—— 1976 [1954], *The Young Hegel: Studies in the Relations between Dialectics and Economics*, translation Rodney Livingstone, Cambridge, MA: MIT Press.

—— 1991 [1988], *The Process of Democratization*, translation Susanne Bernhardt and Norman Levine, Albany: SUNY Press.

Luxemburg, Rosa 1968 [1913], *The Accumulation of Capital*, translation Agnes Schwarzschuld, New York: Modern Reader.

—— 1978, 'Letter of March 8, 1917', in *The Letters of Rosa Luxemburg*, edited by Stephen Eric Bronner, Boulder: Westview Press.

—— 2004 [1899], *Social Reform or Revolution*, in *The Rosa Luxemburg Reader*, edited by Peter Hudis and Kevin B. Anderson, New York: Monthly Review Books.

Mandel, Ernest 1962, *Marxist Economic Theory*, London: Merlin Press.

—— 1976, 'Introduction', in *Capital*, Volume I, by Karl Marx, translation David Fernbach, New York: Vintage.

Marcuse, Herbert 1964, *One-Dimensional Man, Studies in the Ideology of Advanced Industrial Society*, Boston: Beacon Press.

—— 2000 [1958], 'Preface', in *Marxism and Freedom, from 1776 Until Today*, by Raya Dunayevskaya, Amherst: Humanity Books.

Marx, Karl 1933, *Critique of the Gotha Program*, New York: International Publishers.

—— 1973 [1857–8], *Grundrisse, Foundations of the Critique of Political Economy*, translation Martin Nicolaus. New York: Vintage Books

—— 1975a [1835], 'Reflections of a Young Man on the Choice of a Profession', in *Marx and Engels Collected Works*, Volume 1, New York: International Publishers.

—— 1975b [1837], 'Letter from Marx to His Father', in *Marx and Engels Collected Works*, Volume 1, New York: International Publishers.

—— 1975c [1839], 'Notebooks on Epicurean Philosophy', in *Marx and Engels Collected Works*, Volume 1, New York: International Publishers.

—— 1975d [1841], 'Difference Between the Democritean and Epicurean Philosophy of Nature', in *Marx and Engels Collected Works*, Volume 1, New York: International Publishers.

—— 1975e [1842], 'Comments on the Latest Prussian Censorship Instruction', in *Marx and Engels Collected Works*, Volume 1, New York: International Publishers.

—— 1975f [1842], 'Proceedings of the Sixth Rhine Assembly. First Article. Debates on Freedom of the Press and Publication of the Proceedings of the Assembly of the Estates', in *Marx and Engels Collected Works*, Volume 1, New York: International Publishers.

—— 1975g [1842], 'Leading Article in No. 179 of *Kölnische Zeitung*', in *Marx and Engels Collected Works*, Volume 1, New York: International Publishers.

—— 1975h [1842], 'Communism and the Augsburg *Allgemeine Zeitung*', in *Marx and Engels Collected Works*, Volume 1, New York: International Publishers.

—— 1975i [1842] 'Proceedings of the Sixth Rhine Province Assembly. Third Article on the Law on Thefts of Wood', in *Marx and Engels Collected Works*, Volume 3, New York: International Publishers.

—— 1975j [1842], 'The Supplement to Nos. 335 and 336 of the *Augsburg Allgemeine Zeitung* on the Commissions of the Estates in Prussia', in *Marx and Engels Collected Works*, Volume 1, New York: International Publishers.

—— 1975k [1843], *Contribution to the Critique of Hegel's Philosophy of Right*, in *Marx and Engels Collected Works*, Volume 3, New York: International Publishers.

—— 1975l, 'Letter to Ludwig Feuerbach of August 11, 1843', in *Marx and Engels Collected Works*, Volume 3, New York: International Publishers.

—— 1975m [1843], 'Letters from the *Deutsch-Französischer Jahrbücher*', in *Marx and Engels Collected Works*, Volume 3, New York: International Publishers.

—— 1975n [1843], 'Letter to Ludwig Feuerbach of October 3, 1843', in *Marx and Engels Collected Works*, Volume 3, New York: International Publishers.

—— 1975o [1844], 'On the Jewish Question', in *Marx and Engels Collected Works*, Volume 3, New York: International Publishers.

—— 1975p [1843], 'Contribution to the Critique of Hegel's *Philosophy of Right*. Introduction', in *Marx and Engels Collected Works*, Volume 3, New York: International Publishers.

—— 1975q [1844], 'Comments on James Mill, *Éléments de l'économie politique*', in *Marx and Engels Collected Works*, Volume 1, New York: International Publishers.

—— 1975r [1844] *Economic and Philosophical Manuscripts of 1844*, in *Marx and Engels Collected Works*, Volume 3, New York: International Publishers.

—— 1975s [1845], 'Draft of an Article on Friedrich List's Book *Das nationale System der politischen Ökonomie*', in *Marx and Engels Collected Works*, Volume 4, New York: International Publishers.

—— 1975t [1879], 'Excerpts from M.M. Kovalevskij', in *The Asiatic Mode of Production: Sources, Development, and Critique in the Writings of Karl Marx*, edited by Lawrence Krader, Assen: Van Gorcum.

—— 1976a [1845], 'Theses on Feuerbach', in *Marx and Engels Collected Works*, Volume 5, New York: International Publishers.

—— 1976b [1847], *The Poverty of Philosophy*, in *Marx and Engels Collected Works*, Volume 6, New York: International Publishers.

—— 1976c [1847], 'Moralizing Criticism and Critical Morality', in *Marx and Engels Collected Works*, Volume 6, New York: International Publishers.

—— 1976d [1847] 'Wages', in *Marx and Engels Collected Works*, Volume 6, New York: International Publishers.

—— 1976e [1867], *Capital*, Volume I, translation Ben Fowkes, New York: Vintage, 1976.

—— 1976f, *Value Studies by Marx*, translated and edited by Albert Dragstedt, London: New Park Publications.

—— 1978, *Capital*, Volume II, translation David Fernbach, New York: Vintage.

—— 1981a, *Capital*, Volume III, translation David Fernbach, New York: Vintage.

—— 1981b [1844] 'D. Ricardo. *Des Principes de l'économie politique et de l'impôt*, traduit de Constancio etc.', in *Marx-Engels Gesamtausgabe* IV/2. Berlin: Dietz Verlag.

—— 1981c [1844] 'Exzerpte aus Georg Wilhelm Friedrich Hegel: *Phänomenologies des Geistes*', in *Marx-Engels Gesamtausgabe* IV/2, Berlin: Dietz Verlag.

—— 1981d [1845] 'Exzerpte und Notizen 1843 bis Januar 1845', in *Marx-Engels Gesamtausgabe*, IV/2, 301–582. Berlin: Dietz Verlag, 1981.

—— 1983a, 'Letter to Engels of August 1, 1856', in *Marx and Engels Collected Works*, Volume 40, New York: International Publishers.

—— 1983b, *Das Kapital. Kritik der politischen Ökonomie*, in *MEGA²* II/6, Berlin: Dietz Verlag.

—— 1983c [1879], 'Draft Letters to Vera Zasulich', in *Late Marx and the Russian Road: Marx and 'The Peripheries of Capitalism'*, edited by Teodor Shanin, New York: Monthly Review Books.

—— 1985a [1863], 'Letter to Engels of April 9, 1863', in *Marx and Engels Collected Works*, Volume 41, New York: International Publishers.

—— 1985b [1965], *Value, Price and Profit* in *Marx and Engels Collected Works*, Volume 20, New York: International Publishers.

—— 1986a [1857–8], *Outlines of the Critique of Political Economy (Rough Draft of 1857–58)*, in *Marx and Engels Collected Works*, Volume 28, New York: International Publishers.

—— 1986b [1871], 'Drafts of *The Civil War in France*', in *Marx and Engels Collected Works*, Volume 22, New York: International Publishers.

—— 1986c [1871], *The Civil War in France*, in *Marx and Engels Collected Works*, Volume 22, New York: International Publishers.

—— 1987a [1857–8], *Outlines of the Critique of Political Economy (Rough Draft of 1857–58)*, in *Marx and Engels Collected Works*, Volume 29, New York: International Publishers.

—— 1987b [1859], *Contribution to the Critique of Political Economy*, in *Marx and Engels Collected Works*, Volume 29, New York: International Publishers.

—— 1987c [1867], *Das Kapital. Kritik der politischen Ökonomie*, in *Marx-Engels Gesamtausgabe* II/6, Berlin: Dietz Verlag.

—— 1988, *Economic Manuscript of 1861–63*, in *Marx and Engels Collected Works*, Volume 30, New York, International Publishers.

—— 1989a, *Economic Manuscript of 1861–63*, in *Marx and Engels Collected Works*, Volume 31, New York, International Publishers.

—— 1989b, *Economic Manuscript of 1861–63*, in *Marx and Engels Collected Works*, Volume 32, New York, International Publishers.

—— 1989c [1872–5], *Le Capital*, *Marx-Engels Gesamtausgabe* II/7, Berlin: Dietz Verlag.

—— 1989d [1875], *Critique of the Gotha Program*, in *Marx and Engels Collected Works*, Volume 24, New York: International Publishers.

—— 1989 [1875], 'Notes on Bakunin's Book *Statehood and Anarchy*', in *Marx and Engels Collected Works*, Volume 24, New York: International Publishers.

—— 1989f [1879], 'Johann Most. Kapital und Arbeit', in *Marx-Engels Gesamtausgabe* II/8, Berlin: Dietz Verlag.

—— 1989g [1880], 'Notes on the Poverty of Philosophy', in *Marx and Engels Collected Works*, Volume 24, New York: International Publishers.

—— 1989h [1881], 'Notes on Wagner's *Lehrbuch der politischen Ökonomie*', in *Marx and Engels Collected Works*, Volume 24, New York: International Publishers.

—— 1991 [1861–3], *Economic Manuscript of 1861–63*, in *Marx and Engels Collected Works*, Volume 33, New York, International Publishers.

—— 2008, 'Manuskripte zum zweiten Buch des 'Kapitals' 1868 bis 1881', edited by Teinosuke Otani, Ljudmila Vasina and Carl-Ewrich Mori in *Marx-Engels Gesamtausgabe* II/11, Berlin: Akademie Verlag.

Marx, Karl and Freidrich Engels 1976a [1846], *The German Ideology*, in *Marx and Engels Collected Works*, Volume 5, New York: International Publishers.

—— 1976b [1847], *The Manifesto of the Communist Party*, in *Marx and Engels Collected Works*, Volume 6, New York: International Publishers.

Megill, Allan 2002, *The Burden of Reason (Why Marx Rejected Politics and the Market)*. Lanham: Rowman & Littlefield.

Mészáros, István 1970, *Marx's Theory of Alienation*. London: Merlin Books, 1970.

—— 1995, *Beyond Capital*. New York: Monthly Review Press.

Murray, Patrick 1988, *Marx's Theory of Scientific Knowledge*. Atlantic Highlands: Humanities Press International.

Musto, Marcello 2008 (ed.), *Karl Marx's Grundrisse, Foundations of the Critique of Political Economy 150 Years Later*, New York: Routledge.

Negri, Antonio 1984, *Marx Beyond Marx: Lessons on the Grundrisse*. New York: Autonomedia.

—— 1988, 'Crisis of the Planner-State: Communism and Revolutionary Organisation', in *Revolution Retrieved: Writings on Marx, Keynes, Capitalist Crisis and New Social Subjects*, London: Red Notes.

—— 1999, *Insurgencies: Constituent Power and the Modern State*. Minneapolis: University of Minnesota Press.

Neurath, Otto 1973 [1919], 'Experiences of Socialization in Bavaria', in *Empiricism and Sociology*, edited by Marie Neurath and Robert S. Cohen. Dordrecht-Holland: D. Reidel.

—— 2005, *Economic Writings: Selections 1904–1945*, edited by Thomas Uebel and Robert S. Cohen, Dordrecht: Springer Science.

Ollman, Bertell 2003, 'Marx's Dialectical Method is More Than a Mode of Exposition: A Critique of Systematic Dialectics', in *Dance of the Dialectic: Steps in Marx's Method*, Champaign-Urbana: University of Illinois Press.

Paolucci, Paul 2007, *Marx's Scientific Dialectics. A Methodological Treatise for a New Century*, Leiden: Brill.

Paz, Octavio 1974, 'I Speak of the City', in *The Collected Poems of Octavio Paz*, edited by Eliot Weinberger, New York: New Directions.

Peperzak, Adriaan T. 2004, *Elements of Ethics*. Stanford: Stanford University Press.

Plato 1961a, *Republic*, translation Paul Shorey in *The Collected Dialogue of Plato*, edited by Edith Hamilton and Huntington Cairns, Princeton: Princeton University Press.

—— 1961b, *Theaetetus*, translation Francis M. Cornford in *The Collected Dialogue of Plato*, edited by Edith Hamilton and Huntington Cairns, Princeton: Princeton University Press.

Polanyi, Michael 1962, *Personal Knowledge: Towards a Post-Critical Philosophy*, Chicago: University of Chicago Press.

Postone, Moishe 1993, *Time, Labour and Social Domination: A Reinterpretation of Marx's Critical Theory*, Cambridge: Cambridge University Press.

Rockmore, Tom 2002, *Marx after Marxism, the Philosophy of Karl Marx*. London: Blackwell.

Rogin, Leo 1945, 'Marx and Engels on Distribution in a Socialist Society', *American Economic Review*, 35, 1: 137–43.

Rojahn, Jürgen 1985, 'Die Marxschen Manuskripte aus dem Jahre 1844 in der neuen Marx-Engels-Gesamtausgabe', *Archive für Sozialgeschichte*, 25: 647–63.

—— 2002, 'The Emergence of a Theory: The Importance of Marx's Notebooks as Exemplified by Those of 1844', *Rethinking Marxism*, 14, 4: 29–46.

Rosdolsky, Roman 1968, *Zur Entstehungsgeschichte des Marxschen ‚Kapital'*, Vienna: Europäische Verlag.

Sekine, Thomas T. 1990, 'Socialism as a Living Idea' in *Socialist Dilemmas, East and West*, Armonk: M.E. Sharpe.

—— 1997a, *An Outline of the Dialectic of Capital*, Volume 1, London: Macmillan.

—— 1997b, *An Outline of the Dialectic of Capital*, Volume 2, London: Macmillan.

Seneca 1988. *Ad Lucilium epistolae* in *Hellenistic Philosophy: Introductory Readings*, translated and introduced by Brad Inwood and L.P. Gerson. Indianapolis: Hackett Publishing.

Smith, Cyril 2005, *Karl Marx and the Future of the Human*, Lanham: Lexington Books.

Smith, Tony 1993, 'Marx's *Capital* and Hegelian Dialectical Logic', in *Marx's Method in Capital*, edited by Fred Moseley, Atlantic Highlands: Humanities Press.

Trigg, Andrew B. 2006 (ed.), *The Marxian Reproduction Schema: Money and Aggregate Demand in a Capitalist Society*, London: Routledge.

Thomas, Edith 2007, *The Women Incendiaries*, Chicago: Haymarket Books.

Tronti, Mario 1979, 'Lenin in England' in *Working Class Autonomy and the Crisis*, London: Red Notes.

Uchida, Hiroshi 1988, *Marx's Grundrisse and Hegel's Logic*, New York: Routledge.

Index

www.ingramcontent.com/pod-product-compliance
Lightning Source LLC
Chambersburg PA
CBHW072104040426
42334CB00042B/2308